Copyright 2016 Ross-Edison

ALL RIGHTS RESERVED

ISBN-13

978-1535258456

ISBN-10

1535258454

SEVEN TEMPLES ON MALTA

SEVEN TEMPLES ON MALTA

*RED SKORBA *TA' HAGRAT MGARR *KORDIN III
*GGANTIJA *HAGAR QIM *MNAJDRA *TARXIEN

A WALKING TOUR

Hagar Qim, Copyright 2016 Ross-Edison

Hagar Qim, Copyright 2016 Ross-Edison

THE SYMPATHETIC HISTORY
OF THE STONES

"…in the Paleolithic era the Mediterranean Sea was cut into two basins – divided by a tongue of land that joined Tunisia and Italy….Malta and the continental shelf of Sicily were once dry land…a huge area of fairly shallow water lies off Tunisia – but it is separated from Malta by a deep channel…. around 10,000 B.C. some kind of cataclysm changed the face of this part of the world. The land bridge between Tunisia and Sicily sank – leaving the islands of M poking out of the sea."

Society for Interdisciplinary Studies

<u>sis.group.org.uk</u>

Entrance to cave burials at Xemxija, Evans 195

Entrance to cave burials at Xemxija, Evans 1959

Entrane to Western Temple at Skorba, Trump 1966.

TEMPLES OF MOURNING

Entrance to Tarxien. Copyright 2016 Ross-Edison.

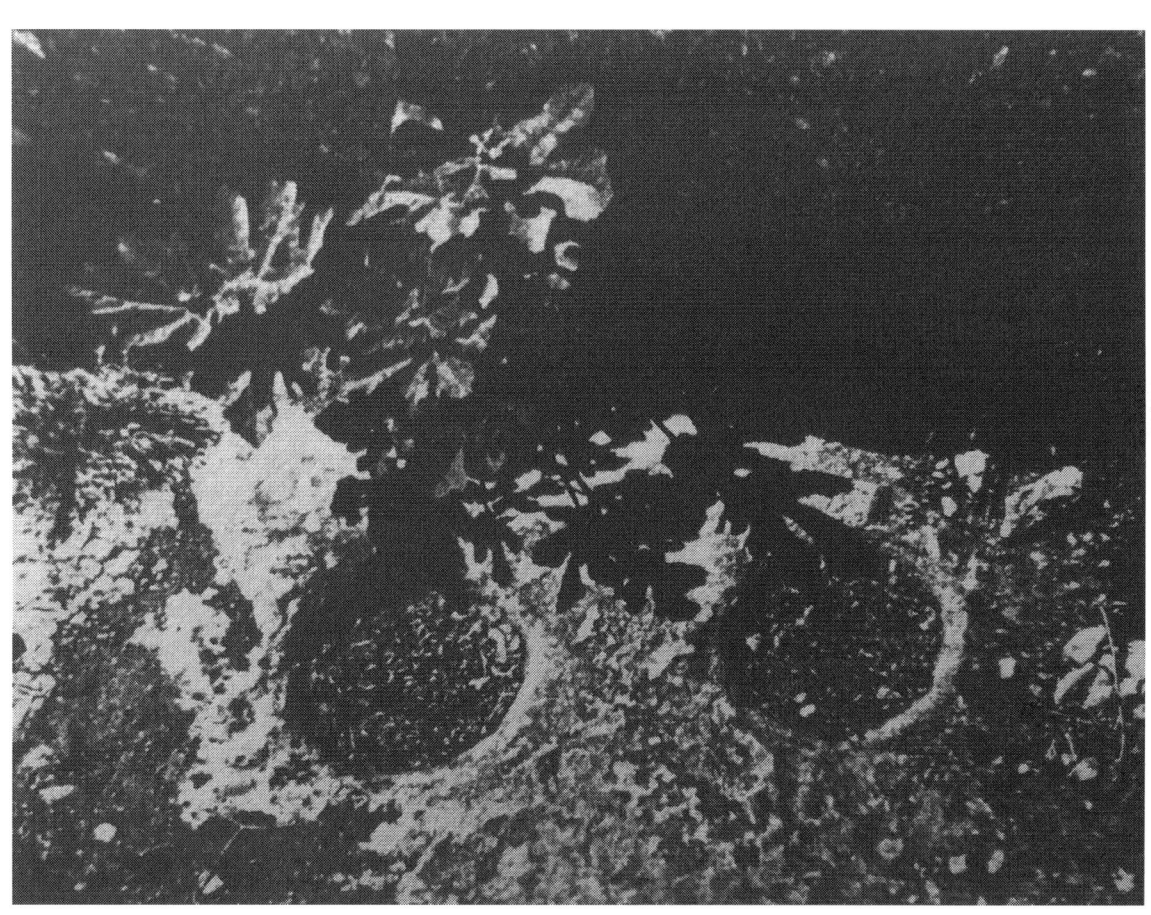

korba, Trump 1966

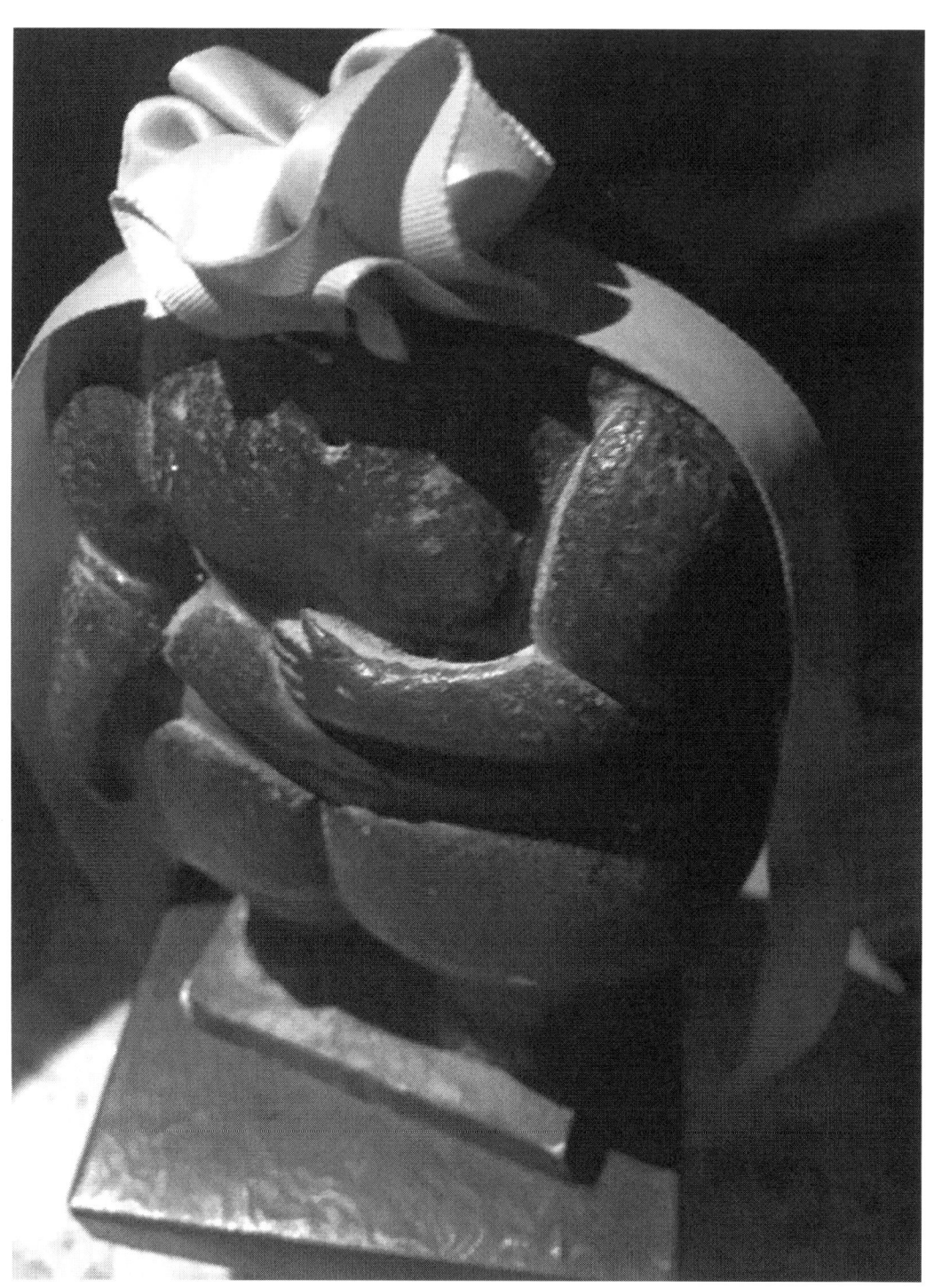

HUT OF THE QUERNS

130 Seashells were found in Hut of the Querns,. Evans 1959

TABLE OF CONTENTS

PREFACE		1
INTRODUCTION		10
CHAPTER ONE	ON THE GREAT MALTA TOUR BUS	145
CHAPTER TWO	INSIDE THE COOL BISTRO	155
CHAPTER THREE	TARXIEN	162
CHAPTER FOUR	RED SKORBA	178
CHAPTER FIVE	XEMXIJA AND TA' HAGRAT	189
CHAPTER SIX	KORDIN III	194
CHAPTER SEVEN	POST-KORDIN III	199
CHAPTER EIGHT	GGANTIJA	200
CHAPTER NINE	HAGAR QIM	210
CHAPTER TEN	MNAJDRA	216
CHAPTER ELEVEN	INSIDE MNAJDRA	219
CHAPTER TWELVE	THE LITTLE HORSES OF MALTA	227
CHAPTER THIRTEEN	IN THE TEMPLE OF MOURNING	230
CHAPTER FOURTEEN	FIRST FEAST OF THE EVENING	231
CHAPTER FIFTEEN	COMING BACK FOR DINNER	234
CHAPTER SIXTEEN	INTO THE DARK	237
CHAPTER SEVENTEEN	THE MOURNING TOUR	240
CHAPTER EIGHTEEN	THE BROKEN CUP	244
CHAPTER NINETEEN	WOMAN OF WOOD	246

TABLE OF CONTENTS

CHAPTER TWENTY	THE ORACLE	249
CHAPTER TWENTY-ONE	ONE ANCIENT EVENING AND ALL THE ANCIENTS WEPT	251
CHAPTER TWENTY-TWO	WHERE DID THEY GO?	254
CHAPTER TWENTY-THREE	"GOOD-BYE, MALTA!"	256
PHOTO CREDITS		263
END NOTES		265

This book is dedicated to the memory of my parents

and to Cuthbert

And you, my father, there on the sad height

...Bless me...with your fierce tears....

Do not go gentle into that good night...

...RAGE AGAINST THE DYING OF THE LIGHT

DYLAN THOMAS, 1954

CUTHBERT

MARCH 30, 2005 – SEPTEMBER 1, 2016

Where did they go?

This book was created for the first-time visitor to the temples on Malta, for the first-time researcher of the megalithic sites, and for anyone who has already fallen in love with the great mystery of prehistoric Malta.

For those who may stop to linger in a half-circle apse inside thick, imposing walls of massive stones, for any who know to listen, the Siren song can be heard, as of old, calling the unwary to come meet death in the underground tombs.

Yet another ancient voice echos and resounds in this book, to be carefully heard, calling and arising from acoustical stones inside an encircling apse, and thus in a thrice the Siren song is hushed as the old sounding stones whisper their ardent message to come back to life.

Walking a connecting path, from tomb to temple, you enter as the ancients did, a gracious open-air courtyard and corridor inside the circle of huge standing stones, so that you feel led, almost helplessly, to wander amid the rubble and ruin.

Suddenly you are no longer standing on a floor of cracked rock, but on a smooth torba floor, as strong and supportive as well-laid cement, and you simply watch as the corbelled curve of the apse wall becomes plastered and painted red, and look there, someone is emerging from deep inside the stones, a sympathetic figure portly and true in robes of pure white, having clambered deftly through a low window that was carefully carved in a large standing stone, but she remains sadly unseen by most visitors because imagination has been constrained today, as inert as a tumbled rock pile from this lost, ancient time.

Nonetheless, for some visitors with rampaging imagination, the heavy-set woman in white approaches, hobbling somewhat on thick, distended ankles toward you, as if she has something important to say.

Such was the process of creating this book.

Lady of Hagar Qim, Copyright 2016 Ross-Edison

Outer wall, Hagar Qim, Copyright 2016 Ross-Edison

Hagar Qim

"On the Eastern side of the temple, the remains of a statue can be seen. It is believed to be the base of two missing 'mother-goddess' statues. A cache of small Mother-goddess statuettes…found under a step inside the temple, is now on display at the Valletta Museum of Archaeology."

ancient-wisdom.co.uk

Legs of Sranding Statue at Hagar Qim, Copyright 2016 Ross-Edison

"Food and drink were carried about in these buildings in exquisitely made jars, cups, and dishes of which the specimens collected during the excavations, and now exhibited in the Valletta museum, are as marvelous as the buildings themselves."

Sir Themistocles Zammit, Excavation Report, Hagar Qim and Mnajdra, 1931/1994

Thermi Pedestal Cup from Tarxien, Evans 1970,

"The variety of shapes of the vases found whole or re-constructed is very remarkable. There were jars and jugs, bowls and basins, pots and cups, ladles and strainers. But the shape that occurs most frequently is that of the bowl."

Professor N. Tagliaferro, Style Classifications from Hal Saflieni Hypogeum, 1910

Hanging bowl from Hal Saflieni Hypogeum, Evans 1959

BOWL FROM HAL SAFLIENI HYPOGEUM

Large shallow bowl from Hal Saflieni Hypogeum, Evans 1959

BOWL FROM HAL SAFLIENI HYPOGEUM

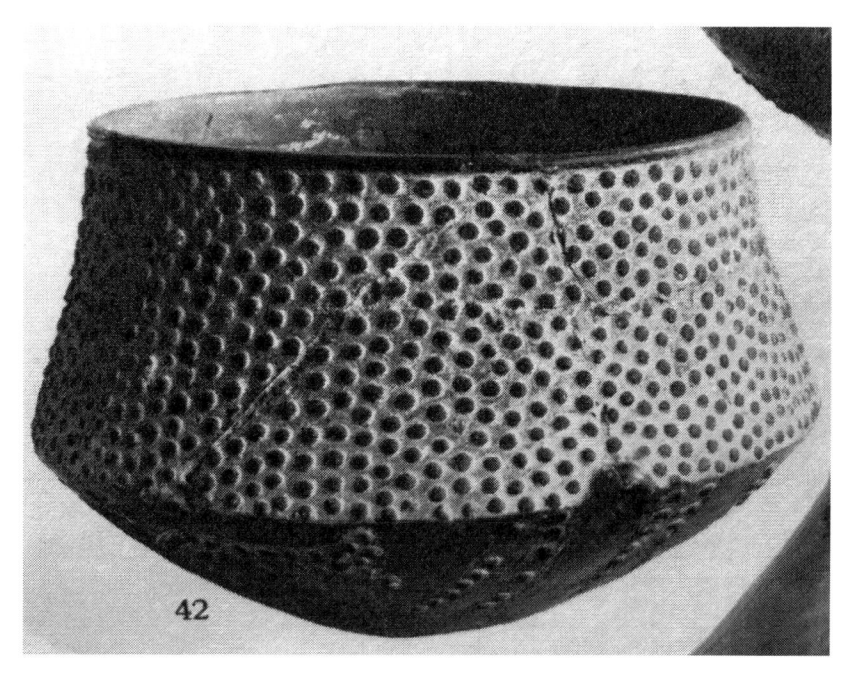

Seudded bowl from Hal Saflieni Hypogeum, Evans 1959

OF ARCHITECTS AND ARTISTS

AND STONE MASONS

"…in the construction…great skill was displayed. Architects Drew elaborate plans, and an army of workmen directed by expert masons quarried the huge blocks and transported them to the appointed place, smoothed, squared them, and laid them with such consummate art…."

Consummate Art

Consummate art of Mnajdra, inner trilithon, Copyright 2016 Ross-Edison

Consummate art at Tarxien, Copyright 2016 Ross-Edison

Tarxien Altar Consummate art,, Copyright 2016 Ross-Edison

Consummate art Corridor, Hagar Qim, Copyright 2016 Ross-Edison

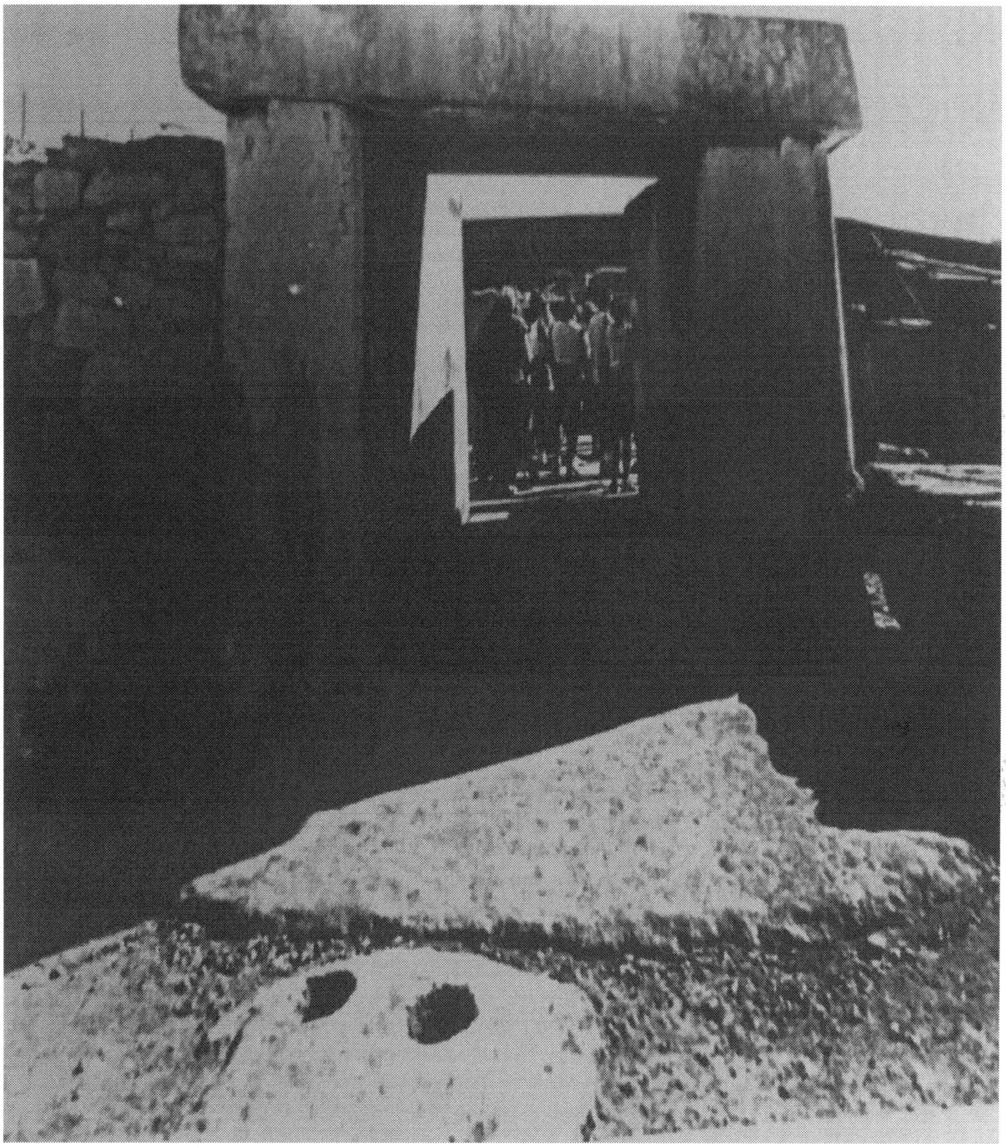

Stones of outer wall, Hagar Qim, Copyright 2016 Ross-Edison.

MOVING THE STONES

'...the minimum hauling party for moving stones upon rollers is two men per ton on level ground, and nine men per ton for hauling up a gradient of nine degrees.'

R.J.C. Anderson, Neolithic Engineering in Antiquity, Vol. XXXV
1961, in Zammit 1931/1994

MOVING THE STONES

MOVING THE STONES

Spiral stone, megalith opposite page, and pillars, inner temple at Tarxien,

Copyright 2016 Ross-Edison

MOVING THE STONES

Entrance trilithon at Tarxien, Copyright 2016 Ross-Edison

Inside the 'Holy of Holies' in Hal Saflieni Hypogeum, Richard Ellis, c. 1910.

"The discovery of the Hypogeum at Paula, whatever may have been the exact use of its mysterious chambers, with their strangely curved walls, adds another and most important testimony to this theory of an early Western Mediterranean civilization (in Sardinia, in the Balearic Islands and in the South-East of Spain, suggest the growth of a civilization never attaining such advanced culture, but persisting through long ages with striking tenacity and individual character, and surviving as a lingering tradition to this day), which Professor Mayr traces from Malta, beyond the limits named above, to the northwestern coasts of France, England and Ireland, and as far North as the Orkney and Shetland Islands."

Newspaper article from the Omaru Mail, New Zealand, 10 June, 1911 \ \ \ \ \

PREFACE

The Iberian walked a few steps apart from the rest of the group, even though the group was his group and the people in it artists he himself had trained. Then he fingered the smooth, cool obsidian in the soft reindeer pouch strapped for safe-keeping across his chest, as if to remind him of something he no longer had the freedom to forget.

It was not just their collective past as wandering vagabond artists that he must keep in mind. It was their onrushing future as artists and stone masons in the new land which they now approached on a footpath down the spine of the Apennines Mountains that ran exposed above the sea all the way to the new land, where they were excitedly headed, and after that the spiny footpath continued over deep waters until the land bridge ended in the shallow waters of a far, far shore.

Too far for the exhausted wander-lust of his companions.

They would settle instead on a misted land they had all glimpsed as one, standing close together in a half circle atop Ragusa Ridge on the large island. From there his entire group had huddled with their cousins, the Sicani, and glimpsed the far, fair land which beckoned them like an irresistible song.

They were walking to it and, once settled in there, would start making their art inside the island caves that would surely be found, all over again.

They had already been told about a huge open cave where newcomers to the island could find immediate shelter.

His one worry was that the sea level was rising. The Sicani warned that they had best leave now. Not that the water was coming up that fast, but it was noticeable now, and if they wanted to walk across the Mediterranean Basin on the land bridge to the beckoning island, their long journey must begin. Otherwise they could go down to the harbor and wait for a broad-bowed sea vessel embarking to the island on the trade routes.

Trade is changing they were told; now other than exotic items people wanted seeds to grow lentils and wheat, and animals not at all wild but passive, such as goats and cows which were in demand and didn't seem to care if they went across the water.

He found this change unnerving.

Then his head filled with images created by his far ancestors, by now so far back in time, and stories the artists told when they taught him and others how to create the animals in the modest glow of candlelight that ameliorated the near darkness, but nonetheless cast shadows, like death flickering on the cave walls and all around them.

In his mind's eye he saw again some of the best work.

On vaulted cave ceilings and walls.

Images of awesome animals that must be hunted.

He remembered the blood colors.

Not real blood, not entirely, not everywhere, but in some images in some places, it *was* part red ochre and part animal blood. Mixed well, then painted into a bright red picture inside a deep cave circle, some blood-like images being difficult to reach until one had crawled through a narrow tunnel that led into a great open chamber with painted red bison appearing like a dream on the low ceiling directly above one's eyes when on one's back in a prone, sleeping position; he recalled another long narrow tunnel which finally opened, to his great relief, inside a spacious circular place of painted images far underground.

Hard going, he recalled.

Had to be taught, skills handed down.

Take his own skills, for example. He could remember his father's tales of their ancient family members who had created so many red ochre and black soot images on inner cave walls, as had *their even more ancient* ancestors who had handed down the skills to them and they to him.

Not everyone can be an artist, they told him.

Almost a curse, they said: you have no choice.

He thought then of some of his goofier brothers and cousins, large men of brawn, and fearless, who had no artistic ability. They avoided his company during a hunt as though he, the artist, was a haunted one, but nonetheless, like all the hunters, they never missed a visit with him into the painted places to become primed on the eve of a hunt.

He painfully remembered how he was otherwise avoided by these jovial kin. As if set aside, doomed to wait a lonely time until the next hunt neared and he was called to bring his candle and tools and ocher to perform the special task. He recalled, however, the good hunts and the savory feasts afterwards where he would always be the first served, and it was the best of the roasted meat, thereby honoring him as the special one of the entire group.

Then a climate change began. The air grew warmer. Ice lost its grip on the land and the frozen crust began disappearing. Water levels in the seas began slowly rising from the melting runoff. Traders began arriving more often on sea vessels but now they brought wheat seeds and barley seeds instead of so much obsidian and flint to make cutting tools in exchange for furs and reindeer skins. And lately the hunts were not as frequent, exchange traders not needing as many furs and skins.

Gradually what the traders wanted more and more were harvested crops in exchange for seeds and passive animals. The large painted cave that was everyone's favorite with the glorious animals on its vaulted ceilings and curving walls was visited less and less. Fertile land to farm kept appearing from beneath the frozen tundra.

The old painted caves so dark and arduous to enter, so important for priming for the hunt, were gradually abandoned in favor of the sunlit fields of farming.

Bewildered by the changes, the young Iberian and his dedicated group of cave artists shouldered their pouches and chipped lithic tools, and moved on.

They had already been told about the big open cave on a lush green island of forests and deer, a cave where people lived and newcomers could immediately find shelter.

Were there other caves there?

Didn't sound like it.

No one mentioned any other caves that weren't filled with water from the sea.

No other caves for domestic dwelling? What would they create on this island of only one cave?

But who even needed to live in the old caves anymore?

Farmers certainly didn't.

Farmers built huts to live in and their animals did not fight or flee but just stood waiting to produce and help produce food, and so the wild animals pictured in the painted caves were no longer urgently hunted for food. The handsome young Iberian felt an unusual fear. Would he and his group continue to see their skills fade in importance and become as abandoned as the painted caves?

For days they had wandered on foot across the land bridge toward the island that they were now fast approaching, already soothing the travelers in a brow-cooling mist from the near-sounding sea, as they approached a land where they would use their skills to move and position large standing stones and decorate them with the dots, holes and circles of the ancient truth they had learned from their ancestors, and carried in their hearts.

Sometimes the young Iberian remembered his grandmother's words. When he was a boy, she would tell him that someday he would be walking to a new land floating in the distant haze of the open sea. He still savored her words:

"There you will make stone circles…" he mumbled *sotto voce* and only to himself.

But then he stopped.

It was embarrassing to say aloud.

Others might hear!

How could he know this, they would ask, or, What *are* you talking about?

For he traveled now with a large mixed group of people he didn't even know: they had simply met while preparing for this journey and embarked together by foot.

Other than his own troop of adventurous Iberian artists moving as a group away from the lands of northern Spain and southern France, there were Sicani farmers walking behind them in brown clothing as colorless as sackcloth, carrying wheat and barley seeds for planting, accompanied by their families and large Ibex goats with the beautiful backward-curving horns. Near them like an escort were people who introduced themselves as coming from the eastern Aegean, along with others from far-away Skae Brae and Orkney.

Two wandering musicians from the Cyclades walked nearby, bringing up the rear, both young men, seeking adventure they said, one of them bearing a harp that looked to be made from a couple of arching Ibex horns shaped into a graceful, curving harp, now securely strapped on like a backpack with strong woven cords, while his friend blew lilting sounds softly with his breath into a perforated, polished bone.

The odds were that the Iberian's utterance about making circles, if overheard by any of these characters would not be understood, not by anyone in this assemblage trekking to the island in the mist across the old land bridge, including his country cousins, the Sicani, from the far Mediterranean south.

So he said it to himself, as he walked along the spine of the earth, against which the rising Mediterranean was already lapping, and in order to finish his thought, he touched the keen obsidian blade of his knife, the cool glassy lump of obsidian, and his cache of red ochre, and finished his grandmother's words about the circles, out loud but softly, so that none would hear that the circles he would build were "…paths for the broken-hearted."

"In all times, men must have been aware

… of feeling the nearness of divine power

in the land and the sea and the welling springs."

John Caskey, Excavations at Lerna, 1952-53,

The American School of Classical Studies at Athens

Cliff top view from Hagar Qim, Copyright 2016 Ross-Edison

Path from Hagar Qim to Mnajdra,Copyright 2016 Ross-Edison

INTRODUCTION

The Mystery of Malta

The great stone temples on the small island of Malta present an enduring mystery. Perhaps no one will ever figure it out. This is because there is no written account, from that preliterate time when the temples were built, no journals, no diary, no letters, no engraved rocks with ancient questions such as those that still illumine the business of Delphi.

In the absence of any written account, how can anyone understand the Neolithic circles on Malta, all 50 of them (and counting) that have been found so far?

This lack of written documentation only means that the trilithon is standing wide open, so to speak, to everyone, for interpretation and understanding, inviting everyone to enter through its standing stones into a circle of Neolithic ruin and an alarming jumble of rocks. The intent of this book is to escort the reader's imagination into the mystery of the megalithic structures built on Malta where today the great standing stones still encircle the ruins that remain.

It is understandable that archaeologists and historians and the interested public would look upon the mysterious circles on Malta with eyes that sought to understand the sites in terms of what is already understood. There are many theories about who the temple builders were and how they used the temples, for example, the temple builders were:

> a death cult; a fertility cult; solstice worshippers; wholesale food distributors; operating arts and crafts schools; chieftains of 'elite rival communities' headquartered in temple fiefdoms across the islands; militants in temple fortresses built atop cliffs by the sea, on the look-out for invaders; managers of 'production centers' in the temple outbuildings where workers made items for local use and for inter-regional trade exchange, such as spun yarn, woven material, sewn clothing, tanned leather, bone and lithic tools, grave goods including amulets and necklaces, and, perhaps, tallow and clay seals put on jars, jugs and amphorae filled in the domestic villages with special Maltese honey for export; and finally, the coup de grace, that the temple builders were obsessive and self-isolating from the Mediterranean trade exchange during the last and lavish period of temple building, in order to obsessively build more and mors.

No doubt about it, these theories, and others, about the temple builders and their use of the temples, are thought-provoking and intriguing, but over-complicate a simple thing.

After all, it was the Stone Age.

Everything was simple.

With simple lithic tools the New Stone Age temple builders smoothed and carved inner apse stones and low step-through windows, in both temple and tomb, and using ropes, rounded stones and pulleys heaved into place the great trilithons and megalithic outer walls.

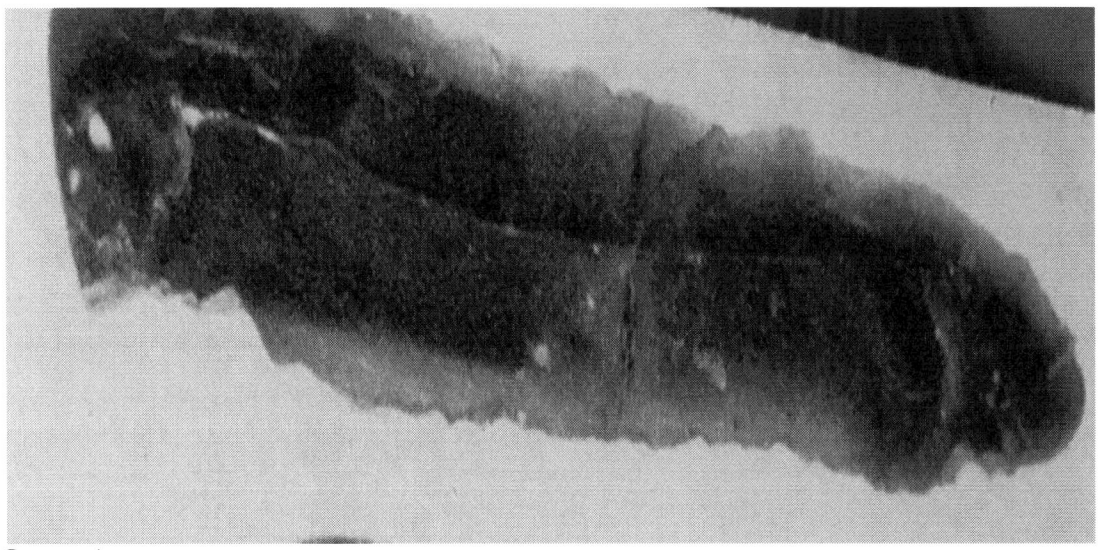

Stone Age Lithic knife, Evans 1959.

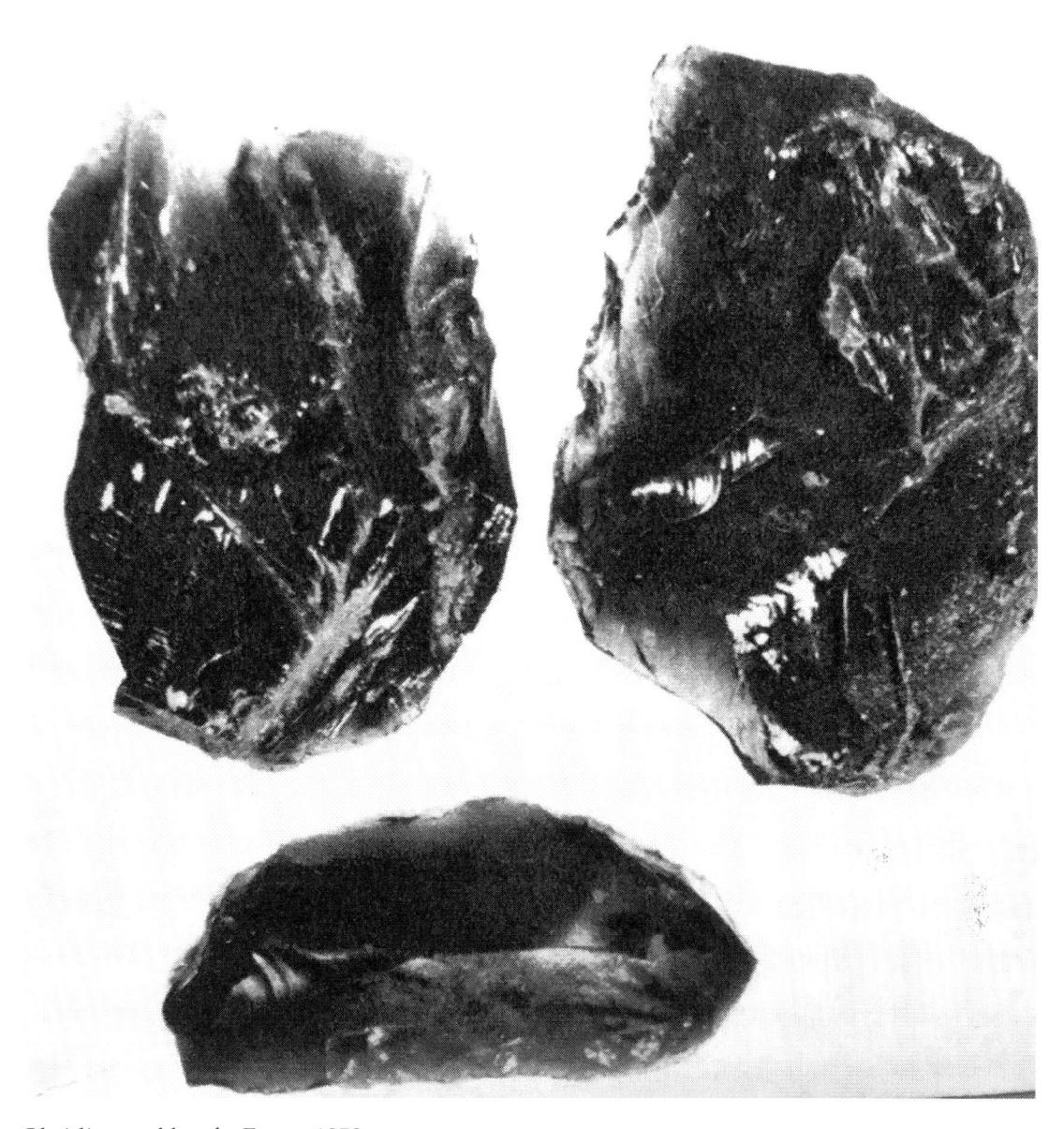

Obsidian and knofe, Evans 1959

STONE AGE LITHIC TOOLS

And simple tools created shell necklaces and amulats.

7. T/S.35, p. 147.

From Evans, 1959

AMULETS

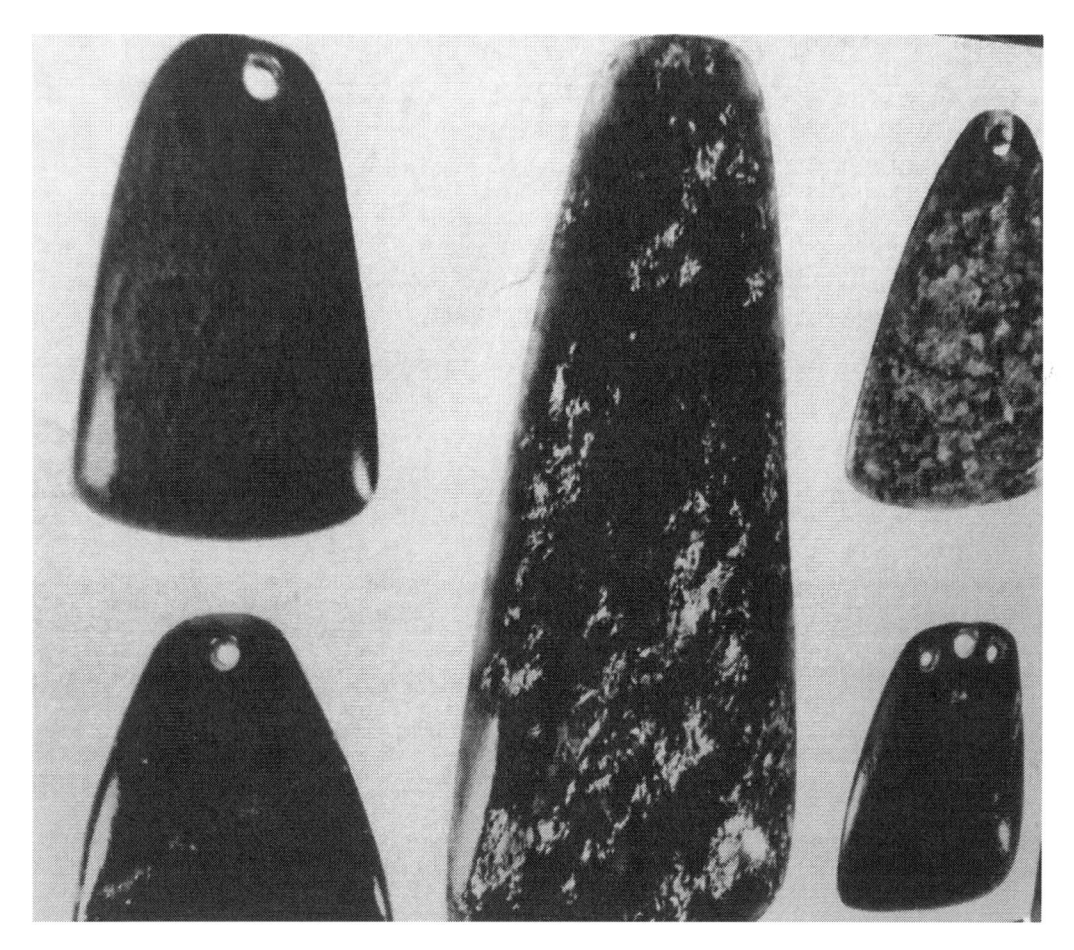

Amulets, grave goods, Evans 1959.

The reason for building the aboveground stone temples close by the underground tombs, is as simple as the lithic tools and the rounded stones that rolled the great stones. This reason is acted out in the Walking Tour that follows, as an imagined scenario one ancient evening inside Hagar Qim.

That scenario, describing one night inside a busy temple, is suggested by the grand *in situ* witnesses -- the clay, ceramic, and lithic items themselves -- discovered whole or fragmented in every site toured in this book, especially at Skorba in the 'Hut of the Querns' and in the great profusion of sherds and figurines found inside the Hal Saflieni Hypogeum, and in excavated finds at Mgarr, Kordin III, Ggantija, Hagar Qim, Mnajdra and Tarxien. Even in the most damaged and plundered sites on Kordin Hill and Mgarr, a great amount of sherds and some intact pottery were found.

The Walking Tour begins one afternoon on the hot summer streets of Valletta and ends one gala evening inside the magnificent Hagar Qim site, in a scenario that is based on archaeological evidence and legendary observations by the early excavators of the megalithic sites, all of which is summarized in five assumptions described below:

The Five Assumptions:

1. The temples replicate the tombs;
2. There is an abundance of pottery, and all the attendant sherds, some of which could be pieced together to form restorable jars, jugs, bowls, lids, ladles, vases, cups, large convex covers for large shallow plates, as well as lithic tools for grinding, found *in situ* in both temple and tomb, although the pottery in the temple appears to differ from pottery in the tomb;
3. So many temples were built;
4. It was easy to come to Malta;
5. Fat Lady figurines and large standing statues of same were found inside the temples.

This intriguing evidence -- the abundant querns, clay, stone and ceramic pottery, the broken sherds and small Fat Lady figurines in addition to a huge nine-foot-high standing statue of same whose damaged remains were found still standing inside the Tarxien temple, as well as damaged, almost unrecognizable remains of large Fat Lady statues still standing at Hagar Qim, the seashells found in temple outbuildings -- and the observant early archaeologists such as Sir Themistocles Zammit, Professor Napoleon Taliaferro, and later, Professor David Trump and Sir John Evans -- together spin this tale. A tale of what might be happening, one ancient evening, inside Hagar Qim.

Here is a sampling of the evidence of what is known.

Replicated Temple-Tombs

Sir John Evans (1971), Professor David Trump (1981) and Sir Themistocles Zammit in his excavation report of 1935 on Hagar Qim (1994), all observed that the temples replicate the tombs.

Sir Zammit notes: "Comparing the interior design from the earlier temples with the cross-section of the Xemxija graves, the similarity is obvious.

"It is possible that the temple builder derived the interior design from the design of grave chambers, so they could practice their rituals in similar surroundings. The strong outer walls give the impression of larger grave caves." (Zammit 1994)

Not only do the temples replicate the tombs but the temples are located nearby.

Red Skorba and Mgarr near Ta' Hagrat are both located near the early Xemxija tombs near St. Paul's Bay; Kordin III and Tarxien are both located near the huge Hal Saflieni Hypogeum; Ggantija is connected by a path from the Brochtoff Circle of burial caves and tombs, and the recently discovered Kercem tombs are also near Ggantija; Hagar Qim and Mnajdra are located near the Ber-Mghaz natural cave tombs, and these two temples are also near the Santa Lucija Hypogeum (where a contemporary cemetery was positioned above the Neolithic tombs, preventing excavation) with the Hal Saflieni Hypogeum about five miles away (a 90-minute walk or pony ride) from Hagar Qim and Mnadjra.

Sir Zammit states the obvious:

"In 1956 some 5,600 years old grave chambers were found near the village Xemxija. These community graves were hollowed out in lobed form to irregular niches (apses), the formed wall projections were supporting the overlying rock.

"Comparing the interior design from the earlier temples with the cross-section of the Xemxija graves, the similarity is obvious. Our knowledge of these early Maltese settlers comes first and foremost from their graves and temples." (Zammit 1994)

But what was the temple-tomb *connection*?

As if the temples are but a reflection.

Like the recent discovery of Kercem on Gozo, perhaps another, as yet unknown Hypogeum, closer to Hagar Qim and Mnajdra will someday be discovered. Meanwhile, the adjacent temples and tombs listed above strongly suggest that the burial sites and the temples were separate but deliberately connected.

"In one case, Brochtorff's Circle at Xaghra on the island of Gozo, the mortuary complex of natural caves was surrounded by a megalithic circle and connected via a ceremonial path…to the Ggantija temple complex about half a kilometer (quarter of a mile) distant." *worldhistory.biz*

It is theorized from imprints made by megaliths that no longer stand, that this pathway from tomb to temple was not a simple walkway but decorated by great stone trilithons and megalithic standing stones along the way to Ggantija temple.

It was important to replicate the tomb experience on the walk to the nearby temple and alsano inside that temple.

For example, inside the Hal Saflieni Hypogeum low, carved burial windows carved like portals opening into recessed places near corridors curving deep into the underground, where tombs of various shapes were hand-cut into the underground limestone, some tomb chambers displaying red spirals painted on ceiling and wall, with some spirals carved into the large standing stones, all making the tombs reflect the massive aboveground temples where low carved windows and red ocher spirals replicate the tombs of Hal Saflieni, so that it is no surprise to find the aboveground temples replicating even the pottery found inside the adjacent underground tombs.

Or replicating some of it.

Because not all of the pottery styles and shapes found in the tombs have been also found in the adjacent temples. One item not always found in the temples is the large, round cover, which appears to be flat or so concave that the cover looks like a large shallow bowl.

Large shallow bowls that also serve as lids or covers for plates found in the tombs were filled with cooked food that had to be covered to protect the food from roaming animals or animal predators who may have gotten into the tombs, because the covered plate of food placed on the burial site would be food for the journey.

After the burial, mourners would walk from the dark, cramped space of the underground tomb to the nearby temple where a prepared cooked feast would be presented as it had been in the tomb, but, in the temple, unlike in the tomb, along with an amphora or two of sweet Maltese wine, the food would be immediately eaten.

Shallow bowl from the Hal Saflieni Hypogeum, Evans 1959.

Food had a different purpose in the tomb.

In the temple, plates of food did not need to be covered (as was necessary to protect it in the tomb), because food in the tomb was not meant to be eaten by the mourners, but mourners who after the burial came into the temple would consume there the prepared food of the mourning feast.

The food and pottery used inside the temple thus had a different purpose from the food and pottery used inside the tomb. Pottery is the speaking voice of the temple builders, their clear indication of the meaning and use of their temples. The evidence is in the great profusion of pottery and sherds, the grinding querns and mortars left behind on the outbuilding floor.

Pottery and Querns

"Food and drink were carried about in these buildings in exquisitely made jars, cups, and dishes of which the specimens collected during the excavations, and now exhibited in the Valletta museum, are as marvelous as the buildings themselves." (Zammit 1931/1994, at Hagar Qim and Mnajdra)

A huge amount of pottery has been found in every site. Even the badly damaged sites have yielded their fair share of pottery and fragmented sherds. This very profusion of pottery suggests why the temples were built and how they were used.

Therefore, an introduction to the great abundance of Neolithic pottery found inside the seven sites and adjacent tombs is called for, with the expectation that the ancient meaning and use of the megaliths might come clear.

For the meaning and use of the megalithic structures on Malta have long been obscured by confusion. This is because an historical overlay of much later Classical Greek temples circa 500 B.C. has been superimposed over the more ancient Maltese sites in a time gap of thousands of years. Libation holes are a prime example of confused epochs. Classical Greeks many thousands of years after the Neolithic temples were being built on Malta did have altars in their temples, with rituals, male priests, female oracles, and written accounts of their existence by notable historians of the day such as Pausanias, the redoubtable travel writer, who visited the altars at oracle sites all over ancient Greece, in his *Tour of Greece*, written in the 2nd Century A.D. and noting such phenomena as libation holes into which milk, honey, wine or sacrificial animal blood would be poured as an offering or gesture of good will to the deity of earth, or to honor and nourish a beloved deceased.

Although no one can say when or where the idea of libation holes was first used, this thinking does not fit the simple stone circles on Malta whose symmetrical twin holes usually on the ground in temple forecourts but also in outer stone walls and inside the temples remain a mystery.

Above page, Entrance to Xemxija burial cave, Evans 1959.

One problem with the idea of Neolithic libation holes arises from holes that are vertical, and not in a position to receive a poured libation.

Vertical twin holes at Tarxien, Copyright 2016 Ross-Edison

The question is: why would vertical twin holes be represented inside the temples?

The answer is not to hold rods and hang drapes.

The answer is not complex, but simple.

The twin holes were the *connection* for Neolithic thinking.

The Xemxija entrance holes into the underground graves, replicated at the temples, tie together the meaning of whole temple-building epoch, Xemxija and other cave burial holes leading underground was the origin of everything. The twinned holes at the temple entrance indicate that inside the temple is where the deceased has gone.

So questions must be asked to simplify a simple thing: what if concealed beneath the historical overlay of a much later time, the Neolithic Maltese 'altars' were actually only stone tables where knives were stored and sacrificial meat was carved, what if no oracles sat in the odd little windows and heard their pronouncements echo from acoustical stones in temple and tomb, what if 'libation holes' were simple reminders of the twin holes of the Xemxjia gravesites and the reason for which the temples were built, and what if the Maltese holes were not used to receive honey, wine or sacrificial animal blood poured through them and into the earth but were only symbols of a mortal destination that must not be forgotten, and what if no rituals were staged inside the great Maltese aboveground structures?

If an Anglican Church-like ceremony featuring male priests in long robes at ritual altars inside the megalithic circles on Malta can be ruled out as anachronistic, how else could the Neolithic megaliths have been used?

Fortunately, for the intrigued imagination of today, the presence of such a large amount of pottery, some being whole or intact pieces but most found in the form of fragmented sherds, that is, pieces of broken pottery as found worldwide at ancient archaeological sites, fractured by the natural drying of the clay and the pressure of earth and time, so many fragments found at each Maltese site, even in heavily damaged sites such as Mgarr and the three forlorn sites of rubble and ruin on Kordin Hill, all serve to imagine the story of what happened inside the huge stone structures.

Although academic and other researchers today still say they wish they could somehow evade the name 'temple' as applied to the Maltese megaliths, such evasion is not possible once the site has been visited. Inside a megalithic structure, a visitor, o academic researcher, experiences a strong sensation that the site *is* some kind of sacred place, a sanctuary, as Sir Temi Zammit declared Hagar Qim and Mnajdra to be:

"Not without a sense of awe one enters the Sanctuary, a rectangular room with double altars in deep recesses…the recess in the left corner of the room contains a double altar…Looking outward…towards the main entrance, one gets a view of the magnificent passage running across the whole building. This passage is lined through with huge uprights…One of these slabs which now lies broken in the outer apse, but which was found in the passage, once formed the lintel of a doorway. " (Zammit 1994)

Therefore, if only for the convenience of continuity, as academic researchers today state, if somewhat reluctantly the megalithic structures are called 'temples' and this book joins them to present a Walking Tour of seven *temples* and the great profusion of pottery found inside them.

To get an idea of the amount of pottery that was found inside the temples and in the nearby tombs, a University of Malta Mathematics Professor, Napoleon Tagliaferro, in his 1910 report estimated that 20,000 sherds had been found by then inside the grand inner chambers of the Hal Saflieni Hypogeum.

Among these sherds at Hal Saflieni was a profusion of bowls: flat-bottomed bowls, carinated bowls, hanging bowls, large shallow concave bowls fitted with large shallow convex lids, and inside the temples along with bowls there were ladles, jars, jugs, cups, amphorae, small plates, stone baking cups for the fire pits carved as at Tarxien, Hagar Qim and Tas-Silg into inner temple floors to serve as cooking platforms, plus there were grinding stones and mortars found in the outbuilding huts, and extremely large tubs discovered *in situ* by Sir Zammit and his team of volunteers at Tarxien, all of which strongly suggest, merely by the sheer volume of items used to prepare and cook food, that the temples were venues for feasting "as seen at Tarxien with its large quantity of feasting refuse." (Malone and Stoddart)

By 1910, as the early excavations continued at various sites, a huge number of sherds and intact pottery items were being found, including pottery and grave goods excavated since 1902 from the great tomb complex, the Hal Saflieni Hypogeum.

It was concerning, however, to the thoughtful Math Professor Tagliaferro, that items and sherds found *in situ* at Hal Saflieni were not being recorded and classified by style and date. This concern was based on an 1852 excavation effort at Hagar Qim and Mnajdra which as its end had boxed up sherds and items for delivery to the Valletta Museum and to the British Museum but, once carted off, the boxes were not seen again, until decades later when the boxes were by chance discovered in a storage room at the Public Library.

Professor Tagliaferro taught math at the University of Malta, was Director of Education for Malta, and served on the Management Committee for the Museum at Valletta along with the archaeology greats of the era such as Sir Temi Zammit. The rare intact pottery and sherds left buried *in situ* and broken by time, in the inner "Holy of Holies" at Hal Saflieni, were finally organized in 1912, classified by style, and ready and waiting to spin the tale of the great megalithic tomb on Malta.

Professor Tagliaferro has recorded for all time the legacy of Malta.

By 1912, only the pottery and sherds from the Saflieni and Tarxien Cultural Phases had been excavated from those inner halls of the Hal Saflieni Hypogeum, an underground that came to be called (again with the vocabulary of later civilization) the 'Holy of Holies.' More pottery items and potsherds were later recovered by Sir Temi Zammit including the upper area at the ancient entrance to the Hal Saflieni tombs dated from far earlier Neolithic Cultural Phases than the 'Holy of Holies' including Zebbug, Mgarr, and Ggantija. Sir Evans in his 1971 Survey summarizes the number of sherds from each Neolithic Cultural Phase found inside the Hal Saflieni Hypogeum:

"Sherd-counts give the following picture:

Zebbug type, 36;

Mgarr type, 21;

Ggantija type, 996;

Saflieni and Tarxien type, 884."

Sir Evans notes:

"Now it is significant that in Tagliaferro's study of the pottery from the Hypogeum…only pottery belonging to the Saflieni and Tarxien phases and to the Bronze Age is described and illustrated. It will be remembered that the work at the Hypogeum began with the excavation of the inner halls…the original entrance being at that time shut off from the rest through a collapse of the roof. The area around the original entrance, that is, the oldest part of the building was excavated last…

"…the elaborate inner halls of the Hypogeum produced only pottery of types assignable to the Saflieni and Tarxien phases and to the Bronze Age. These elaborately carved and painted rooms would therefore have been made during the last phases of the Copper Age…The designs which compose the two painted ceilings are such as are only found on pottery, etc., of the Tarxien phase, and not before, whilst the type of megalithic construction imitated in the carving is not found in the temples themselves before the later part of the Ggantija phase.

"The pottery of the earlier phases came mainly from a heap of potsherds which were lying until 1953 in one of the disused houses above the original entrance to the Hypogeum…the roughly made part of the Hypogeum around the original entrance was in existence for some time before the making of the much more elaborate inner halls and those of the lower storey, which must belong almost entirely to the Tarxien phase. The construction of the monument probably covered almost the whole span of the Copper Age."

Professor Tagliaferro's classifications, with photographs and detailed description of pottery styles found *in situ* in the Hal Saflieni Hypogeum, was a most needed report for understanding the connection between temple and tomb on Neolithic Malta, as he explains in The *Annals of Archaeology and Anthropology, Volume III*, published by the Institute of Archaeology, University of Liverpool, 1910:

"Dr. Albert Mayr, in his valuable work…expresses a regret that no particulars of the numerous fragments of pottery found in or about the megalithic monuments of the Maltese Islands have been made public. The excavations at Hagar Kim brought to light a great number of fragments…Mr. (afterwards Sir) Charles T. Newton …states that during his stay in Malta in 1852 he dispatched two cart-loads of fragments of pottery from Hagar Kim and Mnaidra (sic.) to the Museum of Malta, and adds that he sent some specimens of that pottery in boxes to the British Museum that somehow got lost.

"What became of the cart-loads will never be known.

"No fragments of pottery, either from Hagar Kim or Mnaidra (sic.), were ever exhibited in the Malta Museum between 1852 and 1902. It was only in the latter year…that two baskets full of fragments of pottery, found in a lumber room at the Public Library, were identified…as belonging to that prehistoric monument (Hagar Qim). Those fragments are now exhibited in the Valletta Museum….More potsherds found therein lately by Professor Them. Zammit, M.D., Curator of the Museum, have been added to the collection, and a classification of all of the fragments is at present being made; but so far, no systematic description of them has been published."

Samples follow of sherds found inside the Hal Saflieni Hyposeum all from Taliaferro 1910.

Found inside the Hal Saflieni Hyposeum from Taliaferro 1910.

Hal Saflieni Hypogeum 'Holy of Holies' by Richard Ellis c. 1910

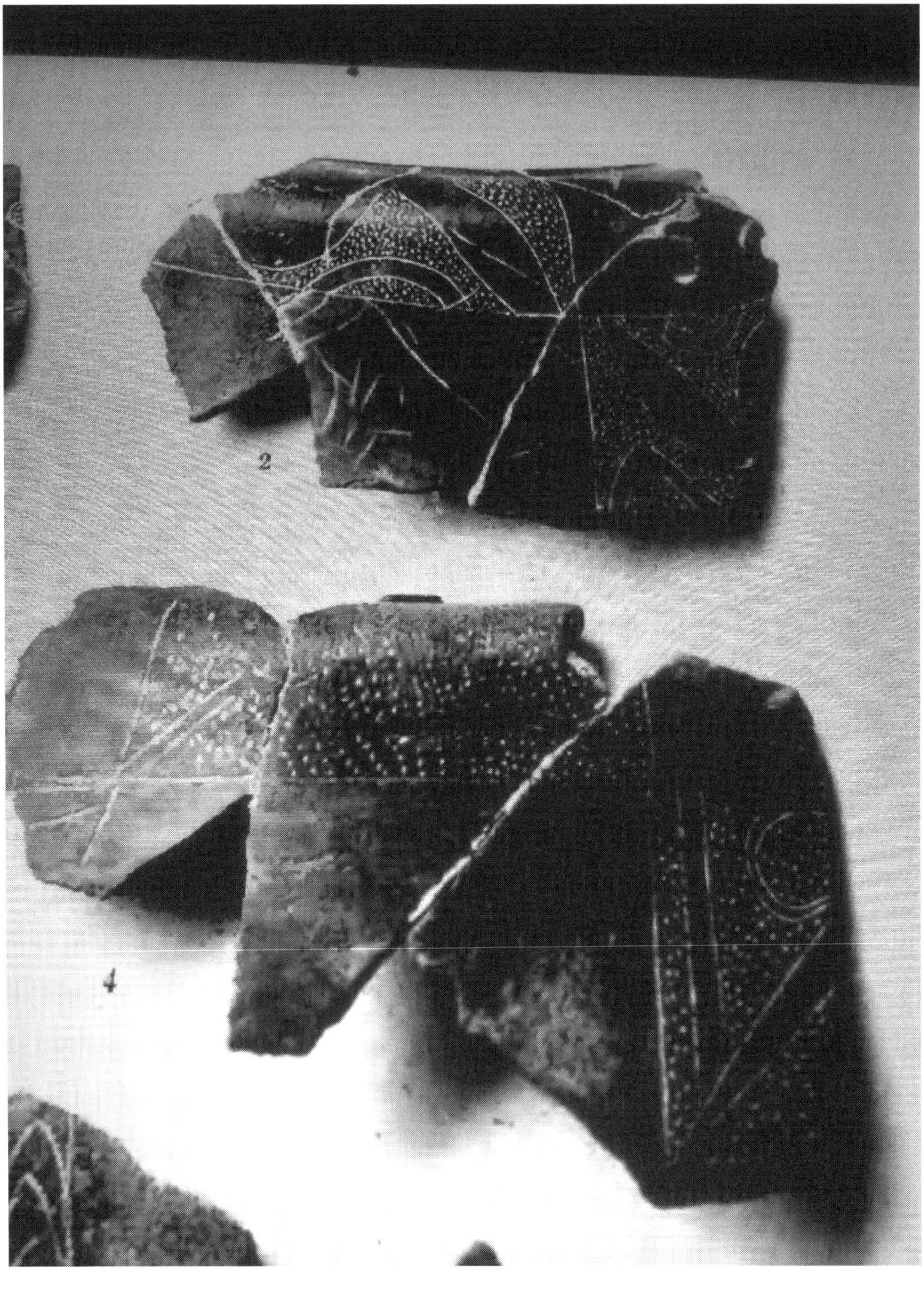

2
4

Found inside the Hal Saflieni Hyposeum from Taliaferro 1910.

Found inside the Hal Saflieni Hyposeum from Taliaferro 1910.

31

Found inside the Hal Saflieni Hyposeum from Taliaferro 1910.

Found inside the Hal Saflieni Hyposeum from Taliaferro 1910.

Found inside the Hal Saflieni Hyposeum from Taliaferro 1910.

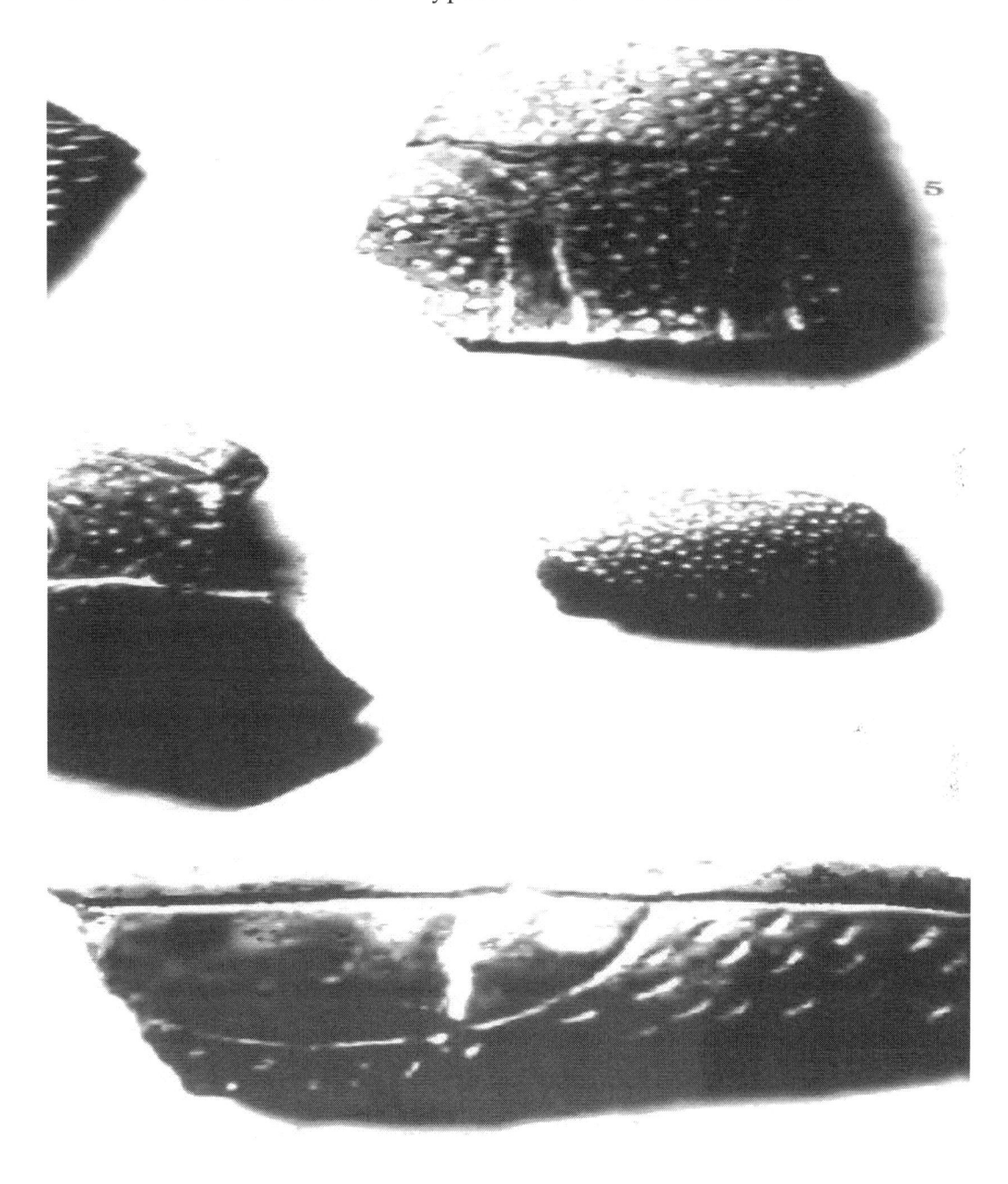

Found inside the Hal Saflieni Hyposeum from Taliaferro 1910.

"Descriptions of whole vases purporting to have been found in or about the megalithic monuments have been given by the late Dr. A.A. Caruana…by La Marmora…by Dr. Albert Mayr…by Mr. J.T. Myres…and by Dr. A.J. Evans. The late Father E. Magri, S.J. described some fragments…at Gozo.

"As most of the pottery connected with the megalithic monuments is found in a fragmentary condition, no notice thereof was taken…(but) described only whole vases. Thus a full description of the Maltese prehistoric pottery is still a desideratum.

"A favourable opportunity for such a work presented itself lately on the occasion of the important discovery of a prehistoric hypogeum at Casal Paula, in a place called 'Hal Saflieni'…it consists of several chambers situated at different levels…

"The variety of shapes of the vases found whole or re-constructed is very remarkable. There were jars and jugs, bowls and basins, pots and cups, ladles and strainers. But the shape that occurs most frequently is that of the bowl.

"There are several of elegant form, plain or decorated in various styles, with rows of projecting studs, polished or burnished or painted red in two shades, others made of black, brown, grey, buff, yellowish-red, or cream-colored ware of various degrees of thickness and fineness, with straight or curved rims, in some cases provided with one or more handles of various shapes, sometimes projecting vertically beyond the rim, in other cases provided with knobs of various shapes in lieu of handles."

Professor Tagliaferro devised a classification of the scant number of the intact or whole pottery, the restorable pottery, and the great piles of potsherds found inside the Hal Saflieni Hypogeum which he estimated at 20,000 pieces. He noted two Categories.

Category I is Unornamented. Category II is Ornamented. This latter Category is extensive, due to the huge number of decorated potsherds found, some restorable or partly restorable by fitting together scattered fragments that composed, for example, a shallow flat tomb bowl and its cover and a hanging lamp.

One item was a large plate, whose fragments were found on two different levels of the Hypogeum, in pieces, however, which fit together to restore most of the plate. The question is why the plate fragments were found in separate areas and levels; was this large plate re-useable in presenting grave goods and re-broken at two or more graves?

Professor Tagliaferro's detailed account of potsherds and whole pottery items might help answer the puzzling questions about all the broken pottery found inside the Hypogeum in the first awkward excavations of 1902 when the accidental discovery of the Hal Saflieni Hypogeum by workmen was finally revealed by a construction company to the university and museum scholars. The Hypogeum was a mess.

"The whole place was nearly full of red earth, stones and rubbish, among which was found a large number of human and animal bones, implements of flint and other stone, some whole vases, a large number of fragments of pottery, a few votive statuettes, a large number of perforated shells, small perforated axes in obsidian and fibrolite, amulets and ornaments, and a considerable number of other interesting objects.

"What struck me most when I began the work of classification, was the extremely limited number of vases which were found whole, whilst the potsherds exceeded twenty thousand in number. This, however, may be accounted for by the fact that…the vases found therein were, as a rule, broken before being placed in the tomb…a common custom to break all the vases used at the funeral as soon as the rites were over. Among the vases that were found whole or only partly broken there were several of minute size, measuring 5 to 8 cm. (2 to 3 inches) in diameter; most of them bowls, some ornamented with incisions filled with white, others plain. They were, very likely, meant as votive offerings.

"As it happens that the Hal-Saflieni hypogeum contains nearly all kinds of pottery and most of the styles of decoration of the fragments hitherto found at Hagar Kim, Mnaidra…Gigantia…and other megalithic monuments, in the Maltese Islands, a study of the pottery found at Hal-Saflieni may be considered as a general study of the prehistoric pottery of the Maltese Islands…and to throw light on the important question of the origin of its first inhabitants."

His detailed list begins with Unornamented Category I.

"Section A

"*Class 1.* "Coarse, buff, reddish or grey ware, unornamented, 2-3 cm. (.79 of an inch to about 1 inch) thick. The colour of the clay varies from an ashy white to a dark grey, and from a dirty red to a reddish brown…They appear to be very primitive.

"Besides a few jars and pots with handles, there are several fragments of large flat bottoms, and handles of various shapes, for large ordinary jars. One such jar, 58 cm. (23 inches) high, 17 cm. (6.5 inches) diameter at the base, 32 cm. (12.6 inches) at the shoulder, with neck 8 cm. (3 inches) high and 17 cm. (6.5 inches) in diameter, has been fully re-constructed.

"No appreciable difference can be detected between some of these fragments and those found by Mr. J.H. Cooke in the 'Ghar Dalam' cavern….However, no inference can be drawn from this resemblance, as the same kind of ordinary pottery for household purposes appears to have been made in Malta in all ages up to the present time...."

After this brief review, Category II, Ornamented Pottery, begins with Sections B to G, Classes 2-26.

"The case is quite different with the decorated pottery," Tagliaferro explains and then details the long list of ornamented pottery found by or before 1910 when this Classification was published.

"Section B. This most primitive style is ornamented with pit-markings, more or less deep. These markings are (a) at first roughly triangular in form, deeply impressed in a coarse thick clay; (b) later, small, round, less deep and nearer to one another, or (c) more or less elongated and distributed in rows, in less coarse clay; (d) at last, these pit-markings are reduced to mere dots or punctures evenly distributed, or filling the ground of incised patterns.

"*Class 2.* Coarse, light grayish ware, 2 cm. (.79 of an inch) thick; decorated with deep, triangular, badly-shaped pit-markings....To this class belongs a large fragment of a very coarse grayish ware decorated with close triangular pit-marking, which reminds us of the wall decorations in several megalithic monuments in the Maltese Islands....

"*Class 3.* Fine grey or buff ware of medium thickness (5-10 mm.) (.20 of an inch to .39 of an inch) decorated with more or less hollow, round, or elongated pit-markings (4-15 mm. or .20 to .59 of an inch in diameter), uniformly distributed...The only shapes of vases which could be determined were those of an interesting bowl formed of black clay decorated with a curvilinear incised band and elongated dots filled with white gypsum, and of a cover decorated in the same style, and found whole....

"Section C

"Rather coarse yellowish or buff-coloured wares; decorated inrelief with the imbricated leaf, the fish-scale, or the scallop.

"*Class 4.* Buff-coloured ware of medium thickness (5-10 mm. or .20 of an inch to .39 of an inch), covered with a fine slip; decorated with a straight or curved ribs or fluting in relief...fragments only, probably of bowls.

Class 5. Coarse reddish ware of variable thickness (8-18 mm.) (.31 of an inch to .71 of an inch), sometimes covered with a fine slip; decorated with overlapping rows of fish-scale ornament in relief. Large jars.

Class 6. Coarse grey or reddish ware, 10-18 mm. (.39 of an inch to .71 of an inch) thick; decorated with large veined leaves in relief, forming scallops. Very large conical vases or jars.

Class 7. Coarse reddish ware, 8-18 mm. (.31 of an inch to .71 of an inch) thick; ornamented with separate overlapping leaves, with round edges in relief.

Class 8. Fine buff-coloured wares of medium thickness (5-19 mm. or .20 of an inch to .75 of an inch), covered with a slip, and ornamented with overlapping rows of long narrow leaves in relief, adjacent to each other but separate.

"Classes 4, 5, 6, 7 and 8," Tagliaferro notes, "include all the varieties of the relief decoration, and, properly speaking, form one large well-marked class which deserves special treatment. This style was applied exclusively to the decoration of vases formed of the local red clay. It seems to have been very primitive, as a large number of the specimens are of a coarse thick ware, and extremely rough workmanship…some specimens…are more refines…Fragments of various degrees of fineness were found at Hagar-Kim, Mnaidra…but so far none in Gozo.

"The fragments are large, as a rule, and show by their curvature that they belonged to large vases. Though the fragments at our disposal are many, it is not easy to make out the shapes of the vessels to which they belonged. But from the total absence of handles, the flatness of the bottoms, and the general aspect of the fragments, it may be safely argued that a considerable number of the fragments formed part of large shallow dishes, or of large conical vessels….There is also a very coarse thick grayish ware, in which the leaves are much smaller (2 cm. or .79 of an inch in diameter), and the rows closer, so that the decoration looks as if it consisted of fish-scales….In a finer variety, of medium thickness (9 mm. or .35 of an inch), the leaves are long (5-8 cm. or 2 to 3 inches) and narrow (3-9 mm. or .12 of an inch to .35 of an inch), with parallel sides, and more projecting semi-circular tip. These leaves are in horizontal rows, and in each row they are simply juxtaposed, without overlapping….

"Section D

"Black, bluish, or red ware; decoration of prominent studs…applied to two or three different types of vases.

"*Class 9.* (a) Dark grey or black…ware, fine and thin (2-5 mm. or .79 of an inch to .20 of an inch inch) bowls, medium sized (12-16 cm. or 4.7 to 6 inches diameter) with short vertical neck (26-40 cm. or 10 to 16 inches broad), and projecting rim, decorated with rows of round studs in relief (3-6 mm. or .12 of an inch to .24 of an inch) in diameter)…The ground is painted white, and the studs are left black, or vice-versa.

"(b) Yellowish red clay ladle, 4-7 mm. (.16 of an inch to .28 of an inch) thick and 13 mm. (.51 of an inch) in diameter, decorated externally with studs (5-7 mm. or .20 of an inch to .28 of an inch in diameter) and provided with a curved tapering handle 14 cm. (5.5 inches) long, decorated with studs on both sides.

"(c) Coarse bluish ware, 6-8 mm. (.24 of an inch to .31 of an inch) thick; fragments of large flat-bottomed basins decorated with studs 8-12 mm. (.31 of an inch to .47 of an inch) in diameter.

"(d) Polished dark red ware, 8 mm. (.31 of an inch); fragments of the neck of a jar, partly decorated with rows of long narrow rectilinear projections (2 x 10 mm.) (0.8 of an inch x .39 of an inch).

"(e) A small 'hanging lamp' (10 cm.) (4 inches) in diameter.

"(f) Some fragments of a large basin about 60 cm. (24 inches) in diameter, of a coarse bluish clay (6-8 mm.) (.24 of an inch to .31 of an inch); are decorated with studs…15 mm. (.59 of an inch) in diameter, and 30 mm. (1.18 inches) distant from centre to centre…The base is flat and plain. An identical sherd was found in the ruins of Hagar-Kim…

"(g) The small fragments of a vessel of a yellowish red fine clay and decorated with studs…the vessel is a fine ladle, the bowl of which measures 10 cm. (4 inches) in diameter. Attached to it is an elegant curved tapering handle decorated with studs on both sides.

"Section E

"Yellow or grey ware, highly polished or burnished, but without ornament.

"*Class 10.* Pale yellow, buff or drab-coloured ware of medium thickness (4-8 mm.) (.16 of an inch to .31 of an inch), covered with a slip and highly polished or burnished, but not ornamented. Fragments of bowls of various sizes.

"*Class 11.* Light or dark grey ware of medium thickness (5-7 mm.) (.20 of an inch to .28 of an inch), highly polished. Bowls, 20-55 cm. (8 to 22 inches) in diameter… This class of burnished ware differs from preceding one in the colour, which is here either dark brown or dark grey. The vases are all bowls. Some have been completely re-constructed; of others only some fragments could be pieced together….

"Section F

"Red ware ornamented in various ways : with rope ornament, incised or in relief, and other band-ornaments.

"*Class 12*. Red ware of medium thickness (5-8 mm.) (.20 of an inch to .31 of an inch), decorated with cords or ropes (8 mm.) (.31 of an inch) wide, in relief.

"A jar of this fabric, 24 cm. in diameter (9.45 inches) and 25 cm. high (9.84 inches), on a base 12 cm. (4.72 inches) in diameter, was re-constructed out of a large number of fragments red on the outside and grey on the inside. It is provided with two vertical handles at its largest diameter. Its lower part, conical in shape, is surmounted by a spherical shoulder. The neck is missing; it was probably conical. It is decorated with a double rope-ornament, incised, running nearly horizontally round the upper part of the shoulder. A single rope-ornament runs also horizontally just above the handles, at an average distance of 8 cm. (3.15 inches) below the other.

"*Class 13*. Red ware of medium thickness (4-8 mm.) (.16 to .31 of an inch) decorated with one or two bands of four or five parallel incised lines. The fragments of red ware included in this class belong, with few exceptions, to basins, conical, or only slightly convex, with a flat base, sometimes provided with a foot-ring. As a rule, these wares have no handles, but their walls are perforated with holes evidently meant for cords or strings. They are sometimes decorated with one or two horizontal bands consisting of four or five parallel incisions in relief running round the neck at a distance of about 3 cm. (1.18 inches) from the brim.

"*Class 14*. Common red ware of medium thickness (4-10 mm.) (.16 to .39 of an inch); the greater part of the sherds are of the same shade of red on both sides, ranging from crimson to vermillion. In other cases, however, they are red on one side and yellowish on the other, or red on the outer side only, the other side being black or dirty grey, which is the natural colour of the clay…

"In this class are included a small number vases of various shapes and sizes. Their clay is covered with a thin slip of finer clay of a more or less deep scarlet…(and the shape of) a small pot with a flat base, conical body, and no rim (was reconstructed).

"*Class 15*. Red ware of medium thickness (4-7 mm.) (.16 to .28 of an inch); painted in darker red. Bowls.

"Among the various styles of decoration of the Hal-Saflieni pottery the painted fabric remained in a very primitive state…nothing but the merest attempt at coloured decoration.

"(a) As a first example may be quoted several fragments of what appears to be a shallow cup. One of them is provided with a portion of a long horizontal handle. All the fragments, which are of a yellowish-red clay, are decorated on their concave side with deep red spots or discs evenly distributed all over the surface.

"(b) A better specimen is a deep bowl 13 cm. (5.12 inches) in diameter with outer surface decorated with two deep-red bands 12 mm. (.47 of an inch) broad, intersecting at right angles at the centre of the curved bottom, and prolonged as far as the neck, thus dividing the outer surface of the bowl into four equal panels.

"(c) In a fragment, apparently belonging to a large bowl 25 cm. (9.8 inches) in diameter, the decoration consists of vertical red bands, 7 cm. (2.76 inches) apart, painted on a yellowish-red ground, and terminating in a deep-red horizontal band running at the top of the neck.

"(d) There are also a few small red cups, the upper half of which is painted in deeper red than the lower half.

"(e) A considerable number of convex fragments of red vases have the outer surface blotted in several places with a large black patch, apparently due to the action of the flames in an open fire, although several of the patches look as if they were painted as parts of a dark red pattern.

"Section G

"Various fabrics and shapes with decoration of incised lines, filled, as a rule, with white or red paint to emphasize the design.

"The motives of the decoration may be classified as follows:

"(a) simplest geometrical elements;

"(b) straight lines drawn at first almost at random, then nearly parallel;

"(c) elegant composite forms, lozenges, triangles, zigzags and lattices;

"(d) curvilinear motives, scrolls and meander bands;

"(e) naturalistic motives, leaves and animals.

Class 16. Light grey ware; granulated; 15-20 mm. (.59 to .79 of an inch) thick. The numerous fragments grouped in this class belong to a very large flat-bottomed vase of conical shape, slightly bulging near the middle part. Its largest diameter, at the top, measures about 60 cm. (23.6 inches) and its smallest one, at the base, 16 cm. (6.3 inches). It is provided near its upper edge with four projections like knobs elongated vertically, 75 cm. (29.5 inches) long and 25 mm. (.98 of an inch) broad; these served as handles. The thickness of the clay varies between 20 and 25 mm. (.79 and .98 of an inch), and from the aspect of the fracture in a certain number of the fragments it appears that this large vase was constructed by horizontal zones or belts, superposed on one another whilst the clay was still soft. The inner surface is blackened almost completely, possibly with smoke. The outer surface is of a drab colour and finely granulated. It is decorated with deep vertical incisions, evidently made with a sharp pointed tool before baking…They terminate at 2 cm. (.79 of an inch) from the rim, which is undecorated.

"These fragments were all found in the chambers of the hypogeum which were discovered in 1902, except one large one which, curiously enough, was discovered in one of the chambers lately excavated.

"*Class 17*. Light grey ware, granulated, of medium thickness (4-12 mm.) (.16 to .47 of an inch) decorated with parallel incisions, sometimes oblique, made before firing, less deep and further apart than those of Class 16… Besides two small bowls, 8 cm. (3.15 inches) and 12 cm. (4.72 inches) in diameter, decorated externally with oblique parallel incisions, only one other vase could be determined out of the sherds. It consists of two large fragments…The base is flat and measures 14 cm. (5.5 inches) in diameter and 8 cm. (3.15 inches) high. The profile is conical, broadened at the rim, with an upper diameter of 24 cm. (9.45 inches). In the interior of the vase, at the center of the base, is attached a quasi-cylindrical knob 2 cm. (.79 of an inch) in diameter and 3 cm. (1.18 inches) high, with a rounded top. The clay is creamy white, and the outside is decorated with vertical incisions terminating in an undulating line running along the upper edge which projects slightly outwards.

"*Class 18*. Grey or brown ware, fine and polished, of medium thickness (4-7 mm.) (.16 to .28 of an inch), decorated with incised ornament of intersecting straight lines, single or double, forming lozenges. The lines are filled with white.

"In this class have been grouped the fragments of several vases, apparently deep bowls with concave shoulders. There are no traces of handles or knobs.

"Class 19. Grey or brown ware, fine and thin (3-5 mm.) (.12 to .20 of an inch): decorated with rectilinear incisions filled with white, forming lozenges, triangles, zigzags, and lattices.

"This class includes a large number of fragments. On one convex fragment…the motive consists of lozenges alternately plain and sub-divided into small lozenges. On others…the incisions are deeper, the lozenges larger, and punctured at the center. There is also a fragment…decorated with six parallel vertical lines, on each side of which are incised adjacent equilateral triangles filled out with punctured dots. On another fragment, apparently a portion of a concave neck…the decoration consists of a broad band round the neck, formed of two parallel horizontal lines, and filled with two rows of fine zigzags.

"On a part of a neck a zigzag of larger size...is formed of sets of four parallel lines deeply incised in relief. The angles of the zigzag are nearly right angles. Other fragments are decorated with panels filled with fine small lattice.

"*Class 20.* Black ware, 3-5 mm. (.12 to .20 of an inch) thick, decorated with incisions filled with white...In this class are grouped small vases, for the most part bowls with concave neck, of fine black hand-burnished clay, 6 mm. (.24 of an inch) thick. It is decorated with curvilinear motives of nearly the same pattern...The incisions are very slight...Neither the design nor the ground has any other decoration.

"*Class 21.* Cream-coloured ware, only 3-5 mm. (.12 to .20 of an inch) thick. Incised meander-bands or curvilinear scrolls, with the contour (of the incisions) painted in red...The ground is painted in cream-white. Several fine specimens of bowls of medium size, 12-20 cm. (4.7 to 7.9 inches) in diameter.

"*Class 22.* Light grey or reddish-brown ware, only 3-8 mm. (.12 to .31 of an inch) thick. Curvilinear motives, incised scrolls, with short oblique strokes on one side, like one half of a 'herring-bone pattern.'

"The vases included in this class are all of the same shape, with rounded body on a ring-base, and conical shoulder and neck, and projecting rim. They differ considerably in size, varying from 45 cm. (17.72 inches) to 22 cm. (8.66 inches) in height, and from 10-30 cm. (3.94 to 11.8 inches) in diameter. Each vase is provided with a pair of horizontal projections perforated with two holes through which passed the suspending cords. The decoration is the same in all. It consists of a curvilinear motive formed, as in the case of the black ware, of a winding scroll. The outlines of the design are fringed with oblique short strokes, forming a 'herring-bone' pattern...Ten vases have been re-constructed, four of which are large and six small. Three others are incomplete.

"*Class 23.* Grey or red, fine and thin ware (1-3 mm.) (.04 to .12 of an inch), decorated with winding scrolls, outlined with incised lines on a ground punctured with dots. Outlines and dots are filled with white.

"The peculiarity of the ware of this class is that the motive of the design, instead of being geometrical as in the preceding classes, is taken from nature. It is a narrow winding leaf in the form of spiral, replacing the scrolls of the previous classes. The ground is filled with punctured dots, and the incisions are made either before or after baking. The shape of the vases...: the lower part is conical, terminating in a small flat base; the upper half is spherical, terminating in a short neck without rim.

"*Class 24.* Black, dark-brown or dark-grey ware, fine but thick (2-18 mm.) (.08 to .71 of an inch), and covered with fine slip. The surface is divided into horizontal panels alternately plain, and decorated with double spindles and winding scrolls. The ground is either (a) filled out with dots or hatches or zigzag, and design plain; or (b) plain, with the design filled out with dots, hatches or zigzag lines.

"This class contains the most interesting among the numerous forms of vases found at Hal-Saflieni, viz., what have been called 'hanging lamps'…Of this particular form of vase a considerable number were found in a more or less fragmentary condition. Fourteen were almost completely re-constructed, whilst of fourteen others, only portions more or less large could be recovered. Of the vessels completely re-constructed the largest measures 57 cm. (22 inches) in diameter, and 35 cm. (14 inches) in height, and the mouth has a diameter of 23 cm. (9.1 inches). The others decrease in size proportionately. The smallest has a diameter of only 7 cm. (2.76 inches), and a height of 4 cm. (1.57 inches). The body of the vases is spheroidal below and conical above; its upper part curves again inwards, and terminates in a slightly convex collar, the inner edge of which forms the mouth of the vessel. The upper part of the conical surface is provided with four small projections perforated horizontally with small holes, through which passed cords by which the vessel was suspended.

"The decoration is as follows: -- A broad band runs round the conical shoulder, and is defined above and below by a horizontal outline. The band is divided into panels by incised vertical lines. The panels are alternately plain and decorated with two incised spirals united by their lower extremities, representing more or less accurately…what appears to me a tulip accompanied with one or two pendulous leaves. The design is filled out with hatches, dots, or zigzags, and the ground is plain, or vice versa. The design is sometimes interrupted by the line which terminates the band, and is parallel to the sharp edge which separates the shoulder from the spherical body. The body has often a decoration different from that of the shoulder, and more care, as a rule, appears to have been bestowed on the decoration of the shoulder than on any other part of the vessel.

"The same motive of decoration, with little variation in the details, is common to all vases designated as 'hanging lamps.' …There is, however, one small hanging lamp, 9 cm. (3.54 inches) in diameter, decorated with studs…

"*Class 25*. Dark brown ware, fine and thin (6 mm.) (.24 of an inch), and covered with a slip. This class is represented only by one convex plate or cover, 25 cm. (9.8 inches) diameter, decorated on the concave side with lightly incised representations of buffaloes, and on the convex side partly plain and partly decorated with curvilinear bands crossed with parallel strokes.

"*Class 26.* (a) Dark grey ware, 8 mm. (.31 of an inch) thick. Convex plate or cover 18 cm. (7.09 inches) diameter, plain on the concave side, and decorated on the convex side with a plain disc at the centre from which radiate six projections like the tentacles of a polypus. The ground is punctured with dots.

"(b) Fine, polished, black, brown, or dark grey ware, covered with a slip, and decorated with curvilinear motives incised and filled with white. Fragments of plates or covers: there are a few covers of the same form and size, but plain."

All told, Professor Tagliaferro's Classes of pottery styles are most valuable because he documents the enormous amount of intact pottery and pottery fragments (reportedly, 20,000 fragments) found in the early excavations of the great burial tomb at Hal Saflieni. These fragments of pottery and whole items of pottery are direct evidence of use of pottery in these tombs, even though some funerary pottery was not used in the temples that adjoined them: this distinction suggests an understanding of the relation between temple and tomb.

As excavations continued on Malta, after Professor Tagliaferro's Classifications report was published in 1910, more and more potsherds and intact or restorable pottery and other *in situ* objects were found at other sites, buried in layers of sediment and soil in abandoned temples, the pottery and potsherds being especially profuse in the temple sites replicating the tombs and some of the pottery found inside them.

Some but not all.

There are some tomb pottery items that are not always replicated in the temples:

1) large slightly concave covers for large shallow convex bowls and plates; and

2) perforated areas beneath the rims of bowls used as hanging lamps.

"The total absence of lamps appeared to me as very strange," Professor Tagliaferro wrote, "in a subterranean building to which daylight had no possible access. No lamps or fragments of lamps of the usual forms…were found among the thousands of potsherds examined.

"It occurred to me, however, after much reflection, that the numerous vases of a peculiar shape, reconstructed wholly or part, and described hereafter, with rounded bodies surmounted by quasi-conical shoulders, and provided with four perforated lateral projections by which the vessels could be suspended, might, after all, be the lamps so long looked for…Unless I am mistaken, there are still perforations in the ceiling of one of the central chambers, 25 mm. (.98 of an inch) in diameter and 75 mm. (2.99 inches) deep, some of which may have served for the suspension of lamps."

"This class contains the most interesting among the numerous forms of vases found at Hal-Saflieni, viz., what have been called 'hanging lamps'...Of this particular form of vase a considerable number were found in a more or less fragmentary condition. Fourteen were almost completely re-constructed, whilst of fourteen others, only portions more or less large could be recovered. Of the vessels completely re-constructed the largest measures 57 cm. (22.44 inches) in diameter, and 35 cm. (13.78 inches) in height, and the mouth has a diameter of 23 cm. (9.05 inches). The others decrease in size proportionately. The smallest has a diameter of only 7 cm. (2.76 inches), and a height of 4 cm. (1.57 inches). The body of the vases is spheroidal below and conical above; its upper part curves again inwards, and terminates in a slightly convex collar, the inner edge of which forms the mouth of the vessel. The upper part of the conical surface is provided with four small projections perforated horizontally with small holes, through which passed cords by which the vessel was suspended."

The large covers found in the Hal Saflieni Hypogeum, which can be taken for shallow convex bowls, are not always found in the temples, as described by Professor Tagliaferro:

"*Notes on Classes 25 and 26*. In these classes are included covers of various sizes found among the potsherds. Only three are whole. The others, having been pieced together more or less completely, give a sufficiently clear idea of the shape and size. The shape is the segment of a sphere, and the diameter of the base in various specimens varies from 7-25 cm. (2.75 to 9.8 inches). The most interesting among them, and perhaps the most interesting object found at Hal-Saflieni, belongs to *Class 25*. It measures 25 cm. (9.8 inches) in diameter and 5 cm. (1.97 inches) in depth, and consists of nine fragments which, having been pieced together, form nearly two-thirds of the whole cover....the only pieces of Maltese pottery decorated with animals.

"The concave part (of one of the covers) is decorated with incised horned quadrupeds…The horns are long and slender, some in the form of a lyre, others thrown backward on the body like the horns of a ram. The animals are of two different sizes. Five large ones, nearly 10 cm. (3.94 inches) long, occupy the central part of the cover, and are distributed near the circumference. The heads are so small that they are barely distinguishable. The bodies are crossed with parallel strokes. The larger quadrupeds have on the lateral part of their body five small elliptical plain spots; the smaller animals have no such peculiarity.

"…Since the above was written, new excavations have been made at Hal-Saflieni, and other parts of the hypogeum are still being discovered. The sherds found so far are more or less similar to those discovered formerly, and belong to one or the other of the twenty-six classes above described. But a large jar, which has been almost completely re-constructed from a considerable number of large fragments found in one of the new chambers deserves to be put apart in a new class, as its style of decoration is composite, and partakes at the same times of *Classes 3, 7, 9 and 20.*" (Tagliaferro 1910)

Professor Tagliaferro's Classifications describe in such valuable detail only one area of only one tomb site. His Classifications are therefore even more astonishing. The extent of the pottery and sherds found in the Hal Saflieni Hypogeum tombs and in even the most damaged of the seven temple sites is noteworthy because the profusion of pottery is making a strong statement. The aim of the Walking Tour in this book is to help define that statement.

As the years of excavation went by, the pottery profusion being found did not abate but continued. Sir Evans some sixty years after the Tagliaferro report did describe "some potsherds of special interest" but his focus was on what he termed "complete" or intact pottery and restorable pottery pieced together from fragments found in the temple sites. Sir Evans presents a master list of pottery styles in *The Prehistoric Antiquities of the Maltese Islands, A Survey*, published in 1971.

What kind of pottery predominated inside the temples?

The Sir Evans Survey of multiple temple sites on Malta presents probable dates for first settlement on the Maltese islands in the great Ghar Dalam cave. The architectural footprint of each of the seven UNESCO World Heritage temples toured in this book followed each other in time, and divided into Cultural Phases.

The Hal Saflieni Hypogeum, the Red Skorba temple prototype, Mgarr at Ta' Hagrat, Kordin III, Ggantija, Hagar Qim, Mnadjra, and Tarxien all fall within set parameters of time and style, known as Cultural Phases, as shown below:

Ghar Dalam	5000 – 4500 B.C.
Red Skorba	4400 – 4100 B.C.
Zebbug	4100 – 3800 B.C.
Mgarr	3800 - 3600 B.C.
Ggantija	3600- 3300/3000 B.C.
Saflieni	3300 - 3000 B.C.
Tarxien	3300/3000 – 2500 B.C.

Dates are from: Bonano, A., Bartolo, J., Mintoff, M., Malta An Archaeological Paradise, M.J. Publications, Valletta, 1993.

This theoretical dating was devised around the mid-1950s based on the early excavations and site work by Sir John Evans, with important adjustments in Sir Evans' Cultural Phases made through the later work of Professor David Trump in his 1961-1963 excavations at Skorba. Professor Trump's finds at Skorba revised Sir Evans' earlier chronology which had placed the Zebbug Phase after the Mgarr Phase. Before the excavation of Skorba by Professor Trump began, Sir Evans believed that Mgarr was older than Zebbug, and for Sir Evans in the mid-1950s, the Red Skorba Phase did not yet even exist.

Professor Trump explains that for simplicity each Cultural Phase is named after a well-known temple, or tomb, constructed within each time frame, and cautioned that some well-known temples are not named as a Phase, but may be dated within another Phase named after a well-known predominant temple. For example, the later temples at Skorba are dated to the Ggantija Phase and not in the far earlier Red Skorba Phase.

In every Phase and in every site, be it temple or tomb, the amazing amount of pottery and the attendant abundance of potsherds, left behind, (recall that Professor Tagliaferro estimated 20,000 potsherds were found BY 1910 inside the Hypogeum of Hal Saflieni) all tell the tale of feasting in the temples. But what about feasting in the tombs?

The pottery tells the tale.

Hal Saflieni Hypogeum

Sir Evans' Survey master list of 1971 describes only 30 items on Professor Tagliaferro's list because Sir Evans listed only items found intact or which could be fully restored from sherds:

11 Carinated Hole-Mouth Bowls, 10 restored, 1 whole or "complete"

2 Covers, 1 restored, 1 complete

1 Open Bowl possibly used as a Cover

1 Bowl with Ring Base

1 Bowl with Low Foot

1 Biconical Pot

1 Footed Jar

2 Footed Vases

1 small Footed Jar

7 Carinated Bowls, 3 restored, 4 complete

2 Miniature Amphorae, 1 restored, 1 complete

Sir Evans describes the carved and lavish inner chambers sometimes called 'the Holy of Holies' where the potsherds described by Professor Tagliaferro were found. Sir Evans notes that the Tagliaferro items described above were all found in the inner 'Holy of Holies' and not in the other areas of the Hal Saflieni Hypogeum such as the ancient entrance aboveground that was still blocked from access in Tagliaferro's day. Sir Evans reports that Sir Zammit observed during later excavations there, that the ancient entrance to the Hal Saflieni tombs, before the entrance was blocked during a 1902 construction project, featured a trilithon and low windows carved in standing slabs (Evans 1971).

See a reconstructed sketch of the ancient trilithon entrance on: heritagemalta.org

The Hal Saflieni Hypogeum perhaps had a modest beginning in natural caves found on the Paola hillside, caves that were used for burials. The expanded use of these natural caves into spacious hand-carved chambers continued from c. 4000 B.C. to the end of the temple building around 2500 B.C.

After 2500 B.C. the underground tombs may have had some uninvited visitors and certainly had its own mysterious and forbidding places. Sir Temi Zammit reported finding a sudden chasm when attempting to go down a set of stone steps from the inner hall leading, or so he assumed, to the bottom third level of the Hypogeum: instead, his downward movement encountered a steep drop-off, and he found himself on a cliff-like edge beyond which no one could go (Evans 1971). And the Hal Saflieni Hypogeum after the temple builders had disappeared apparently had to endure the presence of visiting Bronze Age usurpers who occupied some of Malta's temples and tombs. Professor Tagliaferro reports a metal dagger found inside the Hal Saflieni Hypogeum belonging to the Tarxien Cemetery Phase: there was no metal used on Neolithic Malta and no such weaponry of the temple builders has ever been found.

As the Classification work of Professor Tagliaferro definitively shows, a huge amount of grave goods and potsherds were found. What can these items tell us about why the temple builders carefully replicated the burial tombs?

"Pottery vessels decorated in intricate designs were excavated from the chambers. These may have been used as part of burial rituals or may have also carried grave goods placed close by the deceased. A considerable number of shell buttons, stone and clay beads as well as amulets were also collected during the excavations; possibly worn by the deceased upon burial. Little stone carved animals and birds which may have originally been worn as pendants, were also discovered at the site.

"The most striking finds from the Hal Saflieni Hypogeum are the stone, and clay figurines. These depict human figures which are seated, standing or even lying down. The most impressive of these figures is that showing a woman sleeping on a bed or 'couch', popularly known as the 'Sleeping Lady'…is a work of art in itself portraying a keen eye for detail. The 'lady' is depicted with her right hand clasping a pillow on which her head rests, whilst her left hand is resting gently on her right elbow. The bed she is lying on is slightly concave as though it is bending under the weight of the figure it is supporting." (heritagemalta.org)

Although the Hypogeum of Hal Saflieni remains a somber place of multiple burial sites, corridors leading nowhere or into a chasm, and dissembled skeletal remains, its figurines, pottery and potsherds point out a clear path to understanding why the UNESCO World Heritage temples on Malta were built and how they were used, beginning with the earliest known site, a temple prototype found on a hillside in the farming village of Skorba.

Red Skorba

It was a trail of potsherds, scattered over a hillside in the village of Skorba near Ta' Hagrat, which led Sir Temi Zammit's son, Captain Charles Zammit, to dig a test-trench there in 1937.

A longtime curiosity on the hillside in the farming village of Skorba was the tip of a half-buried megalith. Nearby were potsherds were underfoot in the fields where anyone could see unusually large slabs of quarried limestone forming part of a contemporary wall. The curious megalith could be seen poking upwards like a lone ancient arm of stone, so that long before Captain Zammit's test trench was dug, the megalith protruding from a mound of sediment, topsoil and potsherds, reached up from the hillside toward the sky, pointed like an ancient bookmark to hidden treasure below. If the lonely megalith could talk, it would have been been saying,

"Dig here!"

At that time, however, no one could have guessed that the entire prehistory of Malta lay in wait, in layer upon layer preserved beneath the topsoil and potsherds at Skorba.

Professor Trump later declared that "…this site was not only as important as any of the others for the part it played in uncovering the whole prehistory of Malta, it was more important than all the others put together." on heritagemalta.org

The great importance of Skorba lies in the archaeological stratigraphy whose contents document the ancient settlement of early Malta and how the temples evolved.

There were three most important discoveries among the many discoveries at Skorba:

1. A temple prototype consisting of two conjoined simple ovals;
2. Red slip pottery from an early Neolithic era (4400-4100 B.C.), not known to exist before the 1961-63 Trump excavation, a pottery style not found in the other six sites toured in this book; and
3. 'Hut of the Querns' whose apparently busy activity and date of origin may go further back than the Ggantija Phase (3600-3000 B.C.) to which it was assigned based on the presence of Ggantija-style pottery found *in situ* on the floor of the outbuilding hut. (Trump1966)

Captain Zammit's 1937 test-trench revealed a stone slab which was later identified as a stair step up to the inner area of a Ggantija-era buried temple, but due to limited resources at the time preventing a full-fledged excavation, Charles Zammit's test-trench and items found in it were duly noted before the trench was re-filled and covered over. That left undiscovered, for decades, the Red Skorba time period itself, the prototype oval temple sites, the straight stone wall nearby the ovals thought to be the longest and oldest stone wall found on Neolithic Malta, plus remains of the only domestic dwelling site ever found on Neolithic Malta, and two large temples and outbuildings from the later Ggantija Phase of temple building (3600-3000 B.C.).

Finally, during Professor Trump's 1961-1963 excavation at Skorba, the layers of Maltese prehistory were uncovered, revealing as Captain Zammit had sensed, the entire prehistory of Malta including the oval huts, the stone wall, the red slip pottery, the domestic dwellings, and the two large temples named after their positions, one to the west, named the Western temple, and one to the east, named the Eastern temple, uncovered *in situ* within the excavation area.

"When the East Temple was being cleared, three additional trenches were dug in the field to the east to check that there were no outlying structures like those found on the west. The central one of these (trenches) struck the face of a much earlier wall (of a building). When this building was cleared it proved to be the largest and most puzzling feature of the village…

"The main room is oval, maximum dimensions 8.40 x 5.4 m. internally (27.5 feet x 18 feet), with an entrance at its western end. Its eastern end was damaged by a much later trench…but in part at least the impress of its wall was preserved in the firm fill. South of this room, a smaller D-shaped one (a second oval room) measured 5.60 by 3.20 m. (18 feet x 10 feet). This room had no entrance at the surviving level. Outside these to the east and west were courtyards, probably open to the sky."

The immediate question: how were these simple oval structures used?

The answer is in the floor.

Even though the attendant courtyards were paved with large stones up to 50 cm. (almost 20 feet) in width in the eastern courtyard, and with pebble stones cobbling the western courtyard, the floor inside the ovals was anything but paved. Photographs of the floor inside the oval structure is startling to see because the floor is a rough, undulating surface as if caught by a camera in stop-motion, like stone waves on the bed-rock. See photos of the undulating stone floor in the book, *Skorba*, by David Trump, *A Report for the Society of Antiquaries of London and Heritage Malta* (Trump 1966).

"But the (oval) rooms had no prepared floors, bed-rock apparently having served the purpose despite its great irregularity…Even in its deepest gulleys (of the floor) there was no sign of leveling up with soil or anything else. The substantial sherds of restorable vessels coming from well down in them (the gulleys) would also exclude flooring of organic materials, planking, straw, or fleeces, since decayed. The cobbled surface of the western court sloped down gently to meet the bed-rock in the doorway of the North Room, excluding the possibility of a wooden floor at a higher level." (Trump 1966)

There were half a dozen goat skulls found inside the oval hut, and female figurines, but no hearths, and no human bones.

Hence the oval structures with their unusual flooring of rough, rolling, unpaved, almost undulating bed-rock, and an assortment of female figurines and goat skulls, would not be a comfortable dwelling place but a great abundance of animal bones, and the absence of hearths for cooking, taken together as indicators, strongly suggest that these two oval huts were set aside from daily life activities -- such as cooking and eating – and even walking over the floor would be an abnormal experience.

How then, if not for domestic dwelling, were these two oval structures used?

Their oval shape that replicates the natural burial cave holes of this early time, and the female figurines found inside, suggest a place set aside from domestic activity, as a temple prototype from the early Red Skorba Cultural Phase of 4400-4100 B.C. that foreshadowed the great megalithic temples to come, continuously, over the next thousand years and more until it all ended around 2300 B.C.

Red Skorba Pottery

Sir Evans explained in his 1971 Survey that Professor Trump's surprise find at multi-layered Skorba was the red slip pottery, previously not even suspected to exist. The red pottery style so unique to the early site was named Red Skorba, and became a new Cultural Phase inserted into the early activity on Malta, dating from c. 4400-4100 B.C.

Professor Trump describes Red Skorba pottery items found in each of the two oval structures that were positioned North and South, side by side on the site, but the two ovals were separate rooms, not connected by an entrance:

"A great quantity of broken pottery of pure RSk. (Red Skorba) type, including a number of restorable vessels, was recovered from the level immediately above rock in both rooms…In the North Room were found fragments of figurines, four of terracotta, one nearly complete, and one of stone, all showing the same stylized female figure…Domestic animal bones were in abundance, almost equalling the pottery in volume." (Trump 1966)

Sir Evans in his later Survey of 1971 describes some of the Red Skorba pottery:

"The extensive ceramic material from Skorba is of especial interest because of two ceramic phases (Grey and Red Skorba) which were discovered for the first time on this site and were named after it. It was here too that pottery of the Ghar Dalam Phase (5000-4500 B.C.) was found in undisturbed levels.

"Several of the Red Skorba vases are ladles with the characteristic M-shaped handles…One of these, found in one of the oval shrines of this phase, had wear on the lip which indicated that it had been used by a right-handed person as a ladle.

"A fine biconical vase had a pair of the distinctive trumpet-lugs set vertically just below the rim…Also from the Red Skorba phase, and again from the eastern building, is a fine large carinated bowl decorated with a few incised circles on the carination…

"Finally, there is a squat, globular, necked jar with a pair of perforated horseshoes set high on the shoulder.

The Red Skorba pottery found inside the oval huts suggest that the mourning feast with all the attendant pottery used to prepare and serve food, may have begun in these small oval structures, one of which may have been an outbuilding prep room, which were not domestic dwellings that anyone would want to live in, but by the very unusual floor plan the ovals were deliberately set aside from the everyday activity of daily life.

'Hut of the Querns'

A further statement of how the temples were used is found in a later era at Skorba in the 'Hut of the Querns' where 11 querns and 120 sea shells were found just sitting there, *in situ* on the outbuilding floor. As if work would resume at any moment.

The 'Hut of the Querns' was constructed of mud-bricks built in a rectangular shape. It was not part of other temple outbuildings near the West Temple which dated from the Ggantija Phase of 3600-3000 B.C.

Hence the 'Hut of the Querns' could be older that the Ggantija Phase, perhaps dating back to the Mgarr era of 3800-3600 B.C. or earlier.

What is the significance of the 11 querns and 130 shells found in 'Hut of the Querns' and the busy activity these items imply?

Querns consisted of two stones for grinding, one stone a kind of large bowl and the other stone the actual grinder. See photo of a Skorba quern found in 'Hut of the Querns' in the book, *Skorba*, by David Trump, *A Report for the Society of Antiquaries of London and Heritage Malta* (Trump 1966).

The large pile of seashells was used in making amulets and necklaces for farewell grave goods that would be placed, sometimes in the hands, of the beloved deceased.

"There was a small 'keeping place' outlined in stones just inside the door and another even smaller pit in the eastern corner…which contained 130 shells of Venus sp. and one limpet, very tightly packed. There was no permanent hearth.

"...it was built largely in mud-brick...Fragments of individual bricks were recognized in the debris filling it...The floor was of beaten earth or clay, patched in places with a thin layer of torba.

"The lowest level of fill in it was extremely rich in charcoal and pottery, the latter including two small unbroken vessels and some ten others restorable from the surviving sherds...No less than eleven querns, all of the local coralline limestone, were found here too, most notably a large one with its rubber beside it in the angle of the wall repair.

"Its date is fixed in the Gg. (Ggantija Phase, 3600-3000 B.C.) by the occupation debris on its floor, left to lie there when it was destroyed by fire. Structurally, however, it is obviously older than the temple outbuildings, since these seal off all access to its entrance passage (on the center of the south-east side). It would be tempting to suppose that it was deliberately destroyed to clear the site for the temple. A further point on its date, obvious but important, is that material within its wall-thickness...must be earlier still. Though this is still within Gg. (Ggantija Phase, 3600-3000 B.C.), it shows many details of continuity from Mg. (Mgarr Phase, 3800-3600 B.C.)..."

Seaside Hagar Qim and Mnajdra temples also had outbuildings. Sir Zammit suggested that these outbuildings were used by 'temple attendants.' (Zammit 1994)

What were they doing?

From lithic and bone items found *in situ* in the outbuildings, it is likely that the Hagar Qim outbuildings were in use in similar ways as the 'Hut of the Querns' workshop and a similar workshop located west of the West temple at Skorba. The 'Hut of the Querns' described by Professor Trump is situated north of the West Temple. In these outbuildings and others, various lithic and bone implements were found *in situ*. See photos and lists of *in situ* lithic and bone tools in Abell 2007, on etd.ohiolink.edu.

The work of the 'temple attendants' is suggested by the large number of grinding querns in the apparently busy 'Hut of the Querns' at Skorba and in the other temple outbuildings as well.

As reported by Sir Evans (Evans 1971:37), 120 seashells and 10 querns made of coralline limestone were found in the mud-brick hut with torba flooring located west of the West Temple at Skorba, a workshop similar to the 'Hut of the Querns' dated also to the Ggantija Phase (3600-3000 B.C.) at the Neolithic Skorba site.

What do the many querns and seashells suggest about the use of the temples?

In the magnificent and lavish Tarxien temple, 14 querns were found intact, in addition to fragments of other querns that were found in broken fragments. In addition to the large number of querns, Sir Evans describes 54 complete, almost-complete, and restored items of pottery found at Tarxien, plus 13 decorated "sherds of special interest."

"Numerous querns and rubbers were found during the excavation of the Tarxien temples. Some of these were of local coralline limestone, and these were usually circular in shape; others were of a dark-gray volcanic lava and oval in shape (saddle-querns). Zammit records (1930) that at least 14 of these were found complete, with their upper stones for rubbing, as well as broken examples. The largest querns averaged about 50 cm (almost 20 inches at 19.685 inches) in length, 37 cm (almost 15 inches at 14.566 inches) in breadth and 20 cm (almost 8 inches at 7.87 inches) in thickness." (Evans 1971)

At Kordin III a spectacular trough was found just sittng on the ground near an apse, containing separate spaces for seven individual querns, the container of querns being as big as, and in the shape of, a small boat, kayak or canoe, and smaller querns and mortars were also found.

At Kordin II: There were no complete or restored vases from this structure but an axe amulet of hard gray-green stone was found, plus two items made of bone, 200 pieces of flint and chert, and querns, mortars and rubbers.

Found inside the seaside temple of Mnajdra were a large number of Tarxien Phase pottery items and stone grinders: "The pottery, mostly from Ashby's excavations, which is preserved in the National Museum offers the following picture…4 sherds of Zebbug type, 1 sherd of Mgarr type, 34 of Ggantija type, and no less than 700 of Tarxien type" (Evans 1971) and a quern and various rubbers and grinders made of stone were found in an early excavation in 1909.

In later excavations at Mnajdra, "A number of querns were found, and also pebbles which had been used with them as rubbers. There were a number of mortars and rough stone vessels." (Evans 1971)

In a description of pottery dated to the various Cultural Phases at Skorba, Professor Trump refers to the Zebbug Phase (4100-3800 B.C.) and notes that from this early era,

"Querns of coralline limestone continue freely." (Trump 1966:37)

Professor Trump refers to the early Mgarr Phase (3800-3600 B.C.) at Skorba when reporting that,

"Of coralline limestone were a great number of querns, grinders, and rubbers of various sorts. One hard pebble looked more like a hone than a polisher." (Trump 1966:40)

Food preparation, using querns and mortars for grinding grains and seeds, and using the rough, sloping small stone vessels for baking, was done in the outbuildings to prepare and bake food in these individual baking cups, and presented at the mourning feast in bowls, plates, jugs, jars, ladles and amphorae that temple sherds represent. Bones and obsidian, flint and chert could also be sharpened on querns for a sharp cutting edge for axes and carving knives. Clumps of red ochre would be ground into powder for mixing paint for temple and tomb.

Imagine Sir Zammit's 'temple attendants' busily at work in the outbuildings, perhaps at Kordin III or at a Skorba temple in the Ggantija Phase of temple use, as they worked to grind seeds, chickpeas and grains on large saddle querns to prepare enough food for the mourning feast, or grinding a lump of red ochre into a fine red powder to make paint to touch up an apse wall, or perfecting the smooth beauty of grave goods such as a greenstone axe amulet and the symmetry of a shell necklace.

And as Sir Zammit suggests, a large number of people inside the tombs could not be accommodated for a mourning feast, and so the feast of farewell and celebration of the life of the deceased, was located in another place, a place nearby, reached by a connecting and symbolic path lined with trilithons as at Ggantija, a short walk that led away from the close, dark tomb to an open-air courtyard inside the nearby temple whose outbuilding could amply provide, as at Tarxien, baking cups for 32 people.

The querns in just one temple outbuilding named by its excavators 'Hut of the Querns' thus tell the tale that much prep work was going on there, for use inside the temple: grinding grains and seeds and perhaps imported chickpeas to prepare the reviving food for mourners gathered in the inner courtyard of the temple where the cooking platforms held small sizzling stone bowls in place over pits of fire, stone pits built into the inner courtyard floor, as found intact at Tarxien and Hagar Qim, where the temple fire did not conjure up some kind of exotic Neolithic ritual but was just used to cook food.

Skorba in all its Phases across a thousand years of time presents evidence that pottery and stone tools such as querns were used in a place set aside from everyday domestic life. In the temple prototype from the early Red Skorba Phase, the more complex form of temples to come was forecast in its oval huts, where female figurines reminisent of sculpted Cycladic figures, and pottery, found *in situ* are an obvious early example of stepping beyond the routines of daily life to enter into the mystery and sorrow.

Ta' Hagrat Mgarr

In the University of Malta Library, Sir Themistocles Zammit's excavation report of the Mgarr temple appears in *Bulletin of the Museum, Vol. 1, Nro. 1*, published by the Director of the Museum, Valletta, in 1929 and reprinted in 1935, in which Sir Zammit gives his own account of the finds at the megalithic temple of Mgarr.

Sir Zammit describes the greatly disturbed site:

"*Ta Hajrat* means 'stoney district,' *Hajrat* being the plural of *Hajra*, a stone. In 1916, a mound of large stones emerging from the soil under large carob trees in a field called *Ta Hajrat* was pointed out…The owner of the site informed…that numerous megaliths stood once close to the mound, they were quarried for a number of years in order to clear the field.

"Cartloads of potsherds, found among the ruins, were collected and pounded to dust between large stones to be used for concreting house-roofs in the district."

And just as destructive were the carob trees.

"The ruins suffered considerably from the growth of large carob trees of which the thick roots broke and displaced the stones.

"What survives of the ruins found hidden under the mound, are the walls of two distinct blocks of buildings, the one to the south made of rough megaliths, and a smaller one to the north-east built up of smaller stones.

"It is quite possible that the south-western group of buildings may have served the purpose of a sanctuary in the neolithic period, but the northern block has more the appearance of a group of dwellings with stone walls built up to a moderate height.

"The material which mostly helped to date the site was undoubtedly the pottery. The Maltese prehistoric pottery is happily easy to classify when one is conversant with the collection of material from Hal Saflieni, Hagar Qim, and Tarxien. Although appearing in a great variety of form and decoration, the Neolithic ware is unmistakable.

"Among the most interesting bits of pottery, the following are worth describing:

"Decorated Handle, 'modelled to represent a ram's head with spiral horns';

"Clay Bowls: three miniature clay bowls and two larger ones, a yellowish clay disk, and a model of an amphora were saved from the debris…

"We may say at once that the sherds were recognized as similar to the ware met with in the Maltese islands, at Jigantea, Hagar Qim, Mnaidra, Tarxien, Hal Saflieni, etc.

"From the shallow field in which the ruins stood for thousands of years, no complete vessels were obtained, but the shape of various utensils could well be made out from the larger sherds.

"1. *Plain Black Ware*

"Sherds of this ware were abundant, some of them, better preserved, retained their original shiny surface, the rest, exposed to all sorts of weather, had become dull and gray in color.

"Of the decorated ware, the following types, well represented in the Tarxien and Hypogeum collection, were met with:

"2. *Studded Ware*

"A number of specimens of this type of pottery were obtained…some have comparatively small circular black studs on a polished surface, others have larger and less regular black discoid studs stuck on a surface smeared with a white paste; others have tiny spindle-shaped bands stuck on the surface instead of studs.

"3. *Pitted Ware*

"The pitted ware may be considered as the reversed condition of the studded ware, in as much as a contrast of shadows is in both cases aimed at. Very often, the shadow effect is enhanced, in the pitted ware, by painting the flat surface white, leaving the pits in their original black colour. At Ta' Hajrat, the pitting of the surface is of two varieties:

"A) either the surface is covered with equidistant deep semi-lunar notches, as if produced by a section of a reed;

"B) or the polished surface is impressed with fusiform notches in a slanting direction but parallel to each other. In some cases the notches are far between, in others they are numerous and close to each other.

"4. *Typical Handles*

"If there is a feature characteristic of Stone Age Maltese pottery it is the handle made up of two flat triangular bands attached to the vessel by their base and joined at the apex forming a more or less obtuse angle. Potsherds with handles of this description, numerous at Ta Hajrat, are first class evidence of the use of the building in the best Neolithic period." (Zammit 1929, reprinted 1935)

The disturbed Mgarr site nonetheless revealed to Sir Zammit an abundance of potsherds from all five Neolithic Cultural Phases:

Sir Evans writes:

"The sherds, or at least a large collection of them, found in the original excavations are conserved at the National Museum as follows:

Ghar Dalam type:	8
Zebbug type:	1,006
Mgarr Type:	200
Ggantija type:	200
Tarxien type:	660

For the 1,006 fragments found from the Zebbug Phase (4100-3800 B.C.), "88 have decoration painted in red on a buff ground."

For the 200 fragments found dating from the Mgarr Phase (3800-3600 B.C.), there are 6 fragments painted in a grayish-white paint.

For the 660 fragments found dating from the Tarxien Phase (3300/3000-2500 B.C.), there are "examples of scratched wares, both normal and with 'dot and line patterns' studded, pitted, channeled, and relief-decorated wares."

In his 1971 Survey of whole and restored pottery, Sir Evans lists and describes the following found at Mgarr:

<u>Bowl, restored</u>. Brown ware, only moderately hard-fired, with polished surface, reddish-brown to black color, two narrow lugs set near the flat base, decorated with scratched-line design, height of 4.5 cm (1.77 inches).

<u>Cup, restored</u>. Convex shape, small flat base, coarse reddish-brown ware with three small knobs set below the rim, 4 cm (1.57 inches).

2 Miniature Cups, complete. 1) Irregular shape, with thick walls, dark gritty and well-fired ware, mostly red with black areas, below the rim is an incised horizontal line with vertical incised lines beneath, 3.5 cm (1.57 inches) and 2) Rough dark ware, rough surface, 2 cm (0.787 of an inch).

Miniature Shouldered Bowl, complete. Sides are slightly concave, everted rim, dark, well-fired ware, dark brown to black colors, smooth surface but not polished, 2.7 cm (1.06 inches).

2 Miniature Jars, complete. 1) Brown, soft ware, surface smoothed and polished, 4 cm (1.57 inches) and 2) Flat base, no handles, roughly made, coarse buff clay, unpolished, height 3.4 cm (1.34 inches).

Ram's-Head Handle, part of a Bowl. Fine ware, polished, surface worn at the top, length 8 cm (3.15 inches), head 2.5 cm (almost one inch at 0.984 of an inch).

Even though greatly damaged, with some of the Neolithic pottery ground up long ago and completely destroyed, still the pottery and sherds and the temple model found at Mgarr carry on the oval design and tale of Red Skorba and 'Hut of the Querns' in preparing and cooking food for the mourning feast not inside the tombs but inside the adjoining temple.

Kordin III

Blame it on carob trees flourishing inside the Mgarr temple, blame it on local Maltese grinding up the ancient pottery for roofing material, by the cartload, but great damage occurred at Mgarr.

Nonetheless the damage incurred there pales in comparison to the disturbance of the temple sites on Kordin Hill.

Worse than flourishing carob trees pushing their roots through the floors of the Mgarr temple, worse than Ta' Hagrat locals grinding up the ancient pottery for roofing, was the damage inflicted on the Kordin sites by intruders plundering slabs of quarried limestone. And then there was the bombing of Malta during WWII.

When the protective modern wall of cement blocks, built to surround and protect the Kordin ruins, was partly knocked down by the bombing, intruders could easily enter the site and plunder the already quarried and cut limestone.

Even after the gated and padlocked wall into Kordin III was repaired, Sir Evans in his 1971 Survey notes the ongoing disappearance of whole sites that had been reported by earlier archaeologists, as well as stone walls that disappeared, large stones just gone that had once been the top half of apse walls, and the clay floors and stone steps into inner chambers as reported by archaeologists in the 1800s and early 1900s, but never seen again.

In 1896, Maltese archaeologist Caruana reported finding five temple sites, but by 1908-1909, and in 1913, three of these sites could not be found.

In addition to the disappearing sites, in the 1913 excavation, archaeologists Ashby and Peet did not find the torba floors in Kordin I which they had assumed must have been laid. They further assumed that the earlier excavation by Caruana must have removed the torba floors, "leaving no trace."

In Kordin II, Ashby theorized about an inner entrance to one of the chambers "…but there was no direct evidence to support this, since a stretch of walling is missing here…."

"A rough arc of wall…on the south-west side (of Kordin II) suggests the remains of a second oval chamber (perhaps later mutilated)."

In 1901, "…Mayer speaks of an entirely enclosed space. By Ashby's time, however, part of the north-east wall had disappeared…" in Kordin II.

"To the south (in Kordin II) were the mutilated remains of several other rooms," Sir Evans reports in his 1971 Survey.

In Kordin III, missing or disappeared stones continue a baffling story of human intrusion and the damaging passage of time.

Sir Evans reports:

"To the west of the entrance to room 1 the orthostats of the façade are very much broken, but still *in situ*. Two footing blocks were recognized at the time of the excavation (1913) beyond the point where all traces of the uprights cease. These cannot now be seen."

"The forecourt (of Kordin III) was paved with small slabs of stone of irregular shape…everything points to the probability that the edge of the paving followed a regular curve to meet the façade again at its south-west end. The paving itself had disappeared over much of the western side of the forecourt…The forecourt is now (1958) completely overgrown and it is impossible to make out any details."

Inside the trefoil temple at Kordin III, "…the passage widens to 2.25 m. (7.38 feet), the walls here consisting of two upright slabs, one on each side…The tops of both slabs show the marks of wedges which have been used on them at some relatively recent time for the purpose of quarrying stone."

Inside Kordin III, an apse wall "…consisted of the usual large orthostats…whilst the dividing wall consists of small, roughly rectangular slabs…set on foundation blocks…On top of these was set coursed masonry consisting of rough blocks…One course was preserved in (area) 3 and two courses in (area) 4, when the excavations were made, but they have now almost entirely disappeared."

At Kordin III, "Room 3…must be entered…by a paved passage formed by three pillar-like stones on each side. The middle one of these on each side was set at right angles to the other two and projected at 0.15 m. (0.492 of one foot) into the passage. (The right-hand one had disappeared by 1958.) Complete with its now-vanished lintel, this arrangement would compare with the window-like slabs met with in…Mnadjra and Hagar Qim."

At Kordin III, at "the back of room 3 are three niches…which were not all identical in construction. Two of them…are formed of upright slabs and pillars. The eastern-most…consisted of a covering slab, 1.37 m. (4.49 feet) by 1.01 m. (3.31 feet) by 0.18 m. (0.59 of one foot), supported on two pillars 0.86 m. (2.82 feet) high which stand against the back wall of the apse, but detached from it. The covering slab of this niche was found *in situ*, but was cracked in three places. It has since disappeared.

"Immediately adjacent to the west…is (the second niche) of which the covering slab had disappeared at the time of Ashby's excavation (1913).

"The third niche which lies immediately to the north-west…is a good deal smaller, only about 0.60 m. wide (1.97 feet) and 0.60 m. (1.97 feet) deep. One side is formed by the pillar…which Peet and Ashby thought (almost certainly correctly) to be probably a part of the original structure of the apse wall (1913) whilst the other (side) was formed by three stones piled one on top of the other, the middle one projecting slightly inwards, perhaps to support a shelf. (The three stones cannot now be seen)."

"Ashby (1913) noted the presence in all the chambers of large fallen blocks of stone. Some of those found…had stone wedges underneath them, as though they had been moved comparatively recently. He surmises that they come from the upper part of the apse walls…and in this he is surely correct…"

In the northern temple area, at "…the north-east corner of the room is a doorway 0.73 m. (2.40 feet) in width, with a threshold block 0.23 m. (0.75 of one foot) wide, which was said to be on a level with the rock floor of the room but is now not visible."

"…one reaches an irregular room…whose stone walls, except for the foundations, had already been removed when Peet and Ashby investigated it. The modern boundary wall which runs east-west…was probably built of the material removed from this part of the building (1913). This boundary wall itself has now gone, all but the footings."

There was reported the "remains of two superimposed clay floors. The first was 0.10 m. (0.33 of one foot) to 0.20 m. (0.66 of one foot) thick and 0.75 m. (2.46 feet) to 0.90 m. (2.95 feet) below ground level. Below this came a further 0.08 m. (0.262 of one foot) of clay and soil, and then the second clay floor, 0.02 m. (0.065 of one foot) thick, then another 0.12 m. (0.393 of one foot) of soil, then the rock. At another point a layer of fine black soil with a large quantity of pottery and worked flints was found. Here there was, however, no trace of the clay floors."

Furthermore, to add to the sense of desolation so easily sensed lingering around the Kordin III site, the Royal Navy Detention Barracks, a military prison now made into a museum, still looms over the ancient stones. The Neolithic landscape of Kordin Hill once commanded a spectacular view of the Grand Harbor, but in 1958 a factory was being built that blocked the view of ancient splendor of the harbor and the sea beyond, all of this imparting a kind of mysterious feeling that lingers like grief in the surviving stones themselves.

In his 1971 Survey, Sir Evans describes the devastation on Kordin Hill as he found it in 1958 when he himself excavated the Kordin sites, almost 100 years after a limited excavation in 1840 that, like the Skorba site, Kordin Hill was not further explored at that time.

"Several groups of buildings belonging to the prehistoric period have been noted at various points on Kordin Hill, and have been at one time or another the subject of study and, in some cases, of excavation. Mention was first made of some of these by Leith Adams…in 1870 and by Vassalo…in 1876. The latter remarks that a small area of one of the monuments was excavated in 1840, and that an entrance and apses constructed of large stones were found. Caruana…in 1896…also noted that the terraces of Kordin promontory 'were known long ago to be strewn with the relics of cyclopean structures entombed under mounds of earth and rubbish, which had been allowed to accumulate upon them' and that the task of clearing these remains was undertaken so far back as 1840, but for reasons unaccountable to me the work was abandoned shortly after it was begun.' He drew attention to their importance in his *Report* of 1882… and in his article of 1896…he mentions the existence of five groups, of which he gives the plans of two which he had partly excavated in 1892, and which, he says, are the only ones which 'present any structure.' These are the western and eastern groups, here referred to as Kordin I and Kordin II…

"Some new work was done by Zammit in the western and by Ashby and Peet in the eastern and western in 1908 and 1909…but they were unfortunately unable to locate the other three mentioned by Caruana."

Unable to find Antonio Caruana's other three temple sites, Zammit, Ashby and Peet did, instead, find another temple site to the south of Kordin I and II, a site not identified in Caruana's site descriptions and which was at first named Corrodino South, but came to be called Kordin III.

In May 1909 the first excavation of Kordin III began.

Like the Hal Saflieni Hypogeum, like Mgarr, like Hagar Qim and Mnadjra, the Kordin III site had been terribly damaged, mainly by human intruders in search of quarried limestone, in addition to the ever-flourishing carob trees, and the well-intended clearing of rubbish prior to excavation work.

"It is to be regretted that the Hypogeum at Hal Saflieni has been rifled on more than one occasion, and that the archaeological treasures it contained have been thrown into such a state of confusion as to render its scientific exploration a matter of extreme difficulty. It is also a matter of regret that the clerical duties of the late Father E. Magri, S.J., who was entrusted with the exploration of the hypogeum, prevented him from…the personal supervision of the sifting of the rubbish which nearly filled the hypogeum. The work was entrusted to untrained workmen, and it is only too probable that a considerable number of small objects may have escaped their attention, even supposing that the tedious work…was always done conscientiously."

Like the buried Skorba site, the Kordin III temple was buried beneath a visible "mound of soil and stones from which the tops of a number of larger slabs could be seen emerging." (Evans 1971)

Also much like Skorba, Kordin III when excavated revealed buried temples which were filled, as was Kordin I and II, with sherds, some from Kordin III dating from the early Zebbug Phase (4100-3800 B.C.).

There was no whole, intact pottery found in the Kordin I and II sites. The excavation of Kordin III proved difficult due to "the presence of large, loose blocks of stone in the centre of the rooms, which probably represented the collapsed superstructure."

Even though potsherds were found at Kordin I and II that are "assignable to the Mgarr, Ggantija, and Tarxien phases," due to the damage in the sites, the building dates of Kordin I and II cannot be determined.

"Kordin III is in a rather different category. The pottery now in the Museum from the excavations carried out by Peet and Ashby on the site includes sherds "assignable to the Zebbug, Mgarr, Ggantija, and Tarxien phases (including red-painted fragments of Zebbug type)." A test-trench dug in 1954 revealed five layers of undisturbed pottery, potsherds and other deposits, each underground layer separated by beaten-earth floors:

"The topmost layer consisted of soft, loose earth packed around the stones of the wall, and produced pottery of Tarxien type. Below this came a second level of more compact dark earth 0.10 m. (0.0328 of one foot) deep, with Ggantija pottery. The third level was separated from this by the first of the beaten-earth floors. It was 0.20 m. (0.656 of one foot) deep, consisted of hard dark earth and like the level above contained pottery of the Ggantija type. Below this came the second beaten-earth floor and then a further deposit of hard dark earth, 0.15 m. (0.492 of one foot) deep, containing a mixture of pottery with narrow cut-out patterns (in) Zebbug and Ggantija pottery. Below the third beaten-earth floor the earth continued for a depth of 0.20 m. (0.656 of one foot), ending abruptly at bedrock. This earth was also hard and dark, becoming darker toward the bottom where it was very black. This level produced pottery with both broad and narrow cut-out patterns, which could be regarded as a mixture of types proper to the Zebbug and Mgarr phases."

Like Professor Tagliaferro before him, Sir Evans gives detailed descriptions of pottery styles. But unlike Tagliaferro, Sir Evans describes whole or restored items. From the three Kordin Hill sites, he also cites some sherds "that are of special interest" and objects such as lithic tools and querns:

At Kordin I: There were no complete or restored vases from this structure, but found were a grayish-green axe pendant, a small flint arrowhead, scrapers made of "poor flint or chert" and flakes with triangular points.

At Kordin II: There were no complete or restored vases from this structure but an axe amulet of hard gray-green stone was found, plus two items made of bone, 200 pieces of flint and chert, and querns, mortars and rubbers.

At Kordin III: a restored narrow-neck jar with two handles and two string-hole lugs below the neck, a restored biconical pot, a restored deep carinated bowl with a polished surface colored brown with reddish brown and black decoration, a restored carinated bowl with missing handle, a restored large carinated polished bowl painted red, a restored shouldered pot painted brown to black with a handle, a restored biconical bowl with triangular handle painted a "mottled red, brown and black," and five miniature cups."

Other items found at Kordin III include the big seven-quern trough that is sensational because as big as, and in the shape of, a boat such as a kayak or canoe, and there were also finds of smaller individual querns and mortars for grinding.

A large amount of pottery and sherds from the badly damaged Kordin sites -- so pillaged and damaged by well-intended early excavators, plundering intruders, World War II bombings, and the passage of time -- is cited by Sir Evans in his 1971 Survey:

Zebbug type: 12   (of which 3 are painted)

Mgarr Type: 32

Ggantija type: 164

Tarxien type: 351

Two curious finds at Kordin III include a partial female figurine and 200 pieces of flint and chert…almost all scrapers…and "a small conical stone 57 mm. (2.24 inches) high, 3 cm. (1.18 inches) in diameter at the base. Near the apex are two small, round depressions side by side, each 5 mm. (0.196 of an inch) in diameter and 2 mm. (0.078 of an inch) apart…The object gives the impression of a rough statuette." (Ashby 1913 in Evans 1971)

Ggantija

Torri Tal Gganti

The locals called the place "Torri Tal Gganti" meaning "Tower of the Giants." Island legend had it that Ggantija was built by giants, specifically by a woman giant, in the time when giants lived on Gozo.

Of the seven temples toured here in this book, the Ggantija temple on the island of Gozo is the first known site to be depicted in sketches and paintings in the 1820s soon after the first reeemmmoval of rubbish and sediment from the site.

The giant's stone towers, some poking out of mounds of earth and refuse like the lone megalith at Skorba, and its surrounding stone walls and altars in apses were documented by a German artist visiting from abroad, Charles de Brochtorff, whose many beautiful drawings of the chambers, corridors, and altars of Ggantija in color can be viewed on odysseyadventures.ca.

"It was the first of the Maltese prehistoric monuments to be cleared of the accumulation of earth and debris, which gave the appearance of mounds of rubble with a few upright stones projecting above." (Evans 1971)

The clearance of rubbish and sediment and soil in the 1820s was "…at the instigation of Colonel Otto Beyer, Officer in Charge of the island…The first description of the monument as revealed by excavation was published in Paris the same year…" (Evans 1971) and was entitled *Antediluvian Temple of the Giants (Temple antediluvian des giants)*.

In 1829, W.H. Smyth published sketches of the Gganti site in *Archaeologia*.

In 1836, Alberto de la Marmora published his account of the Gganti site based on his visit there in 1834, and the legendary archaeologist, Albert Mayr, used the Marmora account in his description of the site, citing Marmora's lay-out of Ggantija as sketched by a Maltese draftsman, Mr. C. Busuttil. Noteworthy among the artistic sketches of the Gganti site in the 1800s are "…twenty-one illustrations by a careful artist, C. de Brochtorff, which are preserved in the Royal Library in Valletta…" (Evans 1971)

Like other temple sites, however, excavations at Ggantija started and stopped.

"After its excavation (in 1827) the Ggantija remained for over a century uncared for and open to the depredations of men, animals, and the elements. During this period the condition of the monument deteriorated greatly, and especially many of the interior fittings, which were quite well preserved when the monument was first cleared, fell into decay or disappeared entirely.

"In 1933, however, the land on which the ruins stand was at length appropriated by the Government…A certain amount of clearing and restoration work was also carried out in the interior of the buildings, which were by then in a bad state of neglect and disrepair…and in 1958-9 the rebuilding of the western part of the wall of the terrace in front of the temples led to the discovery of much pottery of the Ggantija and Tarxien types and of part of a square, elaborately decorated, stone bowl." (Evans 1971)

The following potsherds tally compiled by Sir Evans in his 1971 Survey, is based on the excavations at Ggantija by Sir Zammit in 1933 and 1936:

Zebbug type: 22

Mgarr Type: 2

Ggantija type: 145

Tarxien type: 83

In 1954, eight trenches were dug at Ggantija. Trench A contained pottery from Ggantija and Tarxien Phases deposited beneath a torba floor, and at a lower level were found potsherds from the Zebbug and Ggantija Phases. Trench B contained only a few Ggantija-type potsherds but in a lower level of Trench B "a more abundant" deposit of potsherds was found, all of the Ggantija type. Trench C contained Ggantija-type potsherds and a lower level contained only red soil. Trench D was dug inside an apse in the northern temple and "…Here the floor-level was covered by a thin deposit of loose containing sherds of Tarxien type pottery. Below this there was a thin *torba* floor, immediately underneath which was a level of compact dark earth with sherds of pottery belonging to the Zebbug and Ggantija types. In Trenches G and H, "…Pottery was abundant but the only result was to confirm that below the superficial levels, the latest sherds to be found belonged to the Ggantija phase (although sherds of earlier phases were also common)." (Evans 1971)

Although Trench E is not mentioned in Evans' 1971 Survey, Trench F is cited as being excavated behind a niche in the inner temple, with the purpose of seeing if pottery and sherds from a later period than Ggantija type would be found.

"Quantities of sherds of Tarxien type were found here, which abundantly proved the point." (Evans 1971)

To further establish the date of construction of Ggantija, in whole or in part, the platform build outside the two temples as an entrance was examined by removing a section of the modern retaining wall. "This revealed that the platform was built up of large boulders piled on top of one another…though towards the top the stones got smaller and there were quantities of earth between the layers. Mixed in with these were large numbers of potsherds of Tarxien types…Throughout the depth of the whole deposit remarkable quantities of Tarxien sherds were found." (Evans 1971)

Sir Evans in his Survey of 1971 describes some of the *in situ* Ggantija pottery, found whole or restored:

<u>Footed Bowl, complete</u>. Medium-sized with a high footed base, with four semi-circular knobs set at intervals around the shoulder, hard-fired brown ware with highly polished surface, light yellow color with areas of black, foot has vertical parallel-line

decoration, and above the carination is a lightly incised curvilinear decoration, height 12 cm. (4.72 inches). Found in 1937 in the ruins of an altar in the front left apse of the north temple.

Carinated Bowl, restored. Medium-sized bowl with single triangular handle, medium-fired buff ware, smooth surface but unpolished, surface is buff color, interior is gray, this bowl contained 158 sea shells, height 11 cm. (4.33 inches) and maximum diameter is 20 cm. (7.87 inches).

Miniature Bowl, restored. Small bowl with one surviving 'wishbone' handle and the opposite handle restored, fine well-fired red ware with polished surface, the outer surface and inner surface near the rim are red, and the rest of interior is black, height 3.5 cm. (1.377 inches).

Biconical Jar, restored. Small jar of coarse dark brown ware, moderately hard-fired, smoothed but unpolished, upper part is concave with thick rim, lower part tapers to a flat base, decorated with parallel vertical slashes on thick part of rim, and four vertical strips of clay are set on the shoulder with incised horizontal slashes which may have been filled with white paste, height of 11 cm. (4.33 inches).

Spout. Small tubular spout of dark ware with light brown slip, polished.

Hagar Qim

Of the seven temples toured in this book, Hagar Qim presents an ancient *feeling*. For Hagar Qim stirs the emotions in a Romantic way in a most Romantic setting, high upon a clifftop beside the deep blue Mediterranean Sea. Sketches showing the half-buried, curiously Romantic site were drawn when the great Romantic poets, Byron, Shelley and Keats, were flourishing in late 1700s England.

In 1787 sketches of Hagar Qim were published, making the site well-known abroad, drawn by a visiting French artist named Jean Houel. Everyone seeing the drawings wondered what the mounds of earth and huge protruding stones were hiding.

Some legendary visitors later had no doubt that the mounds of earth, sediment and rubbish had been concealing for untold centuries magnificent temples of stone.

"Not without a sense of awe one enters the Sanctuary, a rectangular room with double altars in deep recesses…the recess in the left corner of the room contains a double altar…Looking outward…towards the main entrance, one gets a view of the magnificent passage running across the whole building. This passage is lined through with huge uprights…One of these slabs which now lies broken in the outer apse, but which was found in the passage, once formed the lintel of a doorway. " (Zammit 1994)

Even in its disordered rubble, even under its protective cover, there is still a *feeling* inside the stones at Hagar Qim that embraces the visitor and seems to call forth a fond memory, for in spite of everything that might have conspired to destroy it, such as Bronze Age newcomers and the passage of time, an ancient feeling lingers there in the stones by the sea, especially as sunset embraces the entrance trilithon and paints a vivid red and gold sky over darkening waters.

"The highest stones are visible from Mnajdra on the coast below, whilst to the visitor who approaches by the road from the north-east, they provide a most impressive spectacle." (Evans 1971)

The abandoned temples of Hagar Qim, being so spectacular in beauty, so visible on the cliff top by the sea, were noticed early in the passage of time. They were described in 1647 by Giovanni Francesco Abela, of the Order of the Knights of St. John, in his *Della Descrittione di Malta* where he writes that the large stone structures he had seen on Malta were built by the giants who once lived on the islands. (Stroud 2007)

In 1787 the first known images of Hagar Qim were published, painted by the visiting French artist, Jean Houel, engraver for King Louis XVI, who traveled to Sicily and Lipari as well as the Maltese islands. Houel painted the remains of ancient structures that he saw on his visit, and the resulting work was entitled, *Voyage Pittoresque des isles de Sicile, de Lipari, et de Malta.* (Stroud 2007) One Houel painting shows huge standing stones at Hagar Qim protruding from the buried site, not like Skorba's single stone, but several towering megaliths and segments of an outer wall were visible in the sediment and soil that for centuries concealed the temple's inner walls and apses.

Outer wall of Hagar Qim, Coyright 2016 Ross-Edison

Hagar Qim was described in this condition by travelers to Malta in 1816 and 1836 and then, in 1839, the Governor of Malta, Sir Henry Bouverie, provided funding for clearance of the large and sprawling clifftop site by the sea.

This first work of excavation thus began. It started in November of 1839, lasted for two months, and was written up by Vassallo in 1851. In 1885, archaeologist A.A. Caruana made additional excavations, and based on Caruana's work, a revised site plan by Vassalo was published in 1886 with Caruana's description of the site. In 1901 Albert Mayr made use of the updated Vassalo plan to publish his detailed report on the Hagar Qim excavations to date.

Related excavations were done by Sir Zammit and Peet in 1909-10, and by Ashby in 1910-11 but these were small-scale operations, "…directed mainly to ascertaining whether the plan had been completely uncovered and to obtaining specimens of the pottery from the site, since that unearthed in previous excavations had completely disappeared." (Evans 1971)

After this, some restoration was accomplished at Hagar Qim, but nothing of significance was attempted until after World War II when more extensive restoration was done in 1948 through 1950-51. In 1954, test-trenches were dug by Sir Evans after a new floor-plan of the site had been revised and drawn up in 1952.

"The site is a very extensive and complex one. It consists of a main group of buildings with at least three smaller groups situated not far away from it. The main group is irregular in shape and form and gives the impression of a spontaneous growth as more and more rooms were needed…" (Evans 1971)

From the early excavations of Sir Zammit, Peet and Ashby, Sir Evans observes:

"Not very much pottery from these excavations is preserved in the Museum. Out of a total of 86 sherds, 1 only dated from the Mgarr phase, 2 only from the Ggantija phase, and 71 from the Tarxien phase." (Evans 1971)

In a footnote by Sir Evans, in his 1971 Survey, he asks if the one piece of pottery found at Mgarr was the fragment Ashby had reported finding in his 1913 report.

Furthermore, Sir Evans adds,

"Tagliaferro (Ashby, 1913, p. 72) says that some eighty (80) boxes of sherds were sent to the Museum in 1910, so much must have been lost." (Evans 1971)

Sir Evans does describe the following whole or restored pottery found *in situ* at Hagar Qim, or in the field nearby, and the extraordinary amount of figurines discovered there:

Carinated bowl, restored. A squat biconical pot, with flat base, everted rim and rim-to-shoulder strap handles. Dark grey with black and red-brown flecks and highly polished surface.

Carinated bowl, restored. Has concave sides and convex base, one string-hole handle, buff grey color, smoothed but unpolished, moderately hard-fired, decorated with vertical incisions made before firing, while the base is covered with incised vertical lines and filled with white paste.

Ladle, whole. Medium-size with bent-over handle, made of thick, coarse buff ware with large white and gray grits. Height 4.3 cm. (1.69 inches). Possibly found in a field nearby.

Studded cup, complete. Small, thick cup, asymmetrical shape, oval-shaped mouth, grey color with buff surface, lightly fired, with clay studs of different sizes set close together. Possibly a ladle with a space without studs showing where a handle was attached. Height 4 cm. (1.57 inches). Found in a doorway in 1909.

Miniature dish, complete. Roughly made, gray color with white grits, irregular shape, 1 cm. (0.393 of an inch) in height.

Ram's Head handle, the end of the handle, possibly from a handled bowl, of soft buff color, smoothed but unslipped, 43 mm. (1.69 inches) in height, and 35 mm. (1.37 inches) at base.

Sherd, with applied or moulded decoration in the form of a cross, standing about 1 cm. (0.393 of an inch) above the body of the vase, of soft grey ware, found in a 1910 excavation.

In addition to pottery items made of clay, stone items were found *in situ* at Hagar Qim that could be used for preparing and serving food, including mortars and pestles for grinding grain or spices, large stone bowls to fit in place on the cooking platforms, stone vessels of various shapes and sizes, and the so-called stone 'cups' similar to those found at Tarxien that could have been a cup for drinking but may have been a bowl of irregular shape used for baking or broiling an individual portion.

From the early Hagar Qim excavations, Sir Evans describes:

A large carinated stone bowl, restored. The upper part of the bowl has an asymmetrical type handle, set 16 cm. (6.299 inches) down from the rim, the bowl being 13.5 cm. long (5.3 inches) and 19 cm. (7.48 inches) deep. The width of the bowl at the base is 16 cm. (6.299 inches) and tapers up to 7 cm. (2.75 inches). There is a bead rim at the top of the bowl. The outer surface is rough but the interior is smooth. Found by Sir Zammit in a temple inner apse in 1909.

Fragments of large-size stone vessels. 3 fragments, each from different vessels, one with a thickness of 5.5 cm. (2.165 inches), probably rounded bowls, found in 1910.

Fragments of various sized vessels. 14 fragments found, from a tiny bowl 4.5 cm. high (1.77 inches) and 7 cm. (2.75 inches) in diameter, to a fragment of a large vessel with a thickness of 5 cm. (1.968 inches). Found in 1910.

Stone 'cups' like those found at Tarxien: 32 concave-convex cups made of globigerina limestone. "They are worked with considerable care, especially on the convex side, as if this was to be the visible surface. The depressed surface is very shallow, and they could not possibly have served the purpose indicated by the name.

Four of the examples are fragments only, the rest are complete. Average height 5.5 cm. (2.165 inches). Av. diam. 11 cm. (4.33 inches). Some found in 1910, others in earlier excavations." (Evans 1971)

The depressed side of the cup could have been designed to easily lift out the baked item. Perhaps Hagar Qim, as Sir Temi Zammit suggested, was staffed by a corps of Fat Ladies in white robes who prepared the mourning feast in a temple outbuilding, then baked individual portions in the odd-shaped cups on the stone platforms in the temple and served the mourners in the spacious inner courtyard left open to the sky.

Sixteen Fat Lady figurines are listed in the 1971 Survey, found *in situ* at Hagar Qim.

Mnajdra

The first excavation of Mnajdra was in 1840, yet the site was not fully excavated because deemed less important than the spectacular Hagar Qim temple topping the cliff high above it. Nonetheless, the three temples at Mnajdra much like Skorba held a hidden treasure of information, about Neolithic Malta, with a stunning view of the sea through an ancient trilithon, the best view in Malta, giving an enchanting glimpse of sunsets and in fair weather by day the tiny island of Fifla wavering like a dream in the misted near-distance of a lapis lazuli sea.

"The attractive setting of the Mnajdra remains," Sir Evans writes in his Survey of 1971, "which lie in a small valley close to the seashore between two sections of cliff, gives them a special charm not to be found in any other of the large-scale temples of the islands.

"They consist of a main block which comprises two separate and complete buildings of the usual temple form…and the ruins of a small building already known to exist here…and its connection with the north building of the main block by means of a platform." (Evans 1971)

The two main buildings are similar and each has a separate outer wall. "The whole arrangement, as also many of the details, bear the greatest resemblance to the Ggantija in Gozo…(and)…to the east of the north-east corner of the northern building (of the main block)…lie the remains of a small structure…The building appears to be a small temple of trefoil plan, much smaller than either of the two main buildings." (Evans 1971)

This smaller temple was extensively restored, the remains of its corbelled outer walls appearing similar to Kordin III.

Finally excavations of Mnajdra began. Ashby's work in 1910 and 1913 at Mnajdra discovered an abundance of broken pottery, some of it, in Ashby's words, "in a very rotten condition."

Sir Evans in his 1971 Survey lists pottery items and sherds of special interest found in the 1910 excavations:

<u>Shouldered cup, restored</u>. Tiny flat base, a rolled rim, hard-fired with a little trace of polishing left on the surface. Decorated with branched spirals in each quadrant, scratched, filled with white paste. Height 5.5 cm. (2.165 inches), diameter 8.6 cm. (3.385 inches).

<u>Dish with crinkled rim, restored</u>. Shallow, broad dish, coarse surface with a buff color on the outside, grey inside. Height 12 cm. (4.72 inches), diameter 38 cm. (14.96 inches).

<u>Neck of a very large jar</u>, 24.5 cm. (9.645 inches) high, restored. Unpolished, coarse, buff-grey ware decorated with vertical fluting, some white paste filling remains.

<u>Fragments of a large stone bowl</u>, very large and very thick, 37 cm. (14.56 inches) high and 7.9 cm. (3.11 inches) thick. "Probably had the same shape as the large one at Tarxien…" (Evans 1971) which may be a perfect size and thickness for baking and broiling on a cooking platform inside the inner temple.

As for pottery and sherds found at Mnadjra, in his 1971 Survey Sir Evans writes:

"The pottery, mostly from Ashby's excavations, which is preserved in the National Museum at Valletta, offers the following picture…

4 sherds of Zebbug type,

1 sherd of Mgarr type,

34 of Ggantija type,

and no less than 700 of Tarxien type."

Additionally, a quern and various rubbers and grinders made of stone were found in an early excavation in 1909.

In 1954, ten test-trenches were dug in various places by Sir Evans in his own excavations at Mnajdra, and the following were found:

In Trench A, "a few sherds of Tarxien type" were found beneath a "fairly thick torba floor."

Trench B "produced large amounts of Tarxien type pottery" but no trace of the torba floors reported by Ashby in 1913 were found in 1954.

Trench C cut inside the south temple in the filling between the south wall of an apse and its outer casing, produced, like Trench B, "quantities of Tarxien pottery."

Trench D was cut in the remains of a small apse in a trefoil structure northeast of the north temple. "Here just behind the three slabs which cut off the entrance to this room, there was found a torba floor 5 cm. (1.968 inches) thick, a packing 0.12 m. (0.393 of an inch) thick of hard earth and stones, and then a further 0.25 m. (0.82 of an inch) of red field soil with flecks of charcoal and stones down to bedrock. Little pottery was found in the stone and soil packing, but in the red earth below there was more, all of Ggantija type."

Trench E was cut in a small chamber "…just behind the window-like entrance…(and) below a torba floor 0.15 cm. (0.59 of an inch) was a stratum of stones and loose earth which contained pottery of Tarxien type. Underneath this…was a layer of black earth which contained a number of potsherds all of Ggantija type."

Trench F was cut in the middle floor of the same chamber as Trench E, and found below a torba floor of 10 cm. (3.937 inches) thick, were Tarxien type potsherds.

Trench G, cut inside an apse, disclosed a "…torba floor…5 cm. (1.968 inches) thick and below it came a deposit of earth and stones. This contained sherds of Tarxien pottery of a developed type. The left-hand support of the pitted entrance (to the apse) rested on this deposit…The bottom of the wall slab of the apse also came at about the same level, but below it was a foundation of large boulders, which continued downwards for another 0.40 m. (1.312 inches) to the top of the next level. This was a beaten-earth floor which passed underneath the wall foundation. Below it was about 5 cm. (1.968 inches) of black earth. At the north end of the trench this rested directly on rock, but further to the south there was 10 cm. to 15 cm. (3.937 to 5.90 inches) of reddish soil before rock was reached. The black earth and the red below contained a mixture of sherds, some of Ggantija type, others which appeared to belong to an undeveloped stage of Tarxien phase." (Evans 1971)

Trench H was the only trench cut inside the north temple, confirming the existence of a platform upon which the north temple was built, and, like the platform in front of Ggantija, the Mnadjra platform was built of "…piled-up limestone boulders…(and) a fairly large quantity of sherds were recovered, all of advanced Tarxien types…"

Trenches I and J revealed sherds mostly of Tarxien type, deposited in unsecure layers disturbed by the early Ashby excavations.

Along with the pottery and potsherds found at Mnadjra, "A number of querns were found, and also pebbles which had been used with them as rubbers. There were a number of mortars and rough stone vessels." (Evans 1971)

Food preparation using querns and mortars for grinding and the rough stone vessels for baking, was done in the temple site and served in a profusion of bowls, plates, cups, jugs, jars, ladles and amphorae that the surviving Mnajdra pottery and sherds present.

Tarxien

Just as Hagar Qim still presents a strong citadel of ancient feeling, on its clifftop by the sea, the sprawling Tarxien site presents an ancient and lavish stage for temple activity.

At the Tarxien site, like no other, one can *feel* the bustle.

If a visitor looks closely and listens, standing still, inside ornate courtyards with cooking platforms and apses and spirals and windows of ancient stone, a certain symphony begins to burst out, in all the busyness, sounding the noise and bustle of celebration, of the life of the deceased, and of life itself.

For truly the temples of Malta were *not* built to vicariously experience or exalt the dreary mystery of death, but to affirm ongoing life. At Tarxien even amid the cement restoration of the trilithon entrance, there in an inner temple place the replicated remains of a huge statue of the genial Fat Lady is still standing, while replicated large decorated altars capture the imagination amid the left-over ruins and rubble. The lavish busy floor plan of the Tarxien temple apses says more than any other temple site as echoes of the busy activity there play on.

Sir Evans writes in his 1971 Survey,

"The Tarxien temples, which are the most elaborate group of megalithic remains on the Maltese islands, both architecturally and in their internal decoration, were not known until 1913. In that year, Themistocles Zammit, who was then completing work at the Hal Saflieni Hypogeum, was approached by a tenant of a Government field in the same district (as Hal Saflieni), Lorenzo Despott, who said that he had struck large blocks of stone whenever he dug deeper than usual…At Zammit's request the man dug a trench in his field to demonstrate; as a result, two blocks of stone and a quantity of potsherds, clearly of prehistoric type, came to light."

Delayed by the start of World War I, "…it was not until July 1915 that serious work was started on this epoch-making site.

"From then until 1919, the excavations were pursued regularly each summer, when the whole of the buildings now visible had been exposed…The excavated buildings at Tarxien cover an area of some 5,000 square yards (0.42 hectares). The remains consist, at the present day, (1971) of three separate apsidal buildings on the usual plan, but arranged in a unique relationship to one another, with a smaller, much damaged temple, and some miscellaneous ruins lying to the east. One of the temples in the main group, the middle one, is also unique in possessing three apsidal rooms instead of the usual two found in the later temples.

"The entrance to the entrance temple evidently formed, in the final state of the buildings, the main entrance to the block (of the three temples), if not the only (entrance)…This entrance…having "an ample forecourt in front, which is floored with torba instead of being paved. According to Zammit (in his 1930 report)…this torba extended about 30 m (about 98 feet or 33 yards) outwards from the entrance. It is not now visible." (Evans 1971)

Sir Zammit's Divining Blocks. This forecourt was bounded by an arc-shaped façade with "…a unique feature of 'divining blocks'"…with one at each end of the façade. At the western end of the arc-shaped façade, the divining block was found "…badly damaged, but the eastern one is still fairly well preserved…It consists of a slab of stone measuring 3 m. (9.84 feet) square laid horizontally on the rock. It was originally screened on three sides by upright slabs…That on the left of the block is wedge-shaped, presumably because this was necessary to ensure a perfect fit between this block and the last upright of the façade. In front of the block are the remains of what was probably a sill composed of three horizontal blocks…In the south-east corner of the ledge is a deep conical hole, 0.4 m. (1.312 inches) in diameter and 0.35 m. (1.148 feet) deep. The part of the surface enclosed by this ledge, which is roughly rectangular and measures 1.95 m. (6.397 feet) square, is perforated with five irregularly arranged conical holes. The diameter of the holes at the surface varies between 0.25 m. and 0.35 m. (between 0.82 of one foot and 1.148 feet). They are pierced right through the block into the rock below. A cylinder of stone…with an eye-glass perforation down the center, was found standing in front of this block, and a few yards away lay a heap of over a hundred small stone balls of different sizes."

Whether or not the stone balls and cylinder were "a game" connected in Neolithic times to the divining blocks, cannot be known, but the curious "stand" with a counter-sill featuring the well-known but mysterious Neolithic holes present one of the wonders of Tarxien.

Tarxien poses a complex and meandering narrative that was disrupted and ended in the Bronze Age when the abandoned Tarxien site became a crematory featuring blazing hot fires and actual burials inside the temples of the cremated remains, and a new style of pottery appeared. The complicated floor plan of Tarxien that was occupied by newcomers after 2300 B.C. nonetheless still documents the entire time span of the temple era whose evolution from single apse to six apse is shown in the sketches in Sir Zammit's book, *Malta, The Prehistoric Temples Hagar Qim and Mnajdra*.

In these sketches, the 6-apse floor plan of Tarxien expresses the culmination of 1,000 years of temple building, which appears to have become busier and busier as time wore on at Tarxien, and right up to the end.

Sir Temi Zammit was the first to excavate the sprawling Tarxien site which for centuries was being disturbed by farmers ploughing through the covering topsoil that buried the temples in the Tarxien field.

The buried temples of Tarxien were finally excavated in a simple way when Sir Zammit himself went out to the field with a shovel and dug directly into the buried center of the Tarxien temple complex. Still it would take several years before serious excavations could begin in 1915.

In 1954, Sir Evans cut trenches to continue the excavations. "Six soundings were made, five of them in the main group of buildings, and the sixth in the rear room of the small eastern building.

"Trench A was cut in the half of (an) apse left untouched by Ashby's cutting. The top torba floor here was bounded not by the slabs of the wall but by the rock itself, which had been hollowed out to a depth of 0.90 m. (2.95 feet) over the whole surface. This floor was 0.10 m. (0.328 of one foot) thick. Below it came a packing of stones 0.35 m. (1.148 feet) thick which contained abundant sherds of pottery of the fully developed Tarxien type. Below this again was a thin floor of yellowish torba 0.05 m. (0.164 of one foot) thick, below which was a further 0.15 m. (0.492 of a foot) of earth and stones which rested upon the carefully smoothed bedrock, and which produced potsherds whose shape and decoration were of a cruder kind, though still similar to the Tarxien type…

"Trench D, cut in (a nearby) apse, added nothing, with "…very little depth of deposit.

"Of greatest importance were Trenches B and E."

Trench B was cut into an apse in the middle temple and yielded two distinct floors and "…potsherds of normal Tarxien types…Inside this apse, however, the rock had been hollowed to a depth of 10 cm. to 15 cm. (3.93 to 5.905 inches), and this hollow part was filled with black soil containing large quantities of small sherds of pottery, almost all of Ggantija type, though a very few sherds of the Tarxien phase were also present. A small deposit of black earth filled the space between the somewhat irregular base of the wall stones and the rock…This black soil…produced only sherds of the advanced Tarxien type…"

Trench E revealed stratigraphy similar to Trench B, where five floors down, in black earth just above the bedrock "abundant small sherds all of Ggantija type" were found.

Trench C was cut in the western temple along the north-west wall of an apse. "Sherds of Tarxien pottery of developed types were found in the torba and the soil and stone levels below."

The archaeological question, based on the Ggantija potsherds found, was whether a temple older than the Tarxien Phase of 3300/3000-2300 B.C .had existed at Tarxien.

In 1959, David Trump cut two trenches in the middle temple of Tarxien and found both Ggantija and Tarxien Phase potsherds.

In 1954, a trench cut in the small eastern temple found Ggantija and even older Zeuubg Phase potsherds. "A high proportion of Zebbug sherds" mixed in with Ggantija sherds and the more primitive structure of the small eastern temple suggest that an earlier temple was constructed at Tarxien and in use long before the middle temple and main block of temples were built.

In 1971 Sir John Evans listed in his Survey a profuse amount of Neolithic potsherds recovered from the Tarxien Cultural Phase:

Zebbug type: 15;

Mgarr Type: 2;

Ggantija type: 212;

Tarxien type: 1,652.

In addition to these broken sherds, Sir Evans' 1971 Survey lists 54 complete, or "almost complete" plus pottery restored from sherds found at Tarzien.

Compared to the other six temple sites explored in this book, the Tarxien numbers are large. For Red Skorba, Sir Evans lists 4 items plus ladles; for Mgarr at Ta Hagrat, 8; for Kordin III, 12 ; for Ggantija, 5; for Hagar Qim, 6; but for Tarxien, 54.

Sir Evans describes the 54 complete, almost complete, and restored pottery items from Tarxien, plus 13 decorated "sherds of special interest" and 14 querns found intact, in addition to broken querns.

"Numerous querns and rubbers were found during the excavation of the Tarxien temples. Some of these were of local coralline limestone, and these were usually circular in shape; others were of a dark-gray volcanic lava and oval in shape (saddle-querns). Zammit records (1930) that at least 14 of these were found complete, with their upper stones for rubbing, as well as broken examples. The largest querns averaged about 50 cm. (19.685 inches) in length, 37 cm. (14.566 inches) in breadth and 20 cm. (7.874 inches) in thickness." (Evans 1971)

Sir Evans' 1971 Survey lists the following items from Tarxien:

3 Storage Jars, restored.

1 Handled Jar, complete.

1 Small Jar, restored.

1 Jar, restored.

1 Large Jar, partly restored.

6 Large Amphorae, restored.

2 Small Amphorae, complete.

2 Carinated Hole-Mouth Bowls, restored.

1 Large Bell-Shaped Jar, restored.

1 Large Scale-Ware Basin, partly restored.

12 Carinated Bowls, 1 complete, 3 almost complete, 8 restored.

1 Conical cover (lid), complete.

1 High-Handled Bowl, restored.

1 Strainer Bowl, Carinated, restored.

2 Biconical Bowls, restored.

4 Two-Handled Bowls, restored.

2 Footed Bowls, restored.

2 Flat Dishes, restored.

2 Biconical Cups, 1 almost complete, 1 restored.

1 Spherical Rounded Pot, restored.

1 Miniature Amphora, complete.

1 Miniature Footed Bowl, restored.

1 Miniature Small Bowl, restored.

1 Scoop or Ladle Bowl, almost complete.

2 Fragments of Large Ladles.

1 Shallow Cup on High Foot, complete.

Descriptions of these items in a synopsis of the Sir Evans 1971 Survey follows, to compare with Tagliaferro's Classifications of the Hal Saflieni pottery styles:

3 Storage Jars, restored. 1) Large coil-built biconical jar, coarse brown ware, exterior covered with scale decoration, height 61 cm. (24.015 inches). 2) Large biconical jar, coarse brown ware, exterior covered with scale decoration, height 57 cm. (22.44 inches). 3) Large biconical jar, same as jar described in 2), of coarse brown ware, and exterior covered with scale decoration, height 57 cm. (22.44 inches).

1 Handled Jar, complete. Biconical jar of buff color, height 51 cm. (20.078 inches), fine and hard-fired ware with polished exterior, yellow color, with one triangular handle "rising from the carination" with two crescent shapes on either side of this handle, and four tunnel handles just below the rim. Upper and lower areas have a "deeply incised curvilinear decoration" that was filled in with red ochre.

1 Jar, restored. Coarse brown ware, exterior covered with "all-over scale decoration' with a smoothed interior, height 25 cm. (9.842 inches).

1 Jar, restored. Biconical jar of coarse "gritty" ware, 25 cm. high (9.842 inches) with a rough exterior, smooth interior, color in various shades of brown, with elaborate decoration: a row of vertical notches on rim, four oval stubs or bosses below that on the neck of the jar, each stub having three horizontal notches surrounded by an incised curvilinear design. On the shoulder of the jar are four vertical strips of clay with horizontal notches and, between the tops of these notches are incised semi-circles. Below all of this, the jar is covered with overlapping rows of finger-painted channels.

1 Large Jar, partly restored. Coarse gray ware, around 35 cm. (13.779 inches) in height, unburnished, covered with disks applied against a white background with a series of frames that look like inverted shields.

6 Large Amphorae, restored. 1) Large narrow-necked vase, 48 cm. (18.897 inches) in height with two large tunnel handles opposite each other on the shoulder, neck is high and concave with a narrow mouth, fine and highly polished mainly brown surface with red and black areas of color, otherwise undecorated, found behind an apse at the foot of steps in 1915 by Sir Zammit. 2) Like the amphora in 1) but with irregular shape, surface reddish brown with brown and black areas of color, otherwise undecorated, height 51.5 cm. (20.078 inches). 3) height 47 cm. (18.503 inches). 4) height 46 cm. (18.110 inches). 5) 41 cm. (16.14 inches). 6) 47 cm. (18.503 inches): These latter four amphorae are like those described in 1) and 2). All 6 thought to have been found in 1915 by Sir Zammit behind an apse at the foot of temple steps.

2 Small Amphorae, complete. 1) A well-fired, gritty ware but with a polished surface, dark gray color with areas of reddish-brown and black, decorated with twelve horizontal rows of seed-shaped incisions, filled with white paste, 26 cm. (10.236 inches) in height. 2) Similar to 1) but undecorated, dark gray with black area on one side of the neck, bottom row of incisions forms a circle on the base, 20.5 cm. (8.07 inches) in height.

2 Carinated Hole-Mouth Bowls, restored. 1) Large bowl with beaded rim, yellowish in color, well-fired buff ware with polished surface and curvilinear decoration, with four sets of holes, bowl is 34 cm. (13.38 inches) in height. 2) Very large bowl 55 cm. (21.65 inches) in height, well-fired buff ware with black specks, polished surface decorated with scratched lines, with four sets of holes, found in an apse between a wall and a fixed stone basin.

1 Large Bell-Shaped Jar, restored. Fine medium-grade grey ware, with four sets of holes below the rim, the entire surface decorated with studs on background of white paste, part of jar is missing, present height is 18 cm. (7.08 inches).

1 Large Scale-Ware Basin, partly restored. Large fragments of a huge basin, coarse gray ware but well-fired with a rim created by rolling over the clay, decorated

with overlapping scales, height of 60 cm. (23.6 inches) with diameter of over 1 m. (3 feet and 3.37 inches), found below a torba floor inside an apse by Ashby in 1924.

<u>12 Carinated Bowls, 1 complete, 3 almost complete, 8 restored</u>. 1) Large bowl with triangle handle on shoulder, fine and hard-fired brown ware, highly polished brown to black surface, decorated with curvilinear double-rows of studs on white background, height of 22.5 cm. (8.58 inches). 2) Similar to Bowl 1) but without handle, height 15.5 cm. (6.10 inches). 3) Smaller bowl like 1) and 2) but of dark gray color, with rows of studded decoration and traces of white background, height 9 cm. (3.54 inches). 4) Dark gray in color with red areas, not studded but decorated with criss-crossing scratched lines, height of 15.3 cm. (6.02 inches). 5) Unlike the carinated bowls described above, this bowl has concave sides and a convex lower area on a small flat base, of a fine, dark ware with polished surface and varying colors of brown to black but also encrusted with red ochre, has a plain handle, and interior is entirely painted with red ochre, height 13 cm. (5.11 inches), found beneath a lower torba floor in 1920. 6) A medium-size bowl of gray ware, with a small flat base, scratched lines decoration with traces of white in-filling, height 8.7 cm. (3.42 inches). 7) Bowl with triangular handle on one side and rising from shoulder to half-way up the bowl, of dark gray ware with white in-filling of curvilinear scratched decoration with broad bands of red ochre, inside of handle painted with red ochre, height of 14 cm. (5.51 inches). 8) This bowl has a rim-to-shoulder strap handle, and slightly concave sides on a small flat base, made of a dark ware with a hard-fired polished surface with brown to black areas, decorated with scratched diagonal lines forming triangles, and the lower part of the bowl has a spiral with branching ends, height 7.6 cm. (2.99 inches). 9) A shouldered bowl with round base, a hard-fired gritty ware of buff color, and highly polished surface of light brown to black in color, undecorated, much worn on the interior, with a height of 7.7 cm. (3.03 inches). 10) Similar to previous bowl 9), but with a base serving as a stand, of brown ware with areas of olive gray, brown, and black, no handle, undecorated, height of 10 cm. (3.937 inches). 11) This bowl is like the two previous bowls, with highly polished surface, light brown with some areas of black, no handle, undecorated, height of 9.5 cm. (3.74 inches). 12) A bowl with a small triangular handle on the should and a crescent-shaped embossment on the opposite side, brick-red color on surface, black interior, and a small, flat base, height 10 cm. (3.937 inches).

<u>1 Conical cover (lid), complete</u>. 8 cm. (3.149 inches) in height, probably the lid to the red-brick bowl 12) described above, undecorated.

<u>1 High-Handled Bowl, restored</u>. This is more of a ladle than a bowl with high handle, made of gray-buff ware with polished surface, back of lower handle has a sunken triangle with curvilinear designs, dots, and two incised lines in a V-shape, height with handle 17.5 cm. (6.889 inches).

<u>1 Strainer, restored</u>. This is a carinated bowl with handle and 13 rows of pierced holes in a rounded base, a fine, well-polished ware with dark gray to black colors, height of 6 cm. (2.362 inches).

<u>2 Biconical Bowls, restored</u>. 1) Large bowl of dark ware with white limestone grits. Surface colors of gray-brown to black, well polished, decorated with incised curvilinear designs in branched-volute patterns, height of 10.5 cm. (4.133 inches). 2) Like Bowl 1) but with simpler incised curvilinear design, height of 7 cm. (2.755 inches).

<u>4 Two-Handled Bowls, restored</u>. 1) Hard-fired buff ware with white limestone grits, highly polished part black, part reddish surface, two strap handles of triangle shape, set opposite each other, with two crescent bosses at the shoulder of bowl, height of 18 cm. (7.086 inches). 2) Similar to Bowl 1) but with two string-hole handles, highly polished surface that is brown-gray in color with areas of black, undecorated except for a scratched line and triangle, height of 13 cm. (5.118 inches). 3) Highly polished gray surface, two small triangle-shaped handles set on the shoulders opposite each other, a small semi-circular boss is set on the other two quarters, and below the rim are four sets of drilled holes, a lightly incised curvilinear decoration at the carination, with a height of 8.5 cm. (3.346 inches). 4) Height 13.2 cm. (5.196 inches) and otherwise entirely similar to Bowl 3) described above.

<u>2 Footed Bowls, restored</u>. 1) Height of 11 cm. (4.33 inches), hard-fired gritty ware, yellow color with black flecks, polished surface, with four knobs set on the shoulder. 2) Similar to Bowl (1 but with reddish and black flecks on yellow, the four knobs on shoulders, and decorated with lightly incised curvilinear patterns, 8.5 cm. (3.346 inches) in height.

<u>2 Flat Dishes, restored</u>. 1) Flat-bottomed dish resembling a bowl, not a plate, of hard-fired buff ware with small white limestone grits, interior is polished and exterior is decorated all over with jabbed pits, mottled black to buff colors. 6.5 cm. in height (2.559 inches). 2) Same as dish 1) except the surface color is a mottled brown to black, height of 5.5 cm. (2.165 inches).

<u>2 Biconical Cups, 1 almost complete, 1 restored</u>. 1) Highly polished surface with a flat base, colors from ochreous to black, with exterior covered with deeply incised branching spirals, height of 5 cm. (1.968 inches). 2) A small pot with highly polished interior and fine brown ware whose surface is black and covered with nine rows of jabbed holes filled with white paste, height of 5.4 cm. (2.125 inches).

<u>1 Spherical Rounded Pot, restored</u>. Irregularly shaped, small round pot made of a brown gritty ware, with polished surface, mottled colors of red-brown to black, and

two string holes set opposite to one another just below the rim, with a height of 5 cm. (1.968 inches).

3 Miniature Items: 1 Amphora, complete. 1 Footed Bowl, restored. 1 Small Bowl, restored. 1) Amphora, of fine, hard-fired, buff clay with highly polished surface, scratched curvilinear patterns of double festoons and branched volutes, height of 7 cm. (2.755 inches). 2) Footed bowl, shouldered, on low foot, of light buff clay, polished yellow surface with partly black interior, with a thick rim and four crescent knobs on the shoulder, height of 5.2 cm. (2.047 inches). 3) Small bowl of fine, well-fired buff clay, buff to black surface, polished interior, five rows of jabbed pits above the shoulder and incised volute patters with forked ends on the bottom, height of 4.5 cm. (1.771 inches).

1 Scoop or Ladle Bowl, almost complete. A small open bowl with thick rim that had a long high handle, highly polished interior and rim, the outer surface is cut away and decorated with a row of studs and a layer of white paste in between, maximum diameter of 13 cm. (5.118 inches).

2 Fragments of Large Ladles. Fine ware with polished surface, one ladle is buff ware, the other is gray with orange streaks.

1 Shallow Cup on High Foot, complete. Grey ware, pebble burnished, decorated with areas of dots and on the thickened rim are incised triangles, white paste in the incisions, a triangle handle with a rectangle section running from the middle underside of the cup to the upper part of the foot, total height of 11.5 cm. (4.527 inches) with the cup being 4 cm. (1.574 inches) on the foot of 7.5 cm. (2.952 inches).

Missing in the Evans temple survey is mention of large covers for flat-bottomed shallow bowls or large convex plates, as found in the Hal Saflieni tombs.

Could this mean that large flat-bottomed shallow bowls of cooked food, covered by flat, slightly convex lids, were used in the tombs but not so much, if at all, in the temples?

This suggests that pottery was used in different ways between temple and tomb. Cooked food placed as grave goods in the tombs would be covered to protect from, perhaps, animal predators and to keep the food fresh, that is, fresh for the journey. Inside the temples, however, no need to cover food because it would be immediately served and eaten in the mourning feast. Further evidence in the temples, for preparing and cooking of food for feasting, are the curious stone items, called 'cups' by the archaeologists who found them, inside both Hagar Qim and Tarxien. Thirteen of similar stone 'cups' were found at Tarxien, 32 similar stone 'cups' at Hagar Qim.

Baking bowl from Tarxien, Evans 1970

Sir Evans wondered how anyone could drink from the uneven rim of these cups. But these were not 'cups' for drinking. They were baking dishes made of stone to radiate the heat of the cooking fire. The cups would bake individual servings, for up to 32 people at Hagar Qim, for the partially lowered or lopsided edge made it easy to scoop out and eat the baked appetizer served in the mourning feast.

No cooking or baking would be done in the tombs.

This perhaps points out the different use of pottery in temple and tomb which can be glimpsed at Xaghra, a large burial compound on the island of Gozo, part of which is known as the Brochtorff Circle where some potsherds and intact pottery similar to some items in the temples were found. For example, of all the bowls, and potsherds from bowls, found so far in the Brochtorff Circle:

"Only 14 complete bowls were found from the Brochtorff Circle at Xaghra, although as many as 400 could be present if the full weight of the ceramics is taken into account. In any case, the number is considerably less than the minimum number of individuals (800) buried at the site." *(Malone and Stoddart, Chapter 14 in Mortuary Ritual)*

Some items found in the Xaghra tombs *were* found replicated in the temples or being made in the temple outbuildings, such as the large number of shells in the 'Hut of the Querns' at Skorba possibly being fashioned into grave goods as amulets and necklaces, but some items were in the tombs for a different use.

"Absent in Tas-Silg and found exclusively in funerary contexts are: sub-cylindrical bowls, deep carinated bowls, deep curvilinear bowls, and splay-walled bowls." *(Copat, p.41)*

At the Xaghra Brochtorff excavation, a large number of non-pottery items were also found.

"A further set of items can be considered ornaments...where some 1,000 items have been found. Of these 850 are made of shell; 57 bone, ceramic and stone; 41 are axe pendants from outside the Maltese Islands; and 45 are pseudo-anthropomorphic bone pendants...Chert and flint objects may be more utilitarian in nature. The 267 pieces of flint-chert are...principally large knife scrapers, small scrapers, regular blades, irregular waste flakes with occasional working and retouch, and waste chips." See Malone and Stoddart, *Mortuary Ritual in Prehistoric Malta*, 2009.

The large number of grave goods such as greenstone axe amulets and shell items accompany flint and chert cutting tools, as found in the Xaghra tombs, grave goods which were perhaps used by the deceased, or used by the grave-keepers for attending to the final separating and sorting of skeletal bones. This ritual of skeletal separation has been documented occurring in contemporary rural Greece in the 1970s A.D.

But the separation and stacking of bones would not have been done in the Neolithic temples which did not house any ossuary remains but were built for other activities.

The basic question as suggested by Sir Zammit is:

Who would want to linger in the cramped and unnerving interior of, for example, the Brochtorff Circle at Xaghra where disconnected, ossified skeletal bones, sorted and piled high, perhaps heaped in dissembled piles visible from the edges of a new burial even as the mourners gathered round. How many mourners could be seated at or near the grave? Even in the flickering romantic glow from the hanging lamps, who would want to feast there?

Hence another place was needed.

So many temples were built.

"The necessity to build temples," Sir Zammit observes, "came probably from the growing population's need to participate during rituals, since only few people fitted in the narrow grave chambers, which were also difficult to reach." (Zammit 1994)

In fact, on the small island of Malta, which is 16.8 miles long (27 km) and 9 miles wide (14.5 km), if the 50 temple sites found so far (and counting) could be lined up on a map of Malta, there would be 3 or 4 temples per mile over the length of the island, and 5 or 6 temples per mile across its width. Temples were built in pairs, however, such as Mnadjra near Hagar Qim, so that the actual area covered by temples per mile would be reduced.   Yet the temples did not stand alone. Outbuildings found near the temples, and their contents, suggest that the temples required support activities and were busy places.

But what was the big attraction? What was powerful enough to pull the ancient Maltese and seafaring visitors inside so many temple walls?

Was the big draw into the temple some kind of ritual?

 If so, what was it?

Professor of Mathematics at the University of Malta, Napoleon Tagliaferro, classified the pottery and great multitude of potsherds found within the inner chambers of the Hal Saflieni Hypogeum, and suggested the following ritual:

<u>Ritual breaking of bowls, plates, cups at the gravesite</u>. Professor Tagliaferro does cite the number of 20,000 potsherds found by 1910 in the inner Hal Saflieni Hypogeum. Breaking of pottery such as a cup belonging to the deceased or a favorite plate or bowl could have been a ritual at the grave and replicated in the temple apse. All over the world, however, potsherds are found at ancient archaeological sites, the result of drying clay, pressure from the covering layers of sediment and soil, and the debilitating passage of time. Ritual breaking of pottery in the tomb, still, could have been a farewell act and, if so, contributed greatly to the heaps of potsherds found inside Hal Saflieni Hypogeum as reported by Prof. Tagliaferro in his 1910 list of classifications: "The variety of shapes of the vases found whole or re-constructed is very remarkable. There were jars and jugs, bowls and basins, pots and cups, ladles and strainers. But the shape that occurs most frequently is that of the bowl."

<u>Why so many bowls</u>? Whole "vases" as Professor Tagliaferro called them were the only whole pottery found intact inside the Hal Saflieni Hypogeum. Why was this? Were they protected and not ritually broken because needed to be used over and over again

for presenting grave goods? After a burial, were these items removed for safe-keeping, to be later used again to present grave goods for another burial? Or, did the multitude of bowls have another use as hanging oil lamps?

<u>Repeated ritual use of the same object at another grave</u>. The missing sherd that was being searched for, in restoring a large plate from the upper layer of tombs, was later found in a lower level of the Hypogeum – even though the partly broken plate was found in the upper chamber. How could this have happened? Was this due to repeated use of the large covered flat-bottomed bowl that was partly broken in the upper burial chamber? Some pottery could have been dedicated ritual items for the presentation of grave goods in the tomb, and used over again and again, even if partly broken.

This speculation suggests other questions:

Did the New Stone Age Maltese conduct some kind of ritual that became legendary not just on Malta but in far-flung places around the Mediterranean basin?

What brought visitors to the Maltese temples?

Did mourners come into the temples to enact or watch the symbolic smashing of pottery, as they had, perhaps, seen the family do at the tomb?

The significant amount of whole and fractured pots, jars, cups, ladles, bowls, plates, plus animal bones and fire and soot debris found inside the stone circles, and the number of temples themselves, suggest that there was a great effort made to provide enough structures and sufficient amounts of food, prepared in the temple outbuilding, using much pottery, and querns for grinding seeds and grain, to feast the local Maltese and visitors who would come by sea from around the Mediterranean basin to enter like pilgrims into the great stone circles.

\

Easy to Get to Malta

At first there was the land bridge, and then there was the sea.

People could stand atop Ragusa Ridge in Sicily and on a fair day glimpse the Maltese islands in the near distance. Wavering in the mist like a dream, beckoning.

Many set out for Malta.

"They brought with them crops like barley, two primitive forms of wheat, emmer and club wheat, and lentils. Their boats were large and seaworthy enough for the transport of domestic animals, large cattle, sheep, goats, and pigs, doubtless securely trussed to prevent accidents." (Trump 1972)

Centuries after the temples were built, people were still coming to Malta, quite easily, by sea.

"On 3 June 1780, an Englishman named Patrick Brydone, travelling with two companions, three servants, and several hired boatmen, sailed from Sicily to Malta in a small, oar-driven boat. Mr. Brydone describes the trip:

"'A little after nine (p.m.) we embarked. The night was delightful; but the wind had died away about sunset, and we were obligated to ply our oars to get into the canal of Malta. The coast of Sicily had begun to recede; and in a short time, we found ourselves in the ocean. There was a profound silence, except the noise of the waves breaking on the distant shore, which only served to render it more solemn. It was a dead calm and the moon shone bright on the waters; the waves, from the late storm, were still high; but smooth and even, and followed each other with a slow and equal pace…we had remained near an hour without speaking a word, when our sailors began their midnight hymn….

"'At last they sung us to sleep, and we awoke 40 miles distant from Sicily. We were now in the main ocean, and saw no land but Aetna, which is the perpetual pole star of these seas. -- We had a fine breeze, and about two o'clock we discovered the island of Malta; and in less than three hours more, we reached the city of Valletta.'" (Brydone 1780, 1:216-217, in Robb 2001)

Archaeologist John Robb notes that,

"Brydone's evocative description is interesting for many reasons. It demonstrates that one can row and sail a small, traditional oar-propelled craft across the 100 km strait (62.1371 miles) from Sicily to Malta in less than 24 hours, keeping Mount Aetna in sight the entire way…" (Robb 2001)

It would be short-sighted to assume that prehistoric people who populated the lands touching the various arms of the Mediterranean Sea stayed in place like so many static dots on a map.

When, in fact, Neolithic people could easily travel around by foot and navigable waters were everywhere.

Mediterranean trade boats plied the adjacent sea routes that connected lands around the Boot of Italy, near and far, seeking and delivering exotic trade items. The Boot of Italy is embraced by the various, linking arms of the Mediterranean Sea. (see map on worldatlas.com

Surrounding the great Boot are: 1) the Adriatic Sea on the long eastern side of the Boot linking the Balkans; 2) the Ionian Sea to the southeast of the Boot linking the Greek mainland; 3) the Tyrrhenian Sea on the Boot's west coast linking the volcanic Aeolian islands including Lipari and Pantelleria; and 4) to the east of Italy the Aegean Sea where over 200 islands called the Cyclades (the Greek word for 'circle') include the island of Santorini and the sacred Isle of Delos, birthplace of Artemis and Apollo which the Cyclades islands encircle.

The Ligurian Sea is the fifth arm of the Mediterranean above Corsica and Sardinia where Monaco is located on the landward coast, and also reaches the shores of southern France. The Iberian Sea is the sixth arm of the Mediterranean along the southern coast of Spain which becomes the Balearic Sea around an archipelago of islands including Mallorca and Ibiza, and then heads for the Strait of Gibraltar where it becomes the Alboran Sea.

All of these waterways provided sea routes that inter-connected the Neolithic trade exchange among the lands touching any one of the six sea arms of the Mediterranean, so that travelers coming, from near or far, could by foot or by sea reach southern Italy, then Sicily, and on to Malta situated in the middle of the Mediterranean Sea.

Seagoing trade boats could stick to the Spanish, French, Italian, Balkan, and Greek shorelines as part of trade routes that connected the various seas of the Mediterranean to Malta, directly or indirectly, from all of these Mediterranean places.

Cambridge University Professor, archaeologist John Robb, notes that,

"Malta and Sicily are sometimes inter-visible; Mount Etna in particular can sometimes be seen from Malta, especially during eruptions (Brydon 1780; Trump 1966; 49). Under Neolithic navigational conditions, with small boats or canoes either rowed or sailed, the 100 km. (62 miles) separating Malta and Sicily could have been crossed in one to three days. Travel would probably have taken place during the summer when the sea is calm…Interaction with Sicily and the mainland can actually be demonstrated by traded items…While Maltese items recognizable abroad are limited to sporadic pots…imports into the islands are more visible. Throughout the Neolithic, the Maltese had imported flint from Sicily to supplement the low-quality material available locally…High-quality flint from the Monte-Tabuto area of Sicily was particularly in vogue during the temple period, when it almost completely supplanted obsidian and made serious inroads into the consumption of local chert…

"Obsidian came to Malta from Lipari and from Pantelleria…passing down the coastline of Sicily en route. Polished stone axes were used for clearing land and for shaping timber for houses and boats…'Axe-amulets' pierced for suspension were probably made from axes nearing the end of their use-life…The nearest source for the requisite hard stones (for axes) would have been Calabria and north-east Sicily, although some greenstones may have come from much further away, in the Alpine zone. Almost 200 axe-amulets were found at the Hal Saflieni hypogeum (Evans 1971) and others have been found in temple sites…and imported lava from eastern Sicily was occasionally used for grinding… (Evans 1971), Sicilian alabaster was used for figurines…and semi-precious stones were used for beads (Evans 1971).

"Red ochre is another identifiable import, as none occurs on the islands…(and) specific pottery vessels were used for trading ochre from Sicily to Malta. Ochre was used abundantly in burials (Evans 1971)…(and) to decorate figurines and to make a red paste to decorate incised ceramics. (Evans 1959)

"As the islands became deforested, large old timbers would have become scarce…Timber was needed for the 5-10 m. (16-32.8 feet) spanning-beams supporting temple roofs (Evans 1959) and for boats. Even a relatively small dugout canoe…would have required a straight tree trunk a meter (3 feet) in diameter and 10 m. (32.8 feet) long." (Robb 2001)

Aboard the boats delivering exotic items and raw materials to Malta in its last, lavish building and remodeling Phase of 3000-2300 B.C., as inter-regional Mediterranean trade brought for example ochre, flint, and roofing timber to deforested Malta, there also came the curious incidence of Thermi Ware.

During the entire 3rd millennium B.C. in the central Mediterranean, Greek-Thermi Ware seemed to be everywhere.

At first blush, it must have been a bit puzzling in 1966 and in 1971 when Professor David Trump and Sir John Evans in their published books described sherds of Greek-Thermi Ware being found near or with the much later Tarxien Cemetery style of pottery, even finding two distinct pottery designs (Greek-Thermi vs. Tarxien Cemetery) *on the same jar*, displaying together two distinctively different cultures, styles and chronologies. The confusion had begun.

Professor Trump voiced his own theory about the confusion that came to surround the chronology and provenance of Thermi Ware, namely that,

"This ware is so far the only thing to span the gulf between the Copper Age temple civilization and the Bronze Age cultures which replaced it. Sherds (of Thermi Ware) previously were nearly always associated with TC. (Tarxien Cemetery) material, though never in closed contexts. An exception was a vessel from the Tarxien Cemetery itself, which had Thermi triangles on the lip of a TC. (Tarxien Cemetery) decorated jar." (Trump 1966).

Professor Trump is noting a chronological dilemma: finding the much earlier Greek-Thermi style "nearly always associated with" the Tarxien Cemetery pottery and the Termi distinctive triangular design even incised on a much later Tarxien Cemetery jar.

He further observed that Greek-Thermi Ware items "…were finding their way into Malta through the later Copper Age, but it did not become at all common until the Early Bronze Age when it may even have been copied locally (the TC. jar with dotted triangles on the lip)." (Trump 1966:46)

The confusion of chronology and provenance was well underway.

At first the archaeological discoveries of Greek-Thermi Ware at Skorba and an intact Greek-Thermi pedestal cup found behind an altar at Tarxien were simply reported.

After all, it was Professor Trump from his 1961-1963 Skorba excavations and the work of Sir Evans at Skorba and Tarxien who *named* the distinctive pottery style as 'Thermi Ware.' Both archaeologists confirmed the discovery of two score sherds (that is, 40 sherds) of Greek-Thermi Ware found within Neolithic layers at Skorba, plus the handsome, intact Greek-Thermi cup on a pedestal found at Tarxien behind a heavy stone altar as it was being moved to the Valletta Museum.

Professor Trump cited other imported ware also found in Neolithic layers at Skorba, even though these finds, with the exception of 40 sherds of Greek-Thermi Ware, were scant. Professor Trump as if anticipating the Thermi puzzle to come, suggested that imported pottery could have come to Neolithic Malta by 1) immigration, 2) imitation, or 3) along with the import of raw materials in foreign trade. (Trump 1966)

And thereby, Professor Trump's three-part theory of how Neolithic imports could have come to Malta foreshadowed the tangle of chronology and provenance surrounding Greek-Thermi Ware, versus look-alike Thermi-style Ware, that would continue, to this day in fact, to be found *in situ* on Malta. He wrote that,

"Considering the great quantity of pottery recovered from this site (Skorba), and the rest of Malta, the number of sherds of non-local provenance is remarkably small.

There is a possibility that at least some of the (foreign-style) pieces in styles introduced by immigrants, GhD. (Ghar Dalam), Zb. (Zebbug), and the Bronze Age groups, were made abroad and brought in with the settlers, but there is no way of distinguishing from the later local production…(and) there remain five groups (of imported pottery) which do not seem to have been made in Malta.

"Trefontane. Three sherds from Skorba and two from Santa Verna…

"Diana. One sherd from a level above the Ghar Dalam hut…

"Serra d'Alto. A single sherd of this well known and widespread style…

"Serraferlicchio. Again represented by a single sherd only…

"Thermi. Another group noticed by Evans is far commoner than these, totalling perhaps two score sherds (forty sherds) of Thermi Ware found at Skorba ….They are nearly all sherds of tronco-conic bowls with lips internally thickened. The lip nearly always bears incised standing triangles filled with dots or, more rarely, diagonal hatching. The outside is occasionally decorated with incised designs also. A few sherds possibly of larger bowls or jars with dotted bands are more probably related to these than to the Apennine Ware of Bronze Age Italy. The bowls had flat bases, though a complete one from Tarxien…stood on a high pedestal." (Trump 1966)

Thermi pedestal cup, Evans 1970.

Several accounts of finding the beautiful Greek-Thermi pedestal cup have been given: 1) it was found *behind* the great spiral altar at Tarxien where it had apparently accidentally fallen or been hidden; 2) it was found *inside* the hollow altar; 3) it was *stored inside the hollow stone of the altar until pushed out the back* of the altar as more and more animal bones were placed inside the stone hollow; 4) it was found *inside the wall fill* behind the stone altar when the wall was exposed in the 1958 move of the entire spiral altar into the Valletta Museum. In any case, the handsome cup on a pedestal was believed to be Greek Thermi Ware because its style, chronology and provenance fit into the Late Neolithic Tarxien Phase during Neolithic use of the Tarxien altar when the incised Greek Ware from the settlement of Thermi was still being made.

The Neolithic settlement of Thermi on the Greek island of Lesvos in the Aegean Sea thrived and prospered from 3000 B.C. until 2500 B.C. when, as with Malta, Thermi was abandoned.

Thermi in its heyday was an urban center with rectangular stone structures and protective stone walls with watch towers. Thermi became an economic powerhouse, but with that success came an economic rival, nearby Troy.

In the end, the inhabitants of Thermi, who had built such fabulous domestic and defensive stone architecture, and produced the handsome Thermi Ware pottery, by 2500 B.C. had to flee inland, for survival, so that Greek Thermi Ware after 2500 B.C. was no longer being produced at Thermi on Lesvos.

However, before that, trade of the stylish Thermi Ware, especially the handy pedestal cup with thickened rim and incised triangles, reached far and wide.

The sea arms of the Mediterranean – the Aegean, the Ionian, the Adriatic, and the Mediterranean itself – could have carried the handsome Thermi Ware to areas all around the central Mediterranean in the first half of the 3rd millennium B.C. when Thermi Ware (as Professor Trump and Sir Evans named the unique design) was also being produced at Troy on the Turkish coast on the Aegean Sea just north of Thermi and other nearby settlements could have also produced the Greek style of thick-rimmed cups decorated with incised triangles and lines. The items could have been shipped from Troy and Thermi on long-established direct and indirect trade routes going west, south, and northwest in the sea arms of the Mediterranean.

Thermi Ware was found by archaeologists at Neolithic sites along the east coast of the Aegean Sea at Troy, Thermi, Emporio, and the island of Poliochni to the west of Troy and northwest of Thermi; at Sitagroi and Diklli Tash in eastern Macedonia which was nearby on the Aegean Sea, northwest of Troy; at the inland sites of Radomir and Hotovo in what today is Bulgaria; at Olympia and Lerna on the Greek Peloponessus; at

Steno on the west coast of mainland Greece; at Cetina on the east coast of the Balkan peninsula; on the island of Pelagosa in the middle of the Adriatic Sea; at Navelli and Popoli on the long east coast of the Boot of Italy; at nearby Rodi Garganico and Coppa Nevigata Fontanarosa just south of Popoli; at Casal Sabini and Grottaglia on the Boot *heel* of Italy; at Zungri to the south on the *toe* of the Boot of Italy; at Ognina and Castelluccio on the coast of southern Sicily; and on Malta at Tarxien. (see map, Cazzella, Pace and Recchia 2007)

These locations suggest long-established trade routes that continued from the first half of the 3rd millennium through the second half of the 3rd millennium across the arms of the Mediterranean Sea.

The Aegean Sea must have been a convenient pocket of trade for Troy and Thermi. Direct trade routes from Troy and Thermi could have gone south to Emporio just down the coast, and northwest on a direct route to Sitagroi and Diklli Tash, near and on the Aegean Sea, respectively, in eastern Macedonia. (see map, Cazzella, Pace and Recchia 2007)

The Ionian and Adriatic Seas could have then continued the trade route from Troy and Thermi. An indirect route would have gone northwest from Diklli Tash and drop off for delivery inland to Radomir and Hotovo in what is today Bulgaria, and after that the trade boat would turn southwest and go to Olympia and Lerna on Greek Peloponessus and around the tip of the Peloponessus into the Ionian Sea. Going northwest the trade route could go to Steno, then further north into the Adriatic Sea to coastal Cetina across from the long east coast of the Boot of Italy. From Cetina, it would be a short route across the Adriatic Sea to Navelli and Popoli on the opposite coast along the Boot of Italy. (see map, Cazzella, Pace and Recchia 2007)

From Popoli, trade boats could go southeast to nearby Rodi Garganico and Coppa Nevigata Fontanarosa, then southeast to nearby Casal Sabini and Grottaglia on the Boot *heel* of Italy, and then hug the shoreline south to Zungri on the *toe* of the Boot of Italy. From Zungri, this route could go south to Ognina and Castelluccio on the coast of southern Sicily, and from there on to Malta in the middle of the Mediterranean Sea. (see map, Cazzella, Pace and Recchia 2007)

Easy for Greek-Thermi Ware to get to Malta.

Some researchers today, however, join Sir Zammit in believing that a long sea voyage from the Aegean to Malta was "dangerous" (perhaps impossible) because their seagoing vessels were "frail" and yet, Sir Zammit nonetheless envisions people arriving by sea:

"The early navigators, crossing the Mediterranean, must have been glad of a refuge for the frail crafts, in the first sheltered creek they chanced to reach in their voyages from the Eastern shores.

"This is a good reason why Hagar Qim and Mnadjra are not far from the Zurrieq creek and the Mghalaq cove…why the Tarxien and Kortin (or Cordin) buildings are at a stone's throw from the Grand Harbor. At Gozo, the Jigantia temples, though on high ground, in the Xaghra district, have the sheltered bay of Ramla at the base of the steep hill on which they stand.

"On the eastern shores of Malta, several inlets and creeks scooped more or less deeply in the rocky coast, are usually terraced up to the top, but often rise abruptly as a steep cliff…The fishermen of that district still pull up their boats on the sandy beach in summer and, climbing the hill, reach the Mjar village in about twenty minutes. The name *Mjar* given to the district, is the plural of *Mojra* meaning running water. The largest known spring of the district is now to be found half-way down the hill where it turns the hill into a vast garden…" (Zammit in *Museum Bulletin*, 1929/1935)

The journeys to Malta by sea and the resulting settlements on Malta near the harbors, coves and bays (trade vessels could deliver passengers and also take visitors back home) suggest an easy familiarity with the sea.

"Today one can travel by the Catamaran from Catania to Malta in only 3 hours if the weather is good…(and) a densely wooded small island (316 km$_2$) surrounded by the blue Mediterranean Sea could have enticed…people to choose to live here." (Zammit, 1931/1935)

Neolithic traders in the Mediterranean also chose Malta.

They could routinely dock their boats in the island coves and harbors, delivering and seeking exotic foreign goods and dropping off or picking up passengers. The active engagement of foreign exchange trade with Malta, either direct or indirect, is shown in the archaeological evidence in the temples and tombs, where Malta's need for imported raw materials not found on Malta is evidenced in red ochre decoration, exotic greenstone amulets, and lava from Mt. Etna that made hard-stone rubbers for querns in food preparation.

Trade to Neolithic Malta was lively.

When did it bring Greek-Thermi Ware to Malta?

This question is an interesting element in the puzzle of inter-regional trade to Malta because the Greek-made Thermi Ware which has been found on Malta had to get there somehow.

Before it could be imitated locally, even with local Malta clay, the Greek design had to be delivered to Malta from somehwere.

"As regards Malta, links involving the circulation of the so-called Thermi Ware may have predated the end of the Tarxien Phase of the Maltese later Neolithic (2500 B.C.). J. Evans (1956, 1971) and D. Trump (1966) suggested that this ware may have begun to arrive in Malta well before the TC. (Tarxien Cemetery) Phase (2500–1500 B.C.)…(and) that the connections between this Greek region and Sicily (and from there (to) the Aeolian islands and Malta) may have been direct or via southern Apulia…." (Cazzella, Pace and Recchia, 2007:6).

Neolithic Apulia was the *heel* on the Boot of Italy.

Beginning an easy trade route to Malta.

Discovery of the handsome pedestal cup and sherds at Tarxien that appeared to be Greek-Thermi Ware, however, was the mild beginning of later confusion as to chronology and provenance.

There was confusion from the beginning.

Sir Evans had at first attributed the Greek-Thermi Ware found in Neolithic layers at Skorba to be from the Ggantija Phase (3600-3300 B.C.) because found in statigraphic layers along with Ggantija Phase sherds and pottery. Thermi Ware was later placed by Sir Evans in the Tarxien Cemetery Phase (2500-1500 B.C.).

How could the pottery style make such a big jump forward in chronology?

Determination of the Cultural Phases in which Greek-Thermi Ware appeared on Neolithic Malta was not easy.

"It must be said that 'Thermi Ware' is a misleading definition, as it was assigned to this pottery style making reference to a ceramic type coming from the north-eastern Aegean and dating back to the first centuries of the 3rd millennium B.C.

"Whereas, in the light of the most recent data, this Maltese ceramic style appears to be strongly linked to a peculiar pottery producton characterizing both the Early Helladic III and the Dalmacian period of Cetina, which is well attested in southern Italy and Sicily too in the late 3rd millennium B.C." (Cazzella and Recchia 2012/2013)

This observation throws light on the style-chronology question (how could Greek-Thermi pottery be found with or near Tarxien Cemetery ware?) but the answer would appear clearly and in plain sight when the 3rd millennium B.C. was divided into two halves:

"The ceramic production attributable to an early phase of the Bronze Age should be connected to Thermi Ware. The ceramic style, the best-known form of which is the bowl with a thickened rim and internal decoration (most often consisting of a series of triangles) begins to appear in the north-eastern Aegean in the first half of the third millennium B.C. at Thermi on the island of Lesvos, and at Troy.

"The picture changes in the second half of the 3rd millennium. Discoveries throughout Dalmatia show that the thickened rim bowl with incised decoration was circulating in this area (the Balkans, across from the east coast of Italy). From there, this type of vessel may have made an appearance in the Peloponnese along with other design elements, such as the use of handles surrounded by incised decorations." (Copat, Danesi, Ruggini 2012:48).

The simple divide between the two halves of the 3rd millennium B.C., separating the chronology and provenance of pottery that looked so Greek but wasn't, instead of being simple, was anything but.

As Professor Trump already suspected in his 1966 Skorba excavation report, Greek-Thermi Ware may have been imitated locally, so that the handsome thick-rimmed style decorated with incised triangles looked like Greek Thermi design and became widespread and apparently popular in the central Mediterranean in the second half of the 3rd millennium B.C., but this was long after Greek-Thermi Ware was no longer being made at abandoned Thermi (although the Greek-Thermi Ware could still have been produced after 2500 B.C. at Troy and perhaps also produced at other Aegean and Pelopponese sites).

But not at abandoned Thermi on Lesvos.

Professor Trump had already provided a clue in 1966 when he cited the Tarxien Cemetery jar that showed *both* Greek-Thermi and Tarxien Cemetery design on its rim, which suggested local production, or reproduction, of the Greek-Thermi style, and decades later there was another theoretical clue:

"We may also question the implicit assumption that cultural contact leads automatically to similar pottery styles...Some Neolithic styles, notably Serra d'Alto and Diana wares, were found over broad (Mediterranean) areas because they were probably associated with long-distance trade networks...But if the meaning of ceramic styles subsequently shifted from emphasizing inter-group contacts to emphasizing local identities, then increased contact between societies may well have resulted in heightened local styles." (Robb 2001)

Therefore, the handsome and handy style of the foreign-made Greek pottery, after its initial distribution via the Mediterranean sea routes, may not have lasted as a desired trade item, but an imitated one. Although people may have come to prefer their own locally-made pottery styles, yet due to the handsome and handy look of the Greek-Thermi pedestal cup with lovely triangle patterns incised on thickened rims, whose production on Thermi stopped c. 2500 B.C. anyway, local pottery-makers most likely deftly began to craft for themselves a home-made imitation of the early 3rd millennium B.C. Greek-Thermi style. It would be hard to impossible to pin a date on the time the imitated 'Greek Thermi-style' began. Yet it is known to have flourished in the 2nd half of the 3rd millennium B.C. in central Mediterranean settlements. (see map in Cazzella, Pace, and Recchia 2007)

But what about the stylish Greek-Thermi cup on a pedestal, sealed by time, intact and concealed, inside the inner sanctum of the Neolithic Tarxien temple on Malta?

How did it get there and when?

The Greek-Thermi cup accidentally dropped or hidden behind the altar would be evidence of foreign-made items delivered by inter-regional trade to Malta.

In which half of the 3rd millennium B.C. did the Thermi-style pedestal cup get dropped or hidden at Tarxien?

Was the pedestal cup delivered by inter-regional trade in the first half of the 3rd millennium B.C. from Troy or Thermi or perhaps by a visitor or settler who brought along the pedestal cup to Malta, an "import by immigration" as Professor Trump suggested? (Trump 1966)

Was the handsome Thermi-style cup a later copy perhaps even made of Malta clay?

How did it get behind the spiral altar anyway?

After all, the Tarxien Cemetery inhabitants could well have been inside the Tarxien temple standing at the spiral altar, looking at, or using for their own purposes, the stone altar standing like a useful table with a lower cabinet in which the Thermi pedestal cup could have been stored with the altar knives, and perhaps the Thermi pedestal cup was *found* by the Tarxien Cemetery invaders inside the lower storage cabinet, and then one of them dropped it.

Did it simply roll off the table of the altar and fall behind the heavy stone piece? If so, when?

Or was the Thermi pedestal cup deliberately hidden behind the altar by a temple builder c. 2300 B.C. as the site was being hurriedly abandoned forever?

The Thermi-style cup in any case remained behind the spiral altar at Tarxien and safely out of sight until 1958. To ascertain the time frame, Professor Trump declared that "…the Tarxien pedestalled bowl came from a Tarxien (Phase) deposit into which it could hardly have infiltrated subsequently in one piece." (Trump 1966:46)

Therefore Professor Trump is suggesting a pre-2300 B.C. date of the cup's accidental or deliberate concealment behind the Tarxien altar. But the lingering question is whether the pedestal cup, found intact behind the Tarxien altar, was a Greek import which, somehow, could "span the gulf" between the Late Neolithic Tarxien Phase and the Tarxien Cemetery Phase where the Termi-style was continually being found. Recall that Professor Trump said about Thermi Ware:

"This ware is so far the only thing to span the gulf between the Copper Age temple civilization and the Bronze Age cultures which replaced it. Sherds (of Thermi Ware) previously were nearly always associated with TC. (Tarxien Cemetery) material, though never in closed contexts. An exception was a vessel from the Tarxien Cemetery itself, which had Thermi triangles on the lip of a TC. (Tarxien Cemetery) decorated jar." (Trump 1966).

If the Maltese archipelago went empty for years, perhaps centuries, after the temple builders left it c. 2300 B.C., there would have been no trade exchange with Malta. Inter-regional trade boats would have no reason to come to the empty islands. Any Greek-Thermi items from Neolithic Malta that could "span the gulf" of time before the newcomers took over would be those items hurriedly left behind when the temple builders left the islands around 2300 B.C.

Trade could have resumed after the "gulf" of time when the newcomers to Malta established their presence on the islands, whether years, decades or centuries later.

If the Maltese archipelago did remain empty for an unknown time, there was thus an empty gulf of time before the Bronze Age newcomers arrived on Malta and used, as the archaeological evidence shows, the temples of Skorba, Tarxien and Hagar Qim. The question is: after 2300 B.C., how could Greek-Thermi or imitation-Thermi "span the gulf" of time between the two cultures and be found in Tarxien Cemetery layers, as Professor Trump observed? (Trump 1966)

The temple builders may have left behind some of their Greek-Thermi Ware on the temple floor, as they departed Malta, and the Bronze Age newcomers may have simply picked up the Greek pottery and used it with their own, hence creating the illusion that there was no break in the temple occupation on Malta.

Some theories have suggested that the temple builders did not leave Malta but stayed on with their Greek-Thermi Ware and coexisted with the newcomers, but other theorists think the gulf of time on Malta after 2300 B.C. was empty, perhaps for years or decades, perhaps for centuries. Pottery left from an earlier time, found and re-used, cannot indicate whether the time gap between use of the temples was empty or not.

To address some of these questions, what appeared to be Greek-Thermi pottery or imitated Thermi-style was recently found in or near Tarxien Cemetery deposit layers at the sprawling Tas-Silg temple site, continuing the initial confusion from decades ago.

Researchers using scientific analysis tested a small number of the numerous clay sherds found in various chronological layers at the Tas-Silg site. Only two Thermi-style sherds were tested for clay analysis. Results of the neuron activation tests showed that of the 41 sherds being tested (except for several Phoenician transport amphorae) all were made from local clay. (Mommsen, et al. 2006)

This analysis of this small sample of Tas-Silg pottery fragments does suggest that some of the 'Thermi-style' pottery sherds that were being found in or near Tarxien Cemetery sites in the earlier excavations of Sir Evans and Professor Trump, were likely imitation Greek-Thermi, perhaps even locally produced on Malta from local clay (as the Mommsen group theorized), or produced for export by central Mediterranean settlements such as Cetina and delivered to Malta in the second half of the 3rd millennium B.C. (see trade map in Cazzella, Pace and Recchia 2007 on academia.edu).

The initial confusion from decades ago continued to be chronology and look-alike styles. But the chronology and provenance of Greek-Thermi versus imitation-Thermi is not so much a tantalizing mystery as *evidence* of the inter-regional trade that bought both real and imitation Thermi Ware to Malta's shores.

Finding sherds that *looked like* the handsome Greek-made Thermi Ware in or near Tarxien Cemetery sites was simply misleading, as Sir Evans foreshadowed when he vacillated between placing Greek-Thermi from Skorba in the Ggantija Phase (3600/3300-3000 B.C.) and then deciding to place the Thermi-style as well in the Tarxien Cemetery Phase (2500-1500 B.C.) when the Bronze Age newcomers operated the Tarxien temple as a burial crematorium.

Determining chronology can be a fluid process: recall that it was Professor Trump's finds in 1961-63 at Skorba that caused Sir Evans to reverse his previous dating of the Zebbug Phase as coming *after* the Mgarr Phase, because the Trump excavations showed that Zebbug was older than Mgarr. So too there was the change in placing Greek-Thermi Ware found at Skorba in the Ggantija Phase, that dating being based on finding Ggantija Phase sherds with or near the Greek-Thermi sherds in Neolithic Skorba layers. The Thermi-style was later placed in a time range extending from the Ggantija Phase through the Tarxien Cemetery Phase.

Determining chronology and provenance can be confusing when earlier pottery can be found with pottery of a later time, but the trail of trade that brought the *real Greek-Thermi Ware* to Malta in the first half of the 3rd millennium B.C. clearly cannot end with the 40 sherds found at Skorba or the pedestal cup and sherds at Tarxien but the trail of trade continues to be found, with a great deal of archaeological luck, at the Tas-Silg site today.

There *real Greek-Thermi* pottery was found.

The much-used Tas-Silg temples have history to tell from across the centuries. It is believed to have been originally built by Late Neolithic Maltese during the Tarxien Phase, and after the temple builders abandoned Malta c. 2300 B.C., the Bronze Age newcomers arrived and stayed for about one thousand years until 1500 B.C., followed by the Phoenicians, and finally by the Romans who in turn occupied the four temples at the sprawling Tas-Silg site. In the course of time, Temple 1 at Tas-Silg was dedicated to the Punic goddess Astarte and later to the Roman goddesses Hera and Juno. The intense use over time of Tas-Silg resulted in greatly disturbed areas in the site due to spoliatory events such as plundering or the removing of earlier Neolithic stones for new use or remodeling, as, for example, removing Neolithic stones from the Temple 1 courtyard to make a new cobbled courtyard there for the Phoenicians.

Finding real Greek-Thermi Ware in the midst of the rubble from extensive use and re-use of Tas-Silg, and the resulting large number of pottery sherds from the various cultures who came there, began with recent excavations during 2003-2009.

"The new excavations of the prehistoric layers of Tas-Silg have given us a reliable stratigraphic sequence that extends from the Late Neolithic to the Bronze Age…A total of over 6,500 pottery fragments we have analyzed from a stylistic point of view, taking into account the specific chrono-typological issues in each of the different periods…

"The most widely accepted chronology for the ceramic artifacts of the Temple period was elaborated by Evans and Trump. On the basis of the plans of the different 'temples', Evans put forward the idea of evolution from the less complex three-apse 'temples' (such as at Skorba, Ta' Hagrat and Kordin III) to the temples with a more complex plan (such as Tarxien, Hagar Qim and Mnajdra)…On this basis, and that of the finds of the hypogeum at Hal Saflieni, Evans proposed dividing the Temple period into three sub-phases: Ggantija, Saflieni, and Tarxien…

"Our impression is that this proposed division into phases tends to be too schematic and above-all that the functional difference between 'temple' and cemeteries has not been sufficiently taken into consideration, since it might have affected the presence of different ceramic containers in the two different contexts (Copat, Danesi, Ruggini 2012:39-40)

Style and chronology in and out of context was what complicated from the very beginning the archaeological discoveries of Thermi Ware on Neolithic Malta. Fortunately enough, Late Neolithic layers containing Thermi Ware were preserved in an indisputable context of style and chronology at Tas-Silg.

"Within the sanctuary of Tas-Silg very few Late Neolithic layers are still preserved, due to the unbroken occupation of the site up to the historical periods, as well as spoliatory activities. As a result, less than 450 of the 4,000 ceramic ceramic sherds analysed come from layers relating to this period, while the others are all residual. The Late Neolithic layers have been grouped into 4 sub-phases: the 'before building' phase…which has yielded nearly 50 fragments, the 'building phase'…which has yielded over 80 fragments, the 'use of the sanctuary phase' with nearly 200 fragments, and finally the 'collapse phase'…which has yielded about 100 fragments (Copat, Danesi, Ruggini 2012:47)

The kinds of pottery found in Neolithic layers from the four sub-phases were: carinated bowls 58%, ovoid jars 14%, tronco-conical bowls 9%, carinated hole-mouth jars 7%, globular jars 4%, and shallow curvilinear bowls 4%, plus one single jar and one heart-shaped jar (Copat, Danesi, Ruggini 2012:41).

"As far as the Late Neolithic is concerned, the archaeological deposit was scarcely preserved since the long-lasting use of the buildings had resulted, in many cases, in the partial removal of the original deposit…Nevertheless, in some cases Late Neolithic collapse layers were never removed and we could investigate the deposits underneath which were pretty well preserved as these had been sealed up by the collapses" (Cazzella and Recchia 2012/2013:16-17).

A collapse event could have been a fire, accidental or otherwise set, which by chance secured forever, through the turbulence of time and Phoenician re-use of the Neolithic areas, a Neolithic layer of temple items by burying them in the cinders and ash from the fire, or, the collapse event could have been the wooden roof that caught fire and fell, burying Neolithic items in cinders and white ash, or, perhaps crumbling stones from an old wall simply crumbled and fell, sealing off Neolithic areas in the temple that were apparently never repaired nor mended. Thereby a secure, that is to say, undisturbed, layer of Neolithic pottery and other items was protected inside a temple apse.

A collapse event could have been a fire, accidental or otherwise set, which by chance secured forever, through the turbulence of time and Phoenician re-use of the Neolithic areas, a Neolithic layer of temple items by burying them in the cinders and ash from the fire, or, the collapse event could have been the wooden roof that caught fire and fell, burying Neolithic items in cinders and white ash, or, perhaps crumbling stones from an old wall simply crumbled and fell, sealing off Neolithic areas in the temple that were apparently never repaired nor mended. Thereby a secure, that is to say, undisturbed, layer of Neolithic pottery and other items was protected from further damage or use inside a Neolithic temple apse.

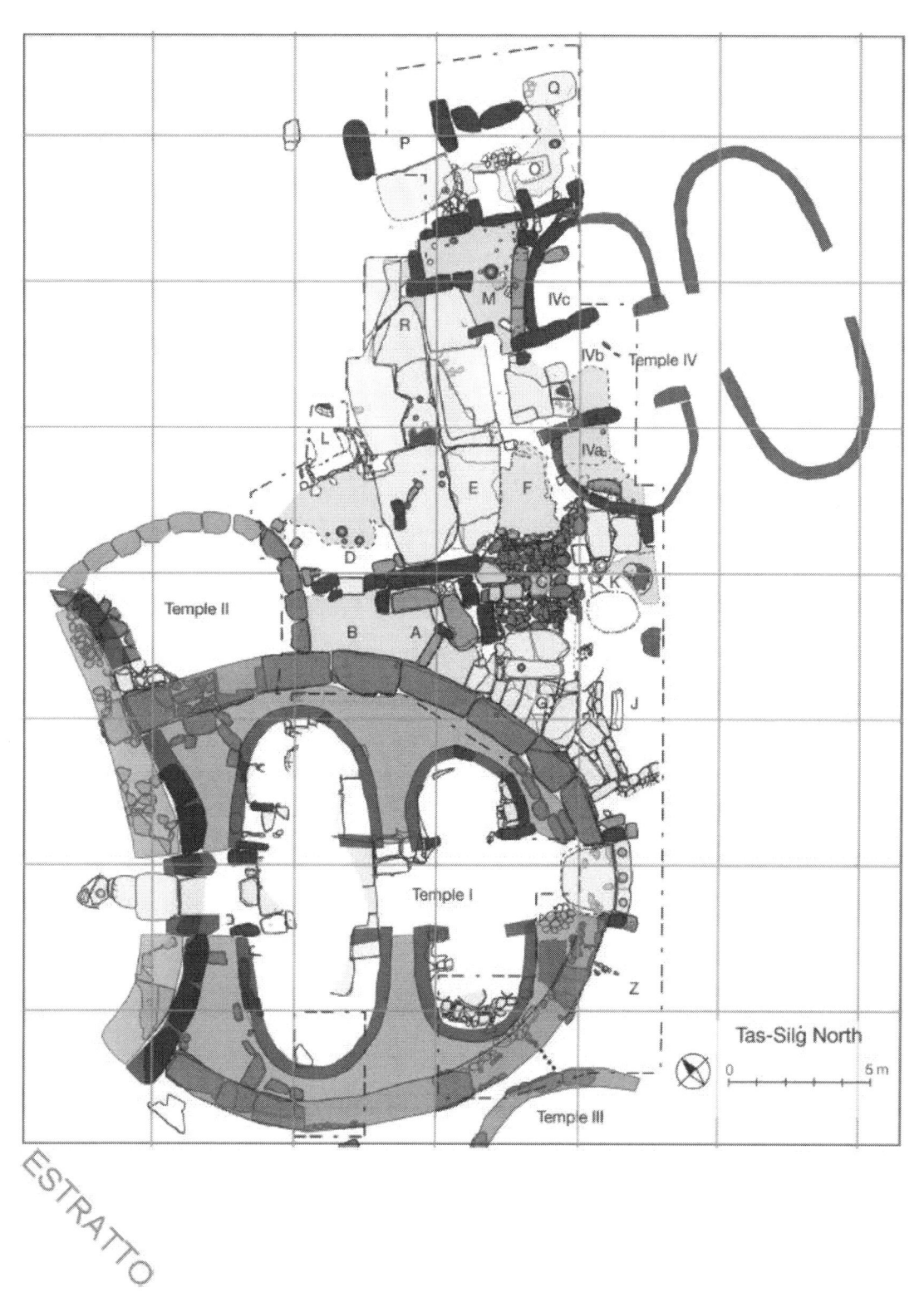

Sketch of temples is from *Tas-Silġ: the Late Neolithic megalithic sanctuary and its re-use during the Bronze Age and the Early Iron Age*, Scienza dell'Antichita, Sapienza Universita di Roma, 2012/2013:19 on academia.edu by A. Cazzella and G. Recchia 2012/2013.

Areas of collapse that were never repaired, occurred in Temple 1 at Tas-Silg, and the collapse events there are dated to 2300-2200 B.C.

"As far as the buildings between Temples I and IV are concerned, the most impressive and uncommon features are a megalithic steps (G) which leads to a raised platform (C) supported by a rubble filling that must have been enveloped by orthostats, now missing…Leading from the north side of the eastern entrance of Temple I, this staircase was tapering-shaped due to the curvilinear conformation of Temple I's enclosure wall. The lower steps form a sort of exedra facing a forecourt (J), which is also overlooked by the raised platform C. The bulk of the rubble supporting the platform divides courtyard J from from both Temple IV and further chambers (A & B) located westwards along the enclosure wall of Temple I…The south edge of courtyard J was likely constituted by the path leading to the eastern doorway of Temple I…A small torba floored room (K) was made in the space between the east side of the platform support and the south side of apse IVA, its shape being therefore irregular. The negative impression of an orthostat, which was probably removed by spoliatory activities, is recognizable on the south side of the room, suggesting a partition between this room and courtyard J. Some Late Neolithic layers were preserved inside the room as well as a circular clay cooking platform…" (Cazzella and Recchia 2012/2013:24).

In the inner Temple 1 at Tas-Silg in sealed Neolithic areas A/B, G/J, I/Z, Greek Thermi Ware was found, see hatch-marked areas in sketch of Temple I where Thermi Ware was discovered (Cazzella and Recchia 2012/2013:30)

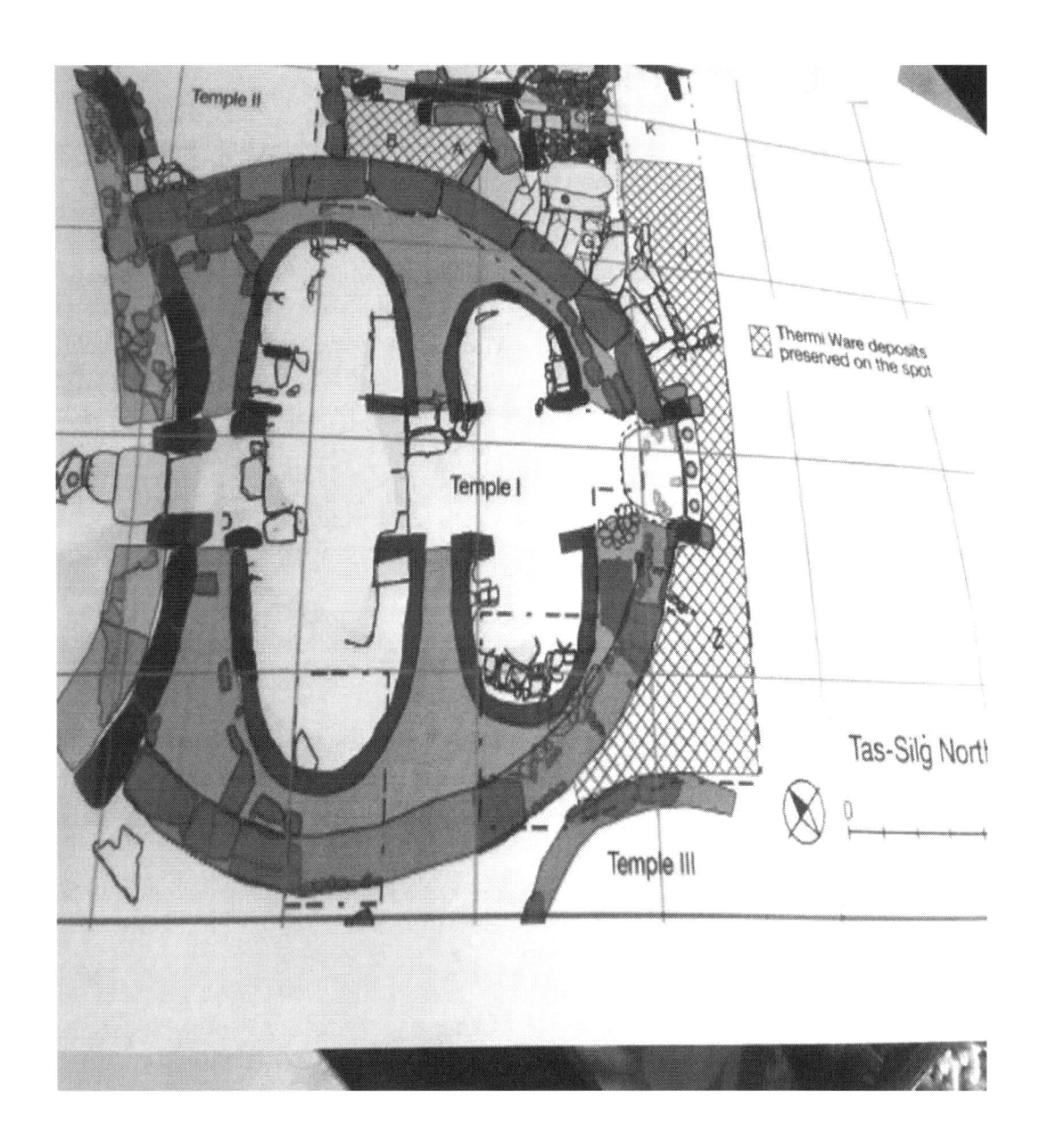

Sketch of Thermi Ware found in Temple I is from *Tas-Silg: the Late Neolithic megalithic sanctuary and its reuse during the Bronze Age and the Early Iron Age*, Scienza dell'Antichita, Sapienza Universita di Roma, 2012/2013:30 on academia.edu by A. Cazzella and G. Recchia 2012/2013.

"…the so-called Thermi Ware which seems to have come into use in association with the late Tarxien pottery production rather than replacing it (Cazzella and Recchia 2012/2013:29).

"According to the stratigraphic sequences unearthed at Tas-Silg, the compresence of Thermi ware and Tarxien Cemetery ware at an early stage of the Early Bronze Age can be discounted" (Cazzella and Recchia 2012/2013:29)

And so, with the recent Tas-Silg Neolithic collapse area findings, how can finding Thermi Ware in or near Tarxien Cemetery deposits be explained?

One explanation is the unintentional finding of the earlier pottery mixed in or near the later Tarxien Cemetery deposits, because, to reiterate,

"Recent research cconducted at the site of Tas-Silg has allowed us to unearth some reliable stratigraphic sequences, within which it is possible to clearly distinguish how some levels of Thermi Ware precede those with Tarxien Cemetery pottery" (Copat, Danesi, Ruggini 2012:48).

Judging from the Neolithc collapse areas in Temple 1, it is likely that the Greek Thermi Ware was an earlier arrival than the collapse date of 2300 B.C. which sealed time inside Temple 1, and it is also likely that all the apparent Thermi Ware found in or near Tarxien Cemetery sites was either imitated-Thermi or Greek-Thermi still in use in the temple from an earlier time. What, is a hungry and thirsty person likely to discard an old but handsome and handy pedestal cup?)

When Professor Trump stated that excavated Thermi bowls, for example from recent finds in the Xaghra Circle, "…were found rarely in temple period contexts, and much more commonly in Tarxien Cemetery deposits," he was overlooking the possibility that, as at Tas-Silg, "…some levels with Thermi Ware precede those with Tarxien Cemetery pottery. The presence of Tarxien Temple pottery in these levels could be due to the unintentional retrieval of older materials…" (Copat, Danesi, Ruggini 2012:48).

This suggests that earlier Greek-Thermi items could have simply *continued being used*, perhaps found in the abandoned temple by the newcomers, and incorporated into their own pottery during the later Tarxien Cemetery phase.

This would explain how Greek-Thermi Ware or look-alike Thermi ware continued to be found in Tarxien Cemetery deposits in the abandoned temples.

Either produced in Thermi or Troy or other nearby Aegean production sites in the first half of the 3rd millennium B.C., or imitated later in localized sites in the second half of the 3rd millennium B.C., the 'Thermi-style' items continually found in later Tarxien Cemetery sites could have simply been old Thermi items incorporated by the Bronze Age newcomers and mixed in with their own pottery style, and, it is known for a fact that the Thermi incised triangles design was found incised on their own later pottery, the two styles found on the same jar, as Professor Trump observed.

In any case, right from the start, the handsome Thermi style that seemed to be everywhere, aroused a continuing confusion of chronology and provenance that could be resolved by the "unintentional retrieval of older materials" in continuous use in the later Tarxien Cemetery sites, or by finding in or near the Tarxien Cemetery sites imitation-Thermi imports from central Mediterranean sites or even made on Malta.

"It must be said that 'Thermi Ware' is a misleading definition, as it was assigned to this pottery style making reference to a ceramic type coming from the north-eastern Aegean and dating back to the first centuries of the 3rd millennium B.C. Whereas in the light of the most recent data, this Maltese ceramic style appears to be strongly linked to a peculiar pottery production characterizing both the Early Heraldic III and the Dalmatian period of Cetina, which is well attested in southern Italy and Sicily too in the late 3rd millennium B.C. (Cazzella and Recchia 2012/2013:29).

Finally from Neolithic Tas-Silg the question of Greek-Thermi Ware vs. the later look-alike Thermi-style being continually found in or near Tarxien Cemetery layers may be put to rest by collapse events which have preserved information from Neolithic layers sealed in time. These undisturbed layers preserve the Greek-Thermi trail of trade to Neolithic Malta that had to occur before the end of the Tarxien Phase when the collapse events occurred at Neolithic Tas-Silg.

Greek-Thermi Ware found undisturbed in Neolithic collapse areas at Tas-Silg, and the imitation 'Thermi-style' that looked so Greek but *wasn't*, but found in or near Tarxien Cemetery layers at Tas-Silg, Tarxien, Hagar Qim, and Skorba, show that in the first half of the 3rd millennium B.C., the inter-regional trade routes, direct or indirect, brought imports of Greek-Thermi pottery to Malta, and the later Thermi-style that imitated it continued to be imported to Malta in the second half of the 3rd millennium B.C. from central Mediterranean settlements such as Cetina or the Peloponnesus (unless locally copied on Malta) (see map in Cazzella, Pace, and Recchia, 2007).

Real Greek-Thermi Ware from afar and local-imitation-Thermi from central Mediterranean sites, or even locally copied on Malta, are a testament to the inter-regional trade that brought the style to Malta in the first place.

Or, as Professor Trump suggested, the inter-regional visitor may have brought the Greek-Thermi cup to the Tarxien altar, for the Thermi-style continued to appear from one provenance or another inside the Neolithic temples in *both halves* of the 3rd millennium B.C., the stylish items "finding their way to Malta" (Trump 1966) because Malta was always easy to get to.

Trade items from Southern France and the Greek settlement of Lerna also made their way to Neolithic Malta on the inter-regional trade routes.

"That the Maltese must from the time of their original settlement have been engaged in active trade…is obvious and easily provable. The geology of the Maltese islands is simple, and they lack many of the resources necessary to a people even in a Neolithic stage of development, such as flint, hard igneous rocks for axes, and red ochre for coloring-matter…Sicilian contacts are clearly attested in the pottery…(and) the black volcanic glass, obsidian is being imported as shown by the piece found at Mgarr, and this is most likely to have come from the Lipari island….

"The contacts…especially some of the Xemxjia material does indicate…south-east Italy, Sardinia, and southern France…Many of the new types of pottery – studded wares, coarse unpolished wares with plastic decoration, etc. – could have been adopted in Malta under the influence of either south-east Italy or southern France, but the bowls with channelled decoration could only have been copied from the latter region (of southern France)." (Evans 1959)

"Further confirmation of trade connections in this north-westerly direction is not far to seek. The tunnel-handle may have been adopted in Sardinia and France from Malta…(and) From Tarxien comes a fragment of a pot with a plastic cordon which is pierced along its whole length with holes at regular intervals. It is quite unlike any Maltese pottery, but identical with a type very characteristic of the culture of southern France and Liguria at this time. In the Hypogeum, moreover, there was found a small bead of greenstone in the shape of two spheres joined together, above which rises a small projection pierced with a hole for suspension. This is an unusual form of bead, known as a 'winged bead', and this example is unique in Malta, though the type is extremely common in the contemporary (Neolithic) cultures of southern France and Liguria.

"To these undoubted imports we might also add the buttons of shell (and, in one instance, of greenstone) of V-perforation, of which one occurs as early as…the Zebbug tombs, and the greenstone axe-pendants (miniature axes perforated at the butt for suspension) which were found in large numbers at the Hypogeum and have turned up sporadically at other sites. Both these types are common to the west and north-west of Malta, in Spain, southern France, and Sardinia, but not so common in Italy and Sicily.

"Thus we can be fairly sure that the Maltese islands were connected by a web of trade relations that were more than sporadic with most of the neighbouring lands of the Western Mediterranean, some of which lay at a considerable distance." (Evans 1959)

That web of trade relations brought a uniquely decorated bone that was found inside the Tarxien temple and also inside the 'House of Tiles' on the Greek island of Lerna dating from Early Helladic I, c. 3200 B.C.

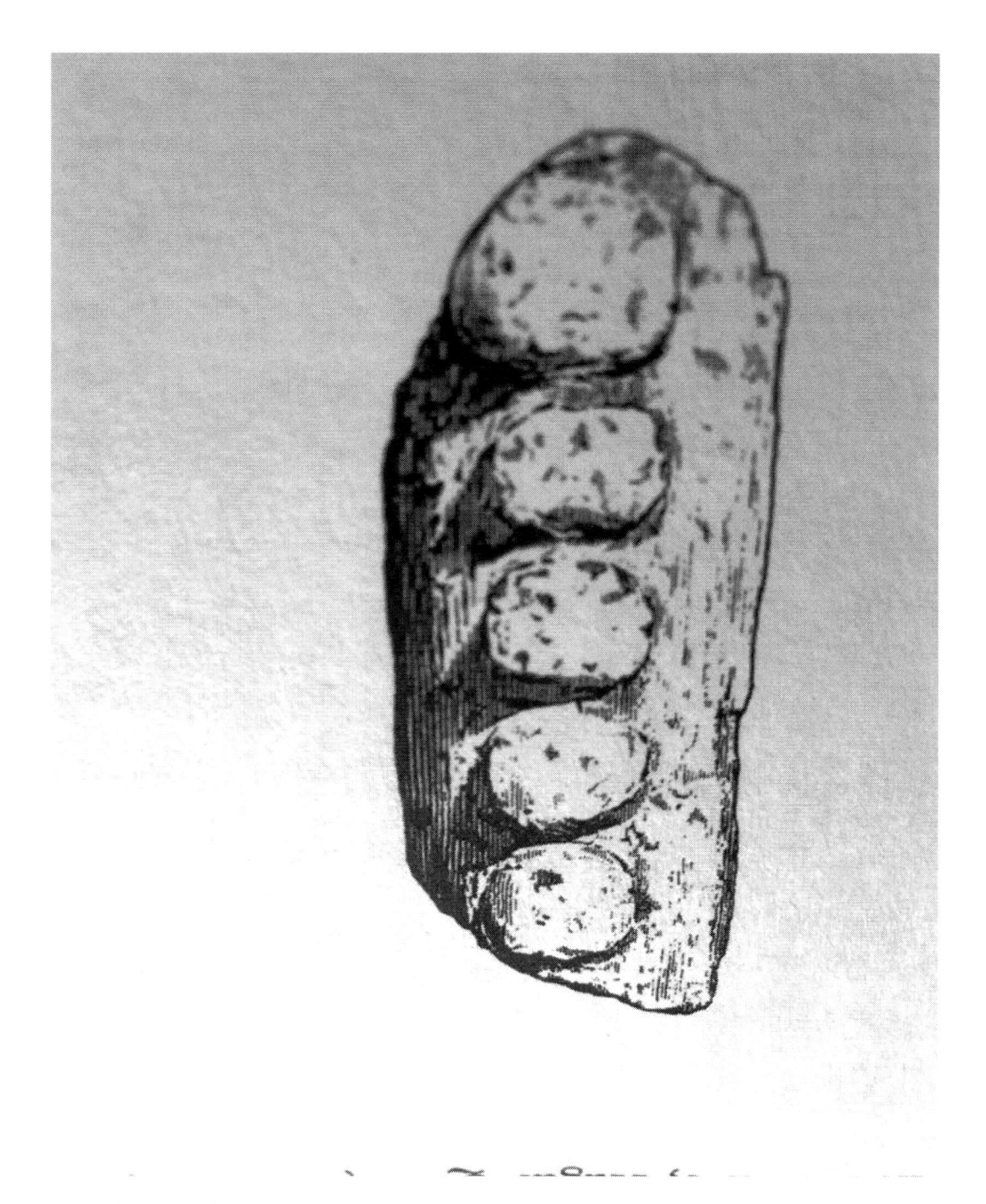

Knobbed bone from Tarxien, Evans 1970.

This elegant bone implement is described in an excavation report on the Lerna settlement (Caskey, 1952-53).

"Among the utensils and miscellaneous implements recovered here is one of special interest, a thin strip of bone, 0.106 m. long (inches), with seven hemispherical knobs on one flat side…The strip is slightly bowed in its length, rounded at its tips, and well polished; otherwise it is undecorated, and it is not pierced for attachment or suspension. There can be no doubt that it belongs to a class of objects already known outside Greece, about which there has been much speculation. Three were found by Schliemann at Troy, one purportedly in debris of the Second Settlement; several others came from tombs excavated many years ago in Sicily; and still another was recovered more recently at Tarxien in Malta.

"Our example from Lerna is, to the best of my knowledge, the only one yet found in Greece. Its finding place…is fixed in the earliest floor deposit that contained Grey Minyan ware, immediately above a stratum in which only Early Helladic pottery occurred. Two successive Early Helladic levels overlay the ruins of the great building which we were seeking particularly to examine." (Caskey 1952-53)

Early Helladic I at 3200 B.C. corresponds to the Tarxien Phase (3300/3000-2500 B.C.) on Neolithic Malta.

How did the uniquely decorated bone get into the Neolithic temple activity of lavish Tarxien? Did it arrive by inter-regional trade? For this decorated bone implement has been found along with Thermi Ware at various central Mediterranean sites (see map in Cazzella, Pace and Recchia 2007 on academia.edu).

Instead of self-isolating Malta in the last and lavish temple-building Phase (3300/3000-2500 B.C.), the Maltese temple builders could *not* self-isolate, because they needed specific import items in order to build, maintain, and decorate the temples, especially needing greenstone for amulets, timber for roofing, red ocher for painting in both temple and tomb, and exotic Greek Thermi pedestal cups and decorated bone implements from Lerna or Troy for use at the Tarxien spiral altar and in the mourning feast.

Why would the inter-regional trade that brought to Malta those necessary items be deliberately cut off? Why would the temple builders withdraw from trade? Especially in the great finale of temple building and remodeling in the final Tarxien Phase?

Only scant evidence of Maltese trade exchange items have been found by archaeologists excavating the Neolithic Mediterranean inter-regional trade sites abroad, but this could simply mean that because some Maltese export items were perishable, they left no archaeological trace. (Robb 2001)

One such perishable export item may have been honey.

The written history of the later Greeks referred to "honey-sweet Malta" and called the island archipelago *Melite* after the Greek word for honey. In the Biblical account of Paul's shipwreck on a Mediterranean island, Acts 28:1 states "…and they knew the island was Melita." (Dengli 2001)

When people could finally write history, ancient Greek lore said the Maltese bees were special. The wild flowers of Malta and Comino especially and other indigenous flowers on trees in the archipelago provided for a special nectar that was legendary in ancient times and is still being made by the bees on Malta today.

The islands still offer to bees a multifloral assortment of flowers, even today in the highly developed land of the archipelago: from the end of May through the end of June and first week of July there are flowers from clover, orange trees, and wild thyme. Wild thyme grows in the north of Malta and on Comino.

Then in the last weeks of August, and into September if there is no heavy rainfall, eucalyptus flowers are in bloom. Even in October, there are flowers when carob trees bloom for the bees to sample (on vassallohistory.wordpress.com).

Did these flowers also bloom in Neolithic times?

Could honey have been a seasonal Maltese export in the Neolithic trade exchange?

If so, how would the honey be shipped? And why would the Maltese transport pots for shipping honey not be found abroad?

Maltese honey in Neolithic times would perhaps be shipped in sealed jars that would go back and forth to Malta for re-fills, as the jars would be special re-fill jars made with lugs below the rim, onto which lugs a tight lid would be screwed in place and then sealed with tallow and clay.

Lugged jar with holes for fastening cover, Evans 1959.

This large 20-inch-tall jug was found *in situ* at Tarxien with lugs placed just below the rim upon which lugs a lid would be fitted. Such a transport jar could be filled with honey. Ready for shipping to far places.

Then, perhaps as the late-summer season wore on, when honey was ready to be shipped even in September and October, the same lugged jars would be sent back to Malta for a re-fill. Transport jars made at Greek Thermi and Troy could have been shipped back and forth in the seasonal Maltese honey trade. Shipping honey would be done in summer and late-summer/early autumn when the seas were calm.

Re-fill honey jars could account for the forty sherds of Greek-Thermi Ware which the Trump excavation found at Skorba, and for other Greek-Thermi Ware found during excavations at the two sprawling Late Neolithic temples at Tarxien and Tas-Silg.

For the temple outbuildings at all three Neolithic temples of Skoba, Tarxien and Tas-Silg, were workshops where lithic, obsidian and flint tools were found that could have been used to secure jars of honey by sealing the lids with heated tallow and clay.

The observation that the temple outbuildings were 'production centers' (along with speculation that the temple outbuildings produced clothing and textiles, as put forth by Sir Zammit, Colin Renfrew and others) can be taken into account here, to illumine a scenario of the Maltese honey export trade.

Some theorists say that based on the huge complex of Phoenician bee hives, still extant today on Malta, it was the Phoenicians who brought bees to Malta well past the Neolithic era, but how can this be proven, and how to imagine a Phoenician trade ship loaded with angry bee hives, being shifted this way and that, as the life in the hives is disrupted and agitated by winds and waves. What sailor or captain would want that cargo?

Ancient Greek accounts describe the 'special' bees on honey-sweet Malta. Were these special bees on the islands when new settlers came trekking in hopeful groups across the old land bridge?

Could there have gathered on beautiful, honey-sweet Malta, embraced by a lapis lazuli sea, a rare admixture of people from far-away places? It would be short-sighted to think that people in Mediterranean prehistory stayed in place and did not move around the adjoining lands and seas, or that trade and visitor interaction by sea in Neolithic times by-passed Malta.

The Neolithic trade exchange did not by-pass Malta, but brought to the island archipelago not just exotic material goods in the trade exchange, but also exotic *ideas*.

"There were no borders for traders, as trade brought accumulation of material wealth and knowledge. Various script systems, 'foreign' languages (initially the names of exotic items) and expertise in technologies were introduced by traders, bringing with them new ideas…concepts travelled as ballast embodied in the traded items, or "in the minds of envoys, merchants, and craftsmen – as an intellectual stowaway" (Dogan and Michailidou on helios-eie-ekt.gr)

Sir Evans noted that Sir Zammit "…imagined Malta as a kind of international 'sacred island' to which shipwrecked mariners came to offer thanks for their survival… (although) the temples have yielded no collection of international nautical *ex votos*. Nevertheless, they have produced, as we have also seen, a fair amount of direct and indirect evidence of contact between the temple-builders and men of other lands, contacts which were made and kept up for purposes of trade in all probability." (Evans 1959)

Trade easily coming to Malta's shores, joining Malta to inter-regional trade routes, dropping off goods and new settlers, or delivering visitors seeking the legendary temples, obviously did not leave Malta isolated from the outside world. The question of Malta's insularity has been described by Cambridge University archaeologist, Professor John Robb:

"Malta in the temple period has almost unanimously been regarded as isolated, turned inward and rejecting contact with the external world…The argument for isolation is built upon four observations. First, the amount of obsidian, which was obtained from Lipari or Pantelleria…drops sharply in the temple period. Secondly, few imported pots have been found on Malta. Third, unlike earlier pottery styles, temple-period ceramics differ markedly from contemporary Sicilian and Italian pottery. Finally, no neighboring peoples made monumental ritual structures similar in any way to the temples (on Neolithic Malta).

"While all of these indicate changed conditions of contact, they must be interpreted within a regional context. Throughout the central Mediterranean, the obsidian trade dropped sharply after the initial Copper Age. Declining obsidian on Malta thus probably reflects not Maltese isolation so much as a general regional trend having to do with a new repertoire of traded objects. Similarly, pottery in general seems not to have been an important inter-regional trade item in the Copper Age. Hence the lack of traded pottery on Malta may not necessarily indicate lack of contact; popular Copper Age trade goods such as ochre and polished stone tools are well-represented on the (Maltese) islands…

"Similarly, while fourth-third millennia pottery on Malta has its own characteristic styles, the same is true of any region throughout southern Italy and Sicily…Hence again, we may be seeing not Maltese isolation from external cultures, but rather a region-wide shift in the scale and texture of the cultural map towards more localized styles." (Robb 2001)

Real-Greek-Thermi Ware and the later look-alike-Thermi Ware found in different time frames inside Skorba, Tarxien and Tas-Silg, all confirm that Malta in the first half of the 3rd millennium B.C. and in the second half remained connected to the active inter-regional trade from near and far, because it was easy to get to Malta, on trade boats bringing exotic items such as elegant knobbed-bone cutting implements and Greek Thermi pedestal cups, the localized copies of these handsome cups coming later, for example from Cetina, as well as bringing building materials to Malta in Late Neolithic days when the temple builders needed obsidian, flint, alabaster, timber, lava and ocher, as the island had none of these, and travelers came as well, desiring to settle on Malta or visit the legendary temples on Malta whose use was well-known all around the Mediterranean basin.

After grave goods such as a cooked meal for the journey, greenstone amulets and shell necklaces were laid at a burial site in the dark underground, the mourners would leave the the tomb and walk to the nearby temple.

And there in the temple, as in the adjoining tomb, the Fat Lady waited.

Photo Courtesy Bradshaw Foundation.

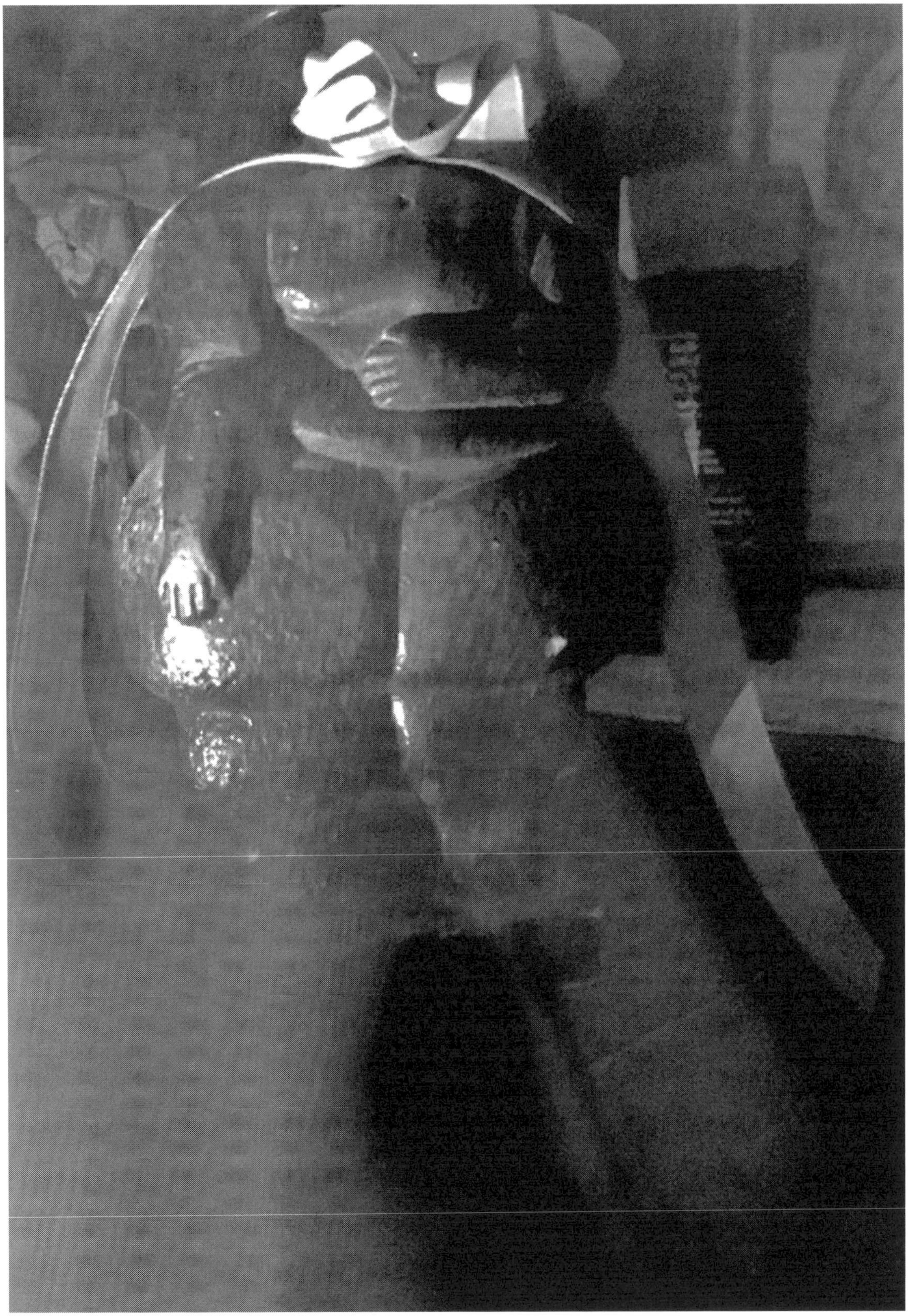

Small Fat Lady Figurines and Large Standing Statues of Same

Found in the Hal Saflieni Hypogeum along with the beautiful Sleeping Lady are the damaged figures of two Fat Ladies sitting side by side on a low couch.

"There is a good example from the Hypogeum and two from Hagar Qim, of which one is the largest and finest specimen known. This figure stands upon a pedestal, the front of which is adorned with rows of drilled holes and painted red." (Evans 1959)

At Hagar Qim temple, seven Fat Lady figurines were found stashed beneath a stone step inside the temple, and at magnificent Tarxien the remains of a clear and definitive statement of the Fat Lady narrative is expressed by a huge standing statue which was 8 to 9 feet tall. It was found badly damaged as if deliberately sliced in half, perhaps by Bronze Age newcomers who may have been taken aback, even startled, perhaps intimidated, by the giant figure looming in the abandoned temple.

Tarxien standing statue, Copyright 2016 Ross-Edison.

Tarxien standing statue, Copyright 2016 Ross-Edison.

Remains of Standing Statue, Hagar Qim, Copyright 2016 Ross-Edison

Clearly the archaeological evidence shows the Fat Lady standing, sitting and sleeping in Neolithic temple and tomb, but why?

What was she doing there?

Photo Courtest Bradshaw Foundation.

Sir Zammit put it bluntly.

"Our knowledge of these early Maltese settlers comes first and foremost from their graves and temples. The objects and furnishings found there, show clearly...the adoration of a corpulent fertility deity." (Zammit 1931/1994)

There is confusion here, however, because the Maltese Fat Lady, a ubiquitous presence inside both temple and tomb, has been widely misperceived as a fertility goddess. Yet some of these 'corpulent' (Zammit 1931/1994) figurines are even questioned as to their gender.

If their gender is in question, how could they be goddesses, particularly female figures representing fertility?

The Fat Lady statuettes and large standing statues of same, found *in situ* in both temple and tomb were there to present a narrative, which was not about fertility.

Her presence in both temple and tomb was that of an older woman, perhaps of a grandmotherly age, having already passed through the prime stages of life including the child-bearing age, whose sturdy figure can hardly represent a state or condition of child-bearing fertility.

But something else.

So it must be asked: if not 'fertility' then, *what*?

What did the Fat Lady represent? How complicated could that be?

After all, this was the Stone Age.

What did the Maltese Fat Lady, one arm folded in acceptance, so similar to the female Cycladic figures, represent to mourners in Malta's Neolithic temples and tombs?

Why was this genial figure even there?

What was the big draw?

Copyright 2016 Ross-Edison.

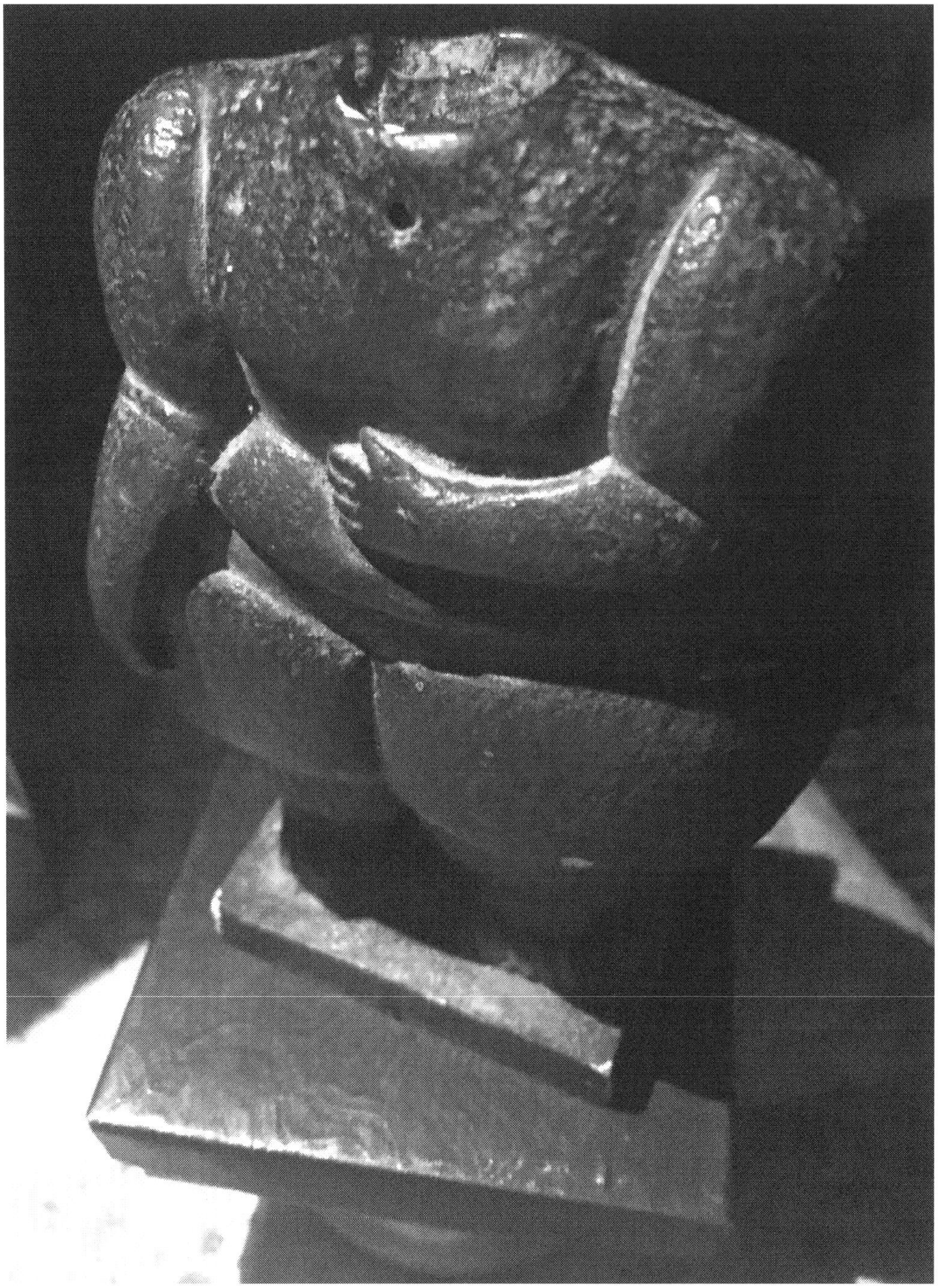

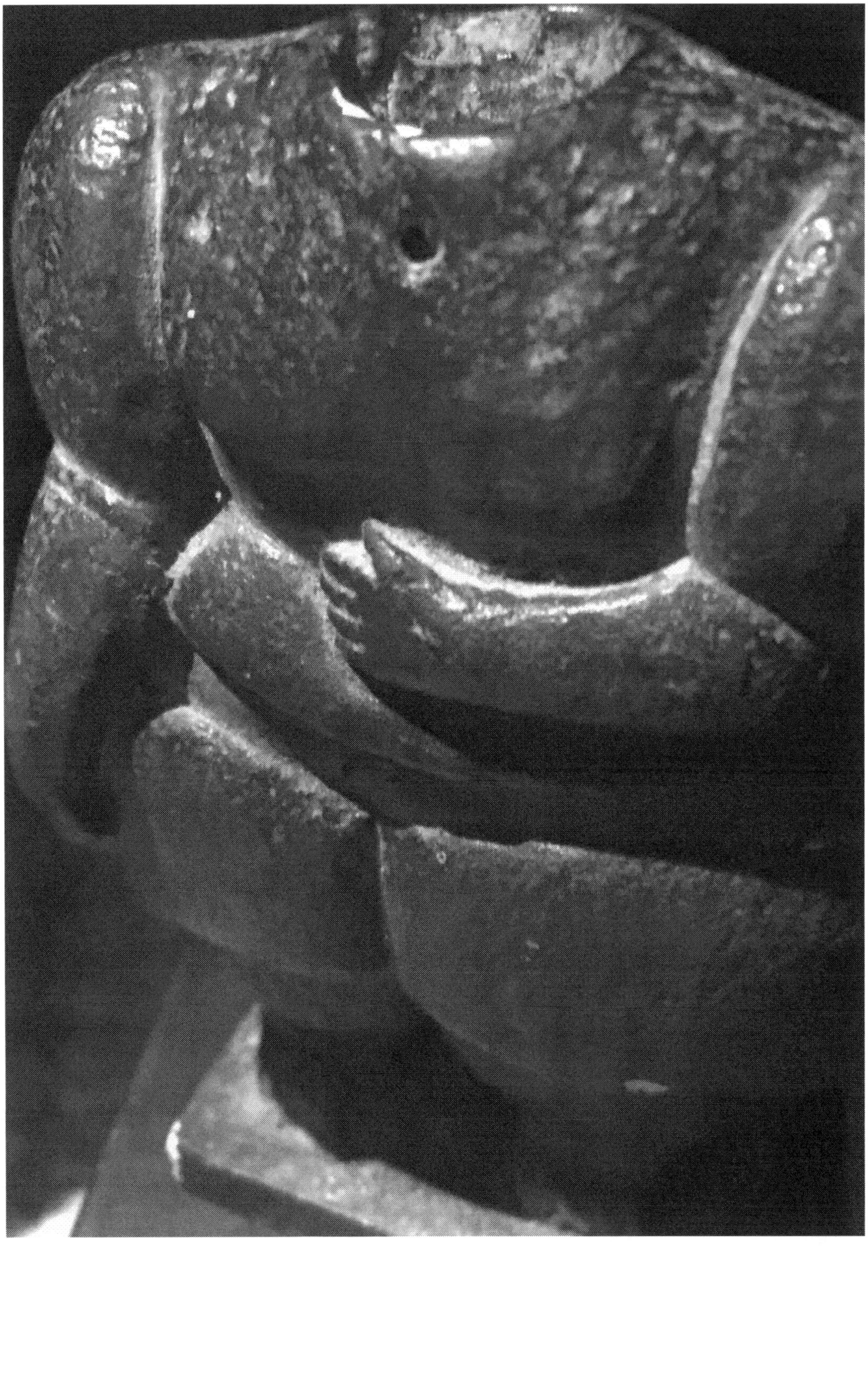

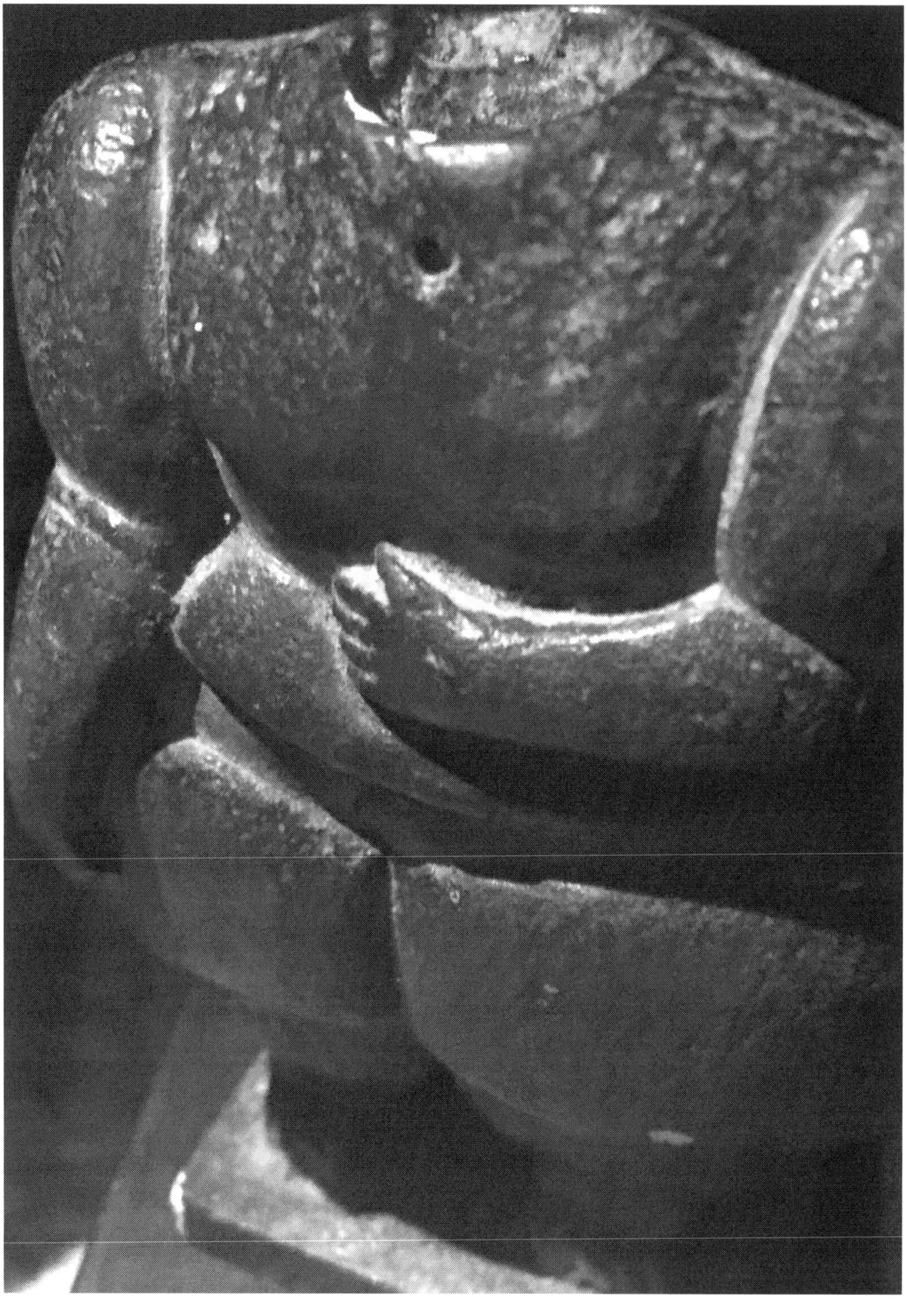

SEVEN OF THESE FIGURINES jusy like these were found stashed together at Hagar Qim, as reported by Sir Zammit in Zammit 1935/1994.

Copyright 2016 Ross-Edison

Copyright 2016 Ross-Edison.

The big draw to the temples on Malta *was* the Fat Lady.

The following scenario has two Norwegian college boys and the Fat Lady herself explaining everything.

The main characters in the story that follows include an artist who is also a stone mason descended from an ancient Paleolithic artist who had led a group of other displaced artists and aspiring farmers across the landbridge from Sicily to Malta, because the artists were no longer needed to paint ochre-red and soot-black images in the priming caves of southern France and northern Spain.

And so, joined on Sicily by wandering musicians from the Cyclades and a few restless souls from Skae Brae and Orkney looking for something to do, the stone mason led artists and aspiring farmers as the waning Ice Age defrosted the Mediterranean, on the landbridge from Sicily to Malta.

Two Norwegian college boys on a group tour have also come to Malta, on a lark really, to ostensibly research the temples, write a paper and get college credit, but mostly looking to have fun, their plan being to dance all night in the legendary Maltese discos, every night, when free vodka flowed, but instead, the tall, blond boys become enamored of *an idea* that is shown to their tour group on their first day on Malta in a slide show at the National Museum in Valletta.

The idea that grabs their young imaginations is abundantly supported by an image in alabaster, and stone, and clay, discovered *in situ* and preserved inside the museum in Valletta, and seen by the Norwegian boys just before their tour progresses through seven of the megalithic UNESCO sites.

As the tour moves along, the boys see with wonder that, long after the temple builders disappeared, the subsequent new inhabitants of Malta in the Bronze Age made use of the strange empty circles and then in turn also left the islands, to the Bronze Age newcomers, then to Phoenicians and next to the Romans, and after that the steady advance of layers of sediment and soil blown by the winds, over time eventually covered most temple sites, leaving just the tips of their tallest standing stones.

The Norwegian boys and their tour group see ancient pots, ladles, cups, bowls, amphorae, jugs and jars from the temples, some restored from sherds fitted back together, and some found intact, on display in the Valletta Museum, as well as tomb pottery and items such as large and slightly convex shallow bowls and their concave covers left in the tombs with grave goods for the dead, mainly cooked food in covered bowls for the journey, greenstone amulets and shell and bead necklaces, all of which are the keys to unlock the mystery of Malta.

The very profusion of these *in situ* objects and items on display in the Valletta Museum, for preparing and serving food for the dead in the tombs, and at the mourning feast in the nearby temple, presents an explanation of why the temples were built, but it is the Fat Lady who shows the Norwegian boys how the temples were used.

And now, the Walking Tour begins.

Street Entrance gate to the Tarxien site, Copyright 2016 Ross-Edison

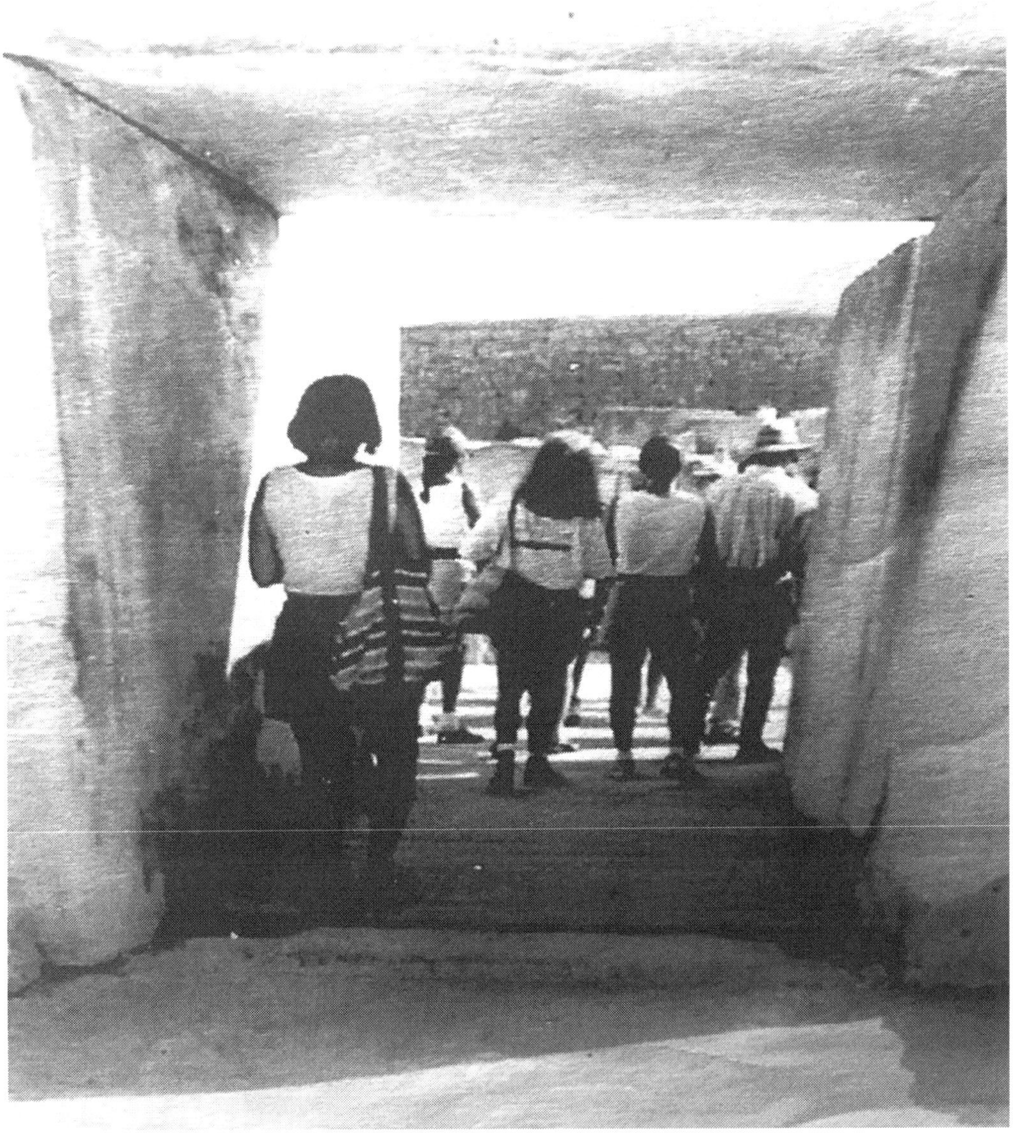

"Why seek ye the living among the dead?"

Luke 24:5, KingJamesBible.org

CHAPTER ONE

ON THE GREAT MALTA TOUR BUS

The big new tour bus opens its gleaming door at the entrance to the National Museum of Archaeology in the heart of the Knights of Malta's 16th-century fortress city, Valletta, and, singly with heavy tread, out comes a troop of bedraggled Germans, Brits, and Norwegian tourists, cameras dangling from their necks, all wearing dress-down casual summertime attire. A beaming Maltese tour guide ushers the diffident group in through the awesome ancient doors of the old stone building and their eyes are immediately filled with dim, cool visions of prehistoric Malta – waiting in timeless patience for arriving visitors in the hallway.

Everyone in the group seems to wake up. After all, it is nine in the morning and many in this tour group are still suffering jet lag. Yet in a trice the group has become tangibly excited, and they are only in the entrance hall.

With a flourish, the museum guide waives the group past the guards at the reception desk (the entrance fee of one Maltese pound was paid by the tour in advance) and pauses before he lets anyone enter the first exhibit room to their left.

With a mysterious little smile, and characteristic Maltese humor at getting to stop such an eager group, the guide with great emotion launches into a brief intellectual summary of the room's collection. Here the group will see *in situ* goddess figurines and large altar stones engraved with pitted dots and mysterious holes and spiral circles – which the attentive group already cranes its necks to see.

"Ladies and gentlemen," the guide begins in a stern tone, "remember: no photographs allowed! This is to protect the sensitive nature of the antiquities. The engravings, statues, pottery and rock carvings which you will now see are delicate. Very delicate! Please! Please, dear sir! You must wait but a few moments more!"

The group shares a collective chuckle as an over-eager tourist is herded back to the fold. Then without skipping a beat, the museum guide continues his breathless, exciting introduction.

"Now, in this room, you are going to see an altar made entirely of carved and dressed stone, and decorated with a spirals frontispiece. These altar stones are many, many centuries old, thousands of years in fact, and everything you see here has been taken from the temple sites. In its place at the site is an exact replica. But what YOU will see here is the real thing!"

The crowd before him murmurs appreciatively, and so, with the smile of some ancient conspirator, he allows them to rush into the first exhibits room.

"But touch nothing!" he calls after them.

"Please! Touch nothing, we beg you!"

What the group sees first is a neatly arranged exhibit of stone slabs. The ancient stones are standing, not encased in temperature-controlled glass cases or any kind of enclosure. The desire to touch them ripples in a gasp of longing through the little crowd. But no one does touch. Instead everyone encircles at a polite distance and stares at the engraved stones.

They see a broad stone table with a little house on top. It's made of carved globerigina limestone. An engraved frontispiece of neat, symmetrical spirals seems to give movement to the stone. Lined up with the spirals and in their midst is an asymmetrical shape that is undecorated, not quite a circle, and not engraved with a spiral design. The museum guide reappears beside them to explain that it is a plug.

"What we have here," he says with endemic Maltese glee, "is a secret compartment. Behind this plug, they found this knife and several others."

He holds the knife up high for all to see and pauses while some 'oohs' and 'ahs' subside, then with great carefulness pulls on clear rubber gloves and bends to dramatically remove the asymmetrical plug and expose a small compartment carved into the deep of the stone.

"This is where they found this knife! You see? But why was it put there? Did they use it for the sacrifice?

"No one knows! But the charred bones of animals were found inside what looks like a little house at the back of the altar. And there was another item found that had fallen behind this heavy stone altar when it was being moved to bring it here to the museum from the inner Tarxien temple. That item which had fallen behind this very altar was the so-called Thermi pedestal cup displayed in this case!"

He unlocks the glass display case and takes out the beautiful Thermi cup for the group to see, holding it carefully for the group to see.

The famous Thermi pedestal cup, Evans 1970.

"Perfect coffee cup," someone says. "Can I buy one of those in the gift shop?"

Everyone chuckles and smiles in agreement,"I want that cup!"

"I call it the 'so-called Thermi cup' because its very existence opened up a mystery: Where was it made? Was it Greek or local? Why was it there? Was it accidentally dropped behind the altar or deliberately hidden as the temple builders fled the island? One theory is that this pedestal cup was merely being stored in the little house on the altar top but as more and more animal bones were added in the little house on the altar top, the Thermi cup was simply pushed out the back of the lttle storage house where it fell to the ground and was not recovered until moving the altar in 1958. None of these speculations can be answered!

"One can only wonder: Is the little house a replica of the large stone temple itself?

"No one knows anything for sure! Nothing was written down! Well, now I let you wander through all the exhibits—in the next room you will see the very knife found inside the spiral altar compartment and pottery found inside the temples and some small figurines of the beautiful Maltese Fat Lady found headless and, some, still stuck upright in the temple floor. Enjoy! And if you have no other questions for me, read the description beside each item you see inside the next room, and meet me in the last exhibit room near the front desk when you are through!"

The over-impressed group spreads out across the small museum.

They come across no more melodrama, no more hidden Neolithic knives, but they do find a large pottery exhibit of domestic jars and cups and lean close to scrutinize the glued-together and chipped clay objects, their great antiquity protected by display in closed glass cases.

From the Red Skorba period, named for the red slip applied to the finished product, the group sees a biconical bowl, its handles set just below the rim and perforated, perhaps for hanging by a woven or plaited cord. A red ladle with a horn-shaped handle looks to the group like a big spoon and they see a smooth place worn almost white on the rim of the ladle's cup where many ancients had sipped.

From the early Zebbug era, they see a large red jar with a dotted design impressed into the clay. Then there is a curious pear-shaped jug with four handles--two placed at mid-center and two near the brim—making it easy to pass from person to person. Next they see a bird's head topping an elongated neck, found broken at the Mgarr site at Ta' Hagrat, which could have served as a ladle or handle for a hefty jar or huge bowl. Next to it is a spacious glazed bowl or large generous cup from the Ggantija period decorated with a curving line in the so-called 'comet relief' design found on pottery inside the Ggantija temple.

Then the tour group comes to the collection of portly hand-sized figurines, standing on thick ankles on little platforms, and next to these mysterious figures is a huge statue of the same figure, only it has been cut off above the knees as if chopped by an axe in a heavy hand.

Near the curious little figurines, which a sign informs are collectively known as the Maltese Fat Lady, the group finds on display an elongated limestone boat-shaped object from the Kordin III site looking for all the world like a bath tub (just the size for washing hands and face before dinner) but some say it's a kayak or canoe or other small boat made of stone until they read the display sign saying it's a quern for grinding, and next to the unusual quern the group sees from the Hagar Qim and Tarxien sites big round stone tubs (just the size for mixing large portions of wine for a gathered group).

In its own glass case nearby resides a small scale model of a perfectly round little limestone building that is completely covered over by a roof.

The group looks around. They have reached the last exhibit room, and there in the doorway stands the museum guide awaiting them.

"Now I would like very much to show you a video," he tells the tour group whose minds are already reeling with ancient images just viewed, tangible objects from disparate sites and times. The group has seen enough.

Seeing their blank faces,, the guide explains,

"We need to see this brief presentation to explain this small roofed model you just saw on display, found *in situ* in the rubble of one of the oldest sites on Malta, Mgarr at Ta' Hagrat."

The tour group stands while the short video is shown. In animated colors worthy of Disney, a small stone structure in the shape of a circle is shown, surprisingly, the guide says, completely covered by a roof.

Temple model from Mgarr, Evans 1970.

The museum guide steps forward with a laser-tipped pointer and calls up the next animated image showing the floor plans of Tarxien and Hagar Qim, slowly rotating side by side.

Pointing to the central corridor inside each temple, he says,

"Although the small Mgarr model shows a roof over the entire structure, the central corridor which passes through all the sites (although it meanders through the added-on wild apse patterns of Tarxien and Hagar Qim) is believed to have been left uncovered. This opening would let the smoke from sacrifice or cooking fires escape through the central open-air passage.

"But the semi-circular side apses *were* well roofed. The small roofed model found intact at Mgarr suggests it. A vaulted stone roof over the entire structure would not be possible to support architecturally, because from an engineering viewpoint, it would be too heavy, but the roof could have been made of wood or limestone slabs could have been supported if laid at intervals on their vertical edge with timber and earth or clay in-filling."

Then the museum guide opens a slim volume and reads aloud from a 1931 report by Sir Themistocles Zammit who excavated the site:

"'Having stone slab roofing is a problem, because limestone slabs can only be used to a maximum span of 2 meters, and if longer than that they break. A temple at the stage of completion would have apses roofed with tree trunks which were covered with quarry stones and the gaps filled with clay. The inside yards between the apses and the trilithon passages were left unroofed." (Zammit 1931/1994)

Now the guide points with the laser tip to the Tarxien temple model, found at the site broken and in pieces that were fit back together, showing to the group where the roofing was and bringing up another slide showing the Tarxien floor plan, how the passageways meander this way and that, often colliding with an unexpected glimpse of crawl-space entry doors or low windows carved in standing stones leading into an adjoining apse or niche chambers that lead nowhere.

"Tarxien is like cave burial chambers built aboveground," the museum guide twinkles at them, "like the catacombs of Rabat and the man-made chambers for the dead carved in the limestone underground of the Hypogeum, don't you think? Don't you think so?"

He brings up a slide of the Tarxien pillar chamber and inner tomb chambers at the Hal Saflieni Hypogeum.

"Cimpare Tarxien inner trilithon to Hypogeum trilithon entrances to grave chambers in the 'Holy of Holies' photo by Richard Ellis, c..1910.".

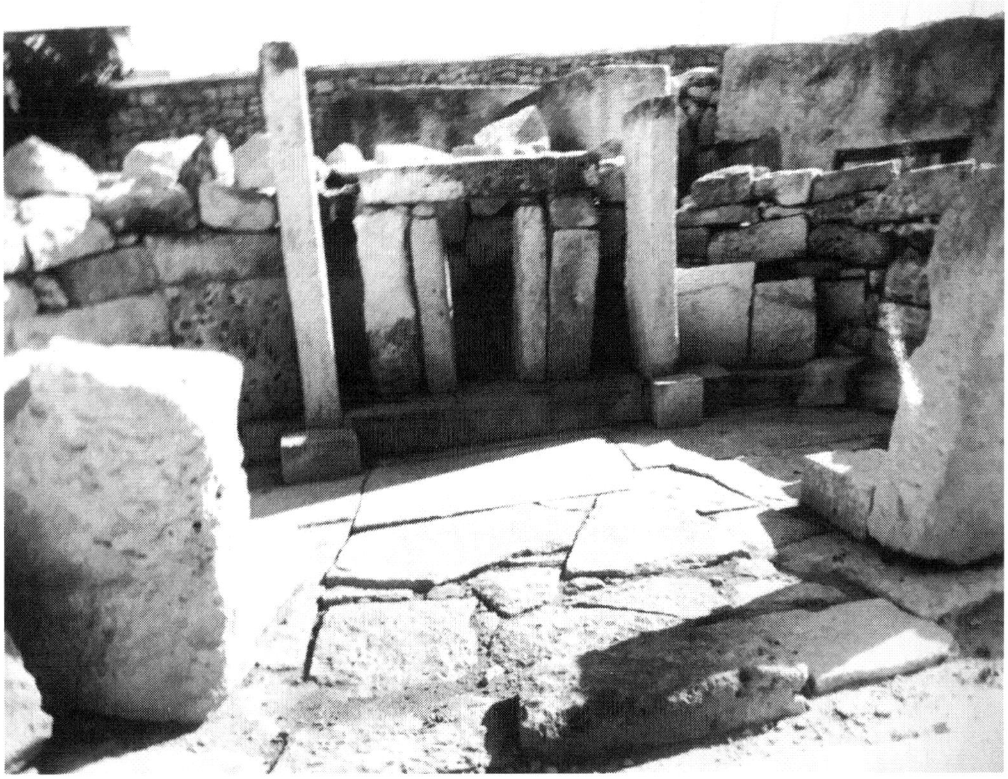

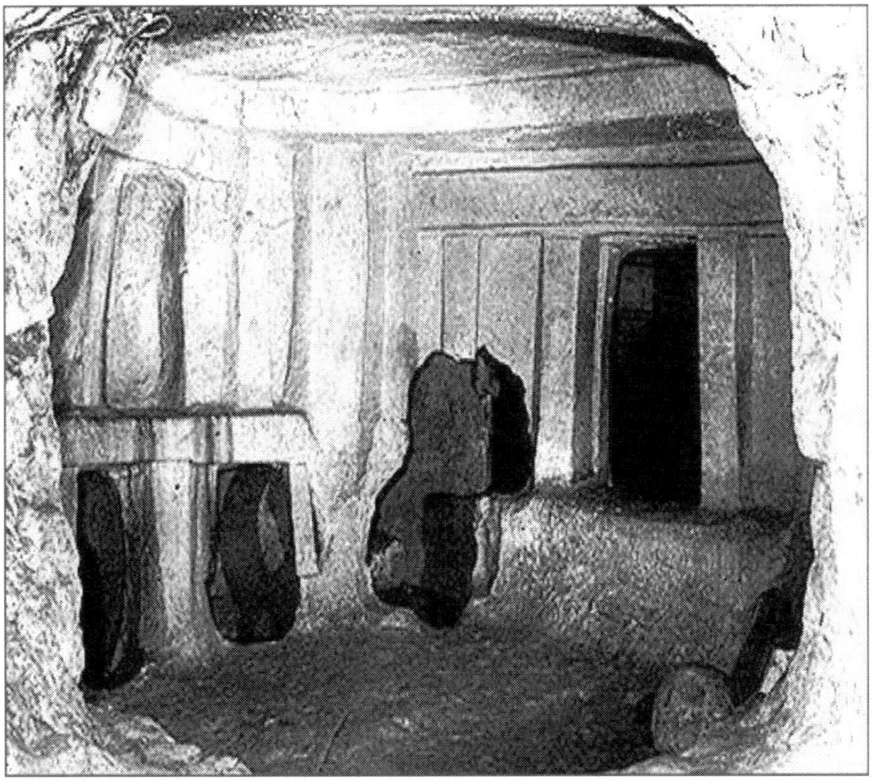

The tour group is tired now and no one responds. They appear somewhat flabbergasted that cave burials and death have been suggested by the temples where they were told no burials were found. They wanted to hear stories about the mystery of the great stones and the ancient symmetry of the stone circles, but now the structures had unexpectedly led them to the sorrow and perplexity of death.

Seeing the group looking a bit stumped and dejected, the museum guide brightly tells them that their tour of the museum is over, and leads them to the museum's huge entrance doors and out to the street. With a burst of chatter, the tour group emerges from the darkened museum into the intense sunshine of late morning. One by one, they line up to re-board the big tour bus, shiny and new, parked and ready to go through the modern-day streets of Valletta.

The museum guide hastens to be standing at the bus door, is soon assisting each tourist up the first step, and to end the morning on an upbeat note, says gaily,

"In the morning you go see the temples!'

The sky is Mediterranean blue, the sun shining bright. Everyone is on the tour bus now, waving and smiling their goodbyes. The genial tour guide is waving back. Malta's natural exuberance is a contagious promise. The mystery of the stone temples remains enticing, and intact.

The Maltese guide disappears back through the great doors of the museum, and the bus starts changing gears to pull away from the curb. One of the Norwegian boys on board sits back in comfort and idly watches passersby on the street, from his vantage point high above them in the bus. Suddenly he sits upright. He has spotted a portly old woman dressed all in white and moving along at a brisk pace on thick swollen ankles.

He gapes.

Hey! Wait a minute! That body, those ankles! Looks like one of those temple figures!

He turns to his seatmate who is eating a candy bar.

"Hey! Take a look at what escaped from the museum!"

The two hurriedly press against the tour bus window, and catch a glimpse of her white dress as the broad-backed Maltese woman moves under an awning, and then she is gone.

The boys start shouting.

"Stop the bus! Let us off!"

Here on the first day of the Malta tour, the group has been given the rest of the day off, to do whatever they want. The tour bus is carrying the group back to the Speranza hotel to go poolside, order lunch, and nap in the sun.

But the Norwegian boys are standing up and announcing, at the top of their lungs, that they'd like to get off the bus and walk around Valletta for a while.

CHAPTER TWO

INSIDE THE COOL BISTRO

The Maltese sun is beating its ancient heat down hard on the fair-haired Norwegian boys. They need some relief.

Since their abrupt exit from the tour bus, the two have rushed, up, down, and around the narrow twisting streets and crannies of Valletta, looking for the escaped museum figure.

They have glimpsed her in several places up and across the busy street where the bus let them off, a heavy-set older woman moving fast on thick, swollen ankles in a white summery dress wrapped like a robe around her broad frame, just after they jumped off the bus, waving their thanks to the startled driver.

Then the boys catch a taunting glimpse of one thick, famous, swollen ankle as it seems to linger almost as if without a body around the corner of a shop while the street twists tortuously sideways uphill, and then the distended ankle joins the rest of her.

She is out of sight.

"There!" the two college boys cry out, in unison, and run across the street to chase the flirtatious summons of an unshapely ankle and the broad figure in white.

Rounding the sharp corner where the street twists up the hill, they are suddenly looking into her dark laughing eyes because she was waiting for them to catch up. Coming so close to the old Maltese woman, the two boys feel embarrassed that she's caught them chasing her, and are not at all amused that she's laughing at them, but instead are unexpectedly frightened of her, waiting there as if to entrap them and ruin their game, and then, sensing their fear, or their rejection, the museum look-alike fondly known as the Maltese Fat Lady turns her broad back on them.

The boys just stare.

Then there beside her appears a small man, wearing strangely enough a three-piece tweed suit, and a striped bow tie. He sports an old-time handlebar moustache and round owl-like glasses. The man is the same height as the Maltese lady. As the two tall boys ponder the appearance of the two short people, they start feeling a bit intrusive when the little man gently takes the lady's arm, like some gallant and protective gentleman from a bygone day.

The Maltese lady turns to the man and says,

"Oh, Temi!"

And with that, the gracious little man folds the little lady's arm in his, scowls at the boys, and runs off with the Fat Lady into the nearest shop.

With a final flash of white, the two little people are gone.

"Come back!" the boys call out in mournful tones.

They rush to the shop window and cautiously peer in, not wanting to startle their prey or the little man, but inside the shop, the two are nowhere to be seen.

The shop owner comes out and closes the shutters.

"What just happened here?" the boys sputter.

"What got into us? Chasing down an old lady who plays tricks on us? And runs off with a little man? Oh, the sun must be melting our *minds*!"

After all, they tell themselves, it's not as if the Fat Lady doesn't *like* us! She doesn't even *know* us! And besides, everyone on Malta is getting ready to go home and take a nap. Why not the Fat Lady?

Why not us?

They give up on what must have been some kind of beguiling daydream, a scenario provoked by the heat of the day.

And it is getting hotter by the minute.

Nonetheless they decide to go wandering around Valletta for a while. Take their minds off this odd escapade with the fleet-footed museum look-alike.

They soon take comfort in the sight of the Grand Harbor sparkling like a Mediterranean jewel far below, and then enter the Valletta Co-Cathedral built in 1573 and completed in 1578 after a great victory in 1565 over the invading Turks of the Ottoman Empire, victory by the young mainly French European noblemen in the Order of the Knights Hospitaller of St. John, otherwise known as the Knights of Malta. The Norwegian boys are over-awed. They are feeling much better. But when the boys enter the great Catholic church, they find themselves walking on tombs.

A Cathedral guide informs them that some 375 knights and officers of the Maltese Order are buried in tombs here beneath the ornate marble floor where they are standing, in the huge, vaulted Co-Cathedral, and now, their imaginations blown, the two exhausted boys are back in front of the museum to wait for the old green Malta bus that for not much of a fare will take them back to the hotel for a swim in the pool, a catered lunch, and a nap.

Something normal, they say to each other.

The old Maltese buses, like a mirage from the 1940s, nonetheless run ceaselessly around the island. The boys wait for the chugging green bus but the debilitating heat makes them forget why they're there and what they're waiting for.

It is almost noon. The intense Mediterranean heat beats down and they wonder where the old woman went.

Then they hear a familiar voice.

Their museum guide from the morning's tour!

"Over here," calls the guide who has just left work for the afternoon. He has easily recognized the tall, slender boys with the bright blond hair. And now he is seeing them melting away in the sun. He quickly advises the pair by pointing to the awning of a dark, cool Bistro just across the street from the National Museum.

Then they all note a strong espresso aroma wafting toward them, its invigorating promise luring everyone to come inside.

"Best go in there now," the museum guide says, "because everything on Malta will close soon for the entire afternoon."

The boys take off at a run, followed by the bemused guide, and the three enter the Bistro's cooling enclosure.

Every seat at every table is taken.

Except one.

There, a handsome young Maltese with dark twinkling eyes and a head full of tousled black curls sat alone at a table, sipping an espresso and beckoning to them.

"Let's go!" said the museum guide and the three start practically hopping over the packed-sawdust floor to thank the young man and take a seat at his table.

Soon everyone is drinking ice water and sipping the intense Maltese coffee. The Norwegian boys feel much better but note the homespun clothing worn by the friendly young man, clothes that look like ancient burlap, perhaps a farmer's clothes, or a common workman's outfit consisting of stained brown trousers and a burlap-brown shirt with pale elbow places worn almost white, all covered by streaks of red and yellow paint, and mud, and then they look at his strong hands, the calloused fingertips, the black-dirt encrusted fingernails. The young Maltese notices their gaze.

"I am a stone mason," he says.

They stare at him.

Stone mason? Like with really big stones?

"And an artist," he paused and they heard him sigh.

"I work out at the temples for the museum," he explained and said he did restoration work and anything that needed to be done to help preserve the ancient sites, including erecting a cover to shield the site from the debilitating forces of sun, wind and rain. Then he smiled at them in such a disarming and beatific way that the boys and museum guide could only smile back.

Yep, the really big stones, the boys figure.

Then they order biscotti for all. The guide adds a large order of hummus, bread, tomatoes, olives and grapes. Their new friend from Malta says he is actually Iberian, but his family has been on Malta for a very long time, and then orders a round of the local red wine for everyone.

The boys look at each other.

"What the heck is Iberian?" they wonder out loud and none too quietly.

Before anyone could be offended, the museum guide says simply,

"Spain."

"Ah," the two say.

And so they sat.

Eating, drinking the sweet dark wine, examining a glassy lump of obsidian that the Maltese artist pulls from the pouch slung across his chest, and then they are all watching the clock because the bewitching hour of one p.m. is fast approaching, and they will be summarily shooed out of the cool Bistro and onto the streets in the high heat of Malta.

Entrance gate to Tarxien, Copyright 2016 Ross-Edison

Trilithon entrance to Tarxien, Copyright 2016 Ross-Edison

CHAPTER THREE

TARXIEN

The big gleaming bus is slowly pulling out of Valletta on the second day of the week-long tour. The group has just heard another lecture at the museum, seen a slide show and an animated revolving floor plan, and is now heading for the ancient Tarxien site.

Their guide holds a microphone and faces the group in the seats before him, but notes two people intently staring out the window – looking for something?

In a loud commanding voice the guide asks everyone to pay attention, please, because they are on their way to the famous Tarxien site. Slowly the two Norwegian boys pull their eyes away from the bus window, in slow-motion, as if in a trance, and look toward the impatient tour guide standing at the front of the bus.

When he can look them all in the eye, the guide says,

"It was 1902 when workmen digging the foundation for a building on a neighborhood Maltese street discovered instead a huge underground burial tomb, unlike any other ever seen on Malta, which would turn out to be a vast bee-hive of cave-like chambers hand-carved three layers deep in the subterranean limestone that underpins all of Malta. Some 7,000 human skeletons were reported buried inside the rock-cut hand-carved chambers of the Hypogeum tombs, some with multiple burials (perhaps family members) entombed in the same chamber.

"Known as the Hal Saflieni Hypogeum, this enormous hand-cut tomb is close to the Tarxien temple which can be seen on a hillside in the near distance only several hundred yards away.

"Inside this giant underground tomb so close to the Tarxien temple were found Fat Lady figurines including the famous Sleeping Lady who is reclined as if dreaming, and also just as at Tarxien temple nearby are found corbelled (curving) stone walls, low-cut windows carved into standing stones and leading to passageways going nowhere, and trilithon entryways leading into an adjacent chamber, or leading nowhere. But unlike the Hal Saflieni Hypogeum, before 2300 B.C. when the temple builders left Malta, there were no burials in the Tarxien temple.

"The temples that we will tour are all temples without tombs.

"No one can explain why the temple builders left Malta or why the inner temple reflects the tombs nearby. All of the temples built on Malta, even though on the inside they may look like the Hypogeum burial chambers, are temples without tombs.

"And just as in discovering the Hal Saflieni Hypogeum, the nearby Tarxien temple was discovered by people digging up the earth. For years, perhaps centuries, farming was going on, right over top of the buried Tarxien site, but plowmen started complaining about bits and pieces of stone turning up in the furrows they turned in the earth for planting, and by 1914 plowmen were running into large stones that were chipping or even breaking the plow blade. The owner of the field decided to contact the National Museum in Valletta.

"The director of the museum at the time was a renowned medical scientist at the University of Malta, Professor Themistocles Zammit, who would later become President of the University of Malta. After being informed by the field's owner about the large buried stones in the field at Tarxien, then-Professor Zammit went immediately to the farmer's field and started digging.

"He reported that a layer of earth that covered the temple appeared burnt, begging the question of whether the temple had been deliberately destroyed, attempting by fire to get rid of the stones, and, that having failed, attempted to hack and saw into oblivion a huge standing statue of the Maltese Fat Lady, the remains of which today can be viewed cut in half above the knees, perhaps in a plan of destruction that didn't work. The burnt ground which then-Professor Zammit reported covering the temple site could have been involved in the Bronze Age newcomers' cremation of their dead. Eventually the whole complex temple site was abandoned by all and buried by time, as the drifting work of wind and storms moved the surrounding sediment and soil overtop of the empty structures.

"If an occupying Bronze Age people did get spooked by the old temple site and its huge standing statues which they wanted gone, how to dispose of standing stones weighing several tons? The answer was to simply use the limestone temples.

"In any case, Sir Zammit went right to the heart of it, unearthing first part of the central courtyard, and "found himself standing in an apse shaped by a half-oval of large dressed standing stones." By 1920 Sir Zammit and his volunteers had methodically and carefully unearthed, and had already begun restoration, on three stone structures with a profusion of apses that comprise the Neolithic site of Tarxien.

"Sir Zammit and his corps of local volunteers found items in the temple site that were just like items found in the Hypogeum. They unearthed small Fat Lady figurines and pottery items such as jars and cups along with larger artifacts such as long-handled ladles, a big round tub, cooking pits in the inner apse courtyards, and decorated stone tables perhaps used as altars with a lower compartment conveniently placed for storage.

"With the exception of the smaller items such as the little figurines and small cups and jars which are not replicated in the site, Tarxien today does display replicas of the artifacts you have seen at the museum. These original items including the spiral altar which you saw yesterday, were removed from the temple for preservation and safekeeping. Let's take inventory now of the original relics found inside Tarxien, items taken directly from the site, those items which we have seen on display at the museum.

"We saw large tubs and pottery including jars, jugs, cups, bowls, small plates and ladles; miniature tabernacles seated on a stone altar decorated with a spiral design; small goddess figurines the size of your hand; large bowls and fonts as if tubs ready for bathing; drilled and pitted designs carved into stones; the stored knife in the altar decorated with spirals and a plug that opens the storage area; and a model temple found in broken pieces but restored to show an example of the unexpected great height of a temple and its roofing.

"Now as we walk through Tarxien temple, see if you can recognize what areas have been reconstructed and look for the replicas of the original items that we have seen in the museum, note the area where they were found, where for centuries they lay, untouched, perhaps covered by the soil of the farm field, since the end of the temple period."

Then the tour guide steps aside and the bus door swings open at the lacy, elegant ironwork gates to Tarxien. The group treks off the bus. They approach the huge trilithon portal which has been reconstructed from the rubble and ruin unearthed by Professor Zammit and his volunteers, a square and stately trilithon now made of cement but still leading into the heart of the temple.

A woman is standing in the center of it with an open golf umbrella. A teenager is standing beside her eating ice cream. No one can get around them. The morning is turning very hot. Some people in the waiting tour start drinking from the *de rigueur* water bottle all travelers are advised to carry.

After a few words from the security guard who was alerted by the tour guide, the teenager runs to the street and finds a trash bin to discard his ice cream, and the woman with the umbrella ambles away. Now the tour group is able to enter the broad central passageway which is common to all the temple sites.

Everyone stops immediately to stare.

They can just see in the near distance the gigantic remains of a Fat Lady statue and the sight has stolen everyone's attention. It's as if the statue has been deliberately cut in half, broken through in a smooth straight cut just above the knees and thighs. The remains of the statue is wearing a skirt. Thick, heavy ankles protrude at the base. Behind the damaged statue, like a Hollywood backdrop, sleek modern office buildings can be seen, dramatically soaring their skyscrapers into the hovering skies.

After that, most of the group take less than an hour to tour the wonders of Tarxien. There are a couple of stragglers though.

As if enchanted, the two Norwegian boys wander off by themselves around the site.

Meanwhile their tour group has dutifully followed the tour guide into the central passage, a corridor which drew them nearer and nearer to a large courtyard area at the far end of which a small structure of slim trilithon pillars sits as if on stage. In front of the stage is a large stone fire pit. The group lingered on its way toward what looked like an inviting little temple house made of slim stone trilithons set in a row, on the stage-like platform which backed up against a wall of rubble. First the group paused awe-struck at seeing the replica of the spiral-and-plug altar where a knife was found stored in a compartment in the midst of whirls of spiral designs.

The group then from behind the ropes had gazed across the inner courtyard to a large replica tub that seems to invite bathing; they had with wonder looked at smooth stone balls laying about near the entrance trilithon that were hand-carved to roll and transport into place the heavy limestone wall slabs, which were now curving around them in some apses; they had puzzled about the step-through windows carved low in large standing stones; and wandered through chamber after chamber of side apses adjacent to each other and reached from the central passage by meandering walkways that sometimes ended up at a niche and a dead-end wall. Their impression was that some apses at Tarxien were hastily added on, then another added yet again, producing an *ad hoc* labyrinth of apses and pathways that obviously had no pre-planned architectural design but just happened.

Now the tour group was getting tired in the hot morning sun and put off by having to stand behind ropes and stare across wooden planks that artlessly spanned an courtyard and across the neatly cut ancient flagstones that smoothly interconnected in front of the little stage. Some felt an urge to take off their sandals and trainers and run across the flagstones barefoot and leap onto the stage.

Almost all reachable areas of the site were roped off though, preventing such tourist activity during the restoration that was going on. No one, short of climbing over the ropes, could get close enough to the stage to see, touch or feel anything. Everyone madly takes photographs anyway.

They had viewed a stone wall revealing the engraved forms of two large animals, namely, two bulls and a cow. After 2500 B.C. when the temple builders disappeared, a Bronze Age culture used Tarxien for their own purposes; then the Phoenicians occupied Tarxien and even the ancient Romans were at Tarxien, leaving Roman artifacts behind them in the field. Everyone wondered aloud just who did the animal carvings and when.

Then the tour group straggles back out the main entrance portal, through the cement trilithon and toward the bus. Their enthusiasm is gone. Tarxien seems a huge mess. Dilapidated. Rubble of a stunted temple.

The group stands for a moment in the hot sun listlessly looking at each other. Where is the magic?

There are, however, two members of the tour group who do not wonder about the magic. They are busy chasing it down. That would be the two tall and slender, blond Norwegian college boys who have gotten conveniently lost from their tour group on this hot sunny morning on Malta.

They are having a great time exploring the confusion of stones, walkways leading nowhere, intriguing apses and stone tables, all roped off, but the boys get close-up anyway, stepping over ropes and blithely eluding the security guard.

It's a grand game.

Their next objective is the off-limits little pillar house on the stage platform, framed by the row of little trilithons. They pause to look across the paved courtyard studded by the stone firepit, to where the little structure sits as if in a stage play, and plot their course.

Then two small Maltese boys push past them. Their fresh young faces are streaked by tears and marked by the grim lines of mourning, the frown of grief. Sounds from a crowd of people in the courtyard open to the sky start rising in a cloud of babble, echoing an exotic mix of languages off the stone walls and along the flagstone walkways and bouncing off the oblong slabs that formed the roofing over the apses and stone tables and the trilithon pillars making a small house on a stage set at the apex of the half-moon courtyard. The little Maltese boys pause near the Norwegian boys in the clutter of stones ropes, boards, and distant little houses.

Trilithon into Tarxien, Copyright 2016 Ross-Edison

INSIDE TARXIEN TEMPLE

Copyright 2016 Ross-Edison

INSIDE TARXIEN TEMPLE

Copyright 2016 Ross-Edison

INSIDE TARXIEN TEMPLE

Copyright 2016 Ross-Edison

INSIDE TARXIEN TEMPLE

Copyright 2016 Ross-Edison

INSIDE TARXIEN TEMPLE

Fire pit Tarxien, Copyright 2016 Ross-Edison

Copyright 2016 Ross-Edison

The Norwegian boys start laughing. They have been manhandling the replicated stone plug in the replicated spiral table which in Neolithic days opened to storage space for a large knife and they almost have it off when they are interrupted by the two little boys with gleaming bronze tans on their sad faces.

"Is this the way to go?" one boys asks.

"Way to go!" the Norwegians say, almost in unison as usual when they are joking, and then they are chanting the sports lingo, "Way to go!" and staring at the odd little duo who look to be about six and eight years old.

"I mean, do we go that way, you know, to get inside?"

The Norwegians look to where the little boy is pointing.

It's the far little structure they themselves want to get into, the little house near a huge tub and the row of slim trilithons on the stage backed up to a crude wall of rocks. We have to get in there, the youngsters are saying.

They get a smile from the older boys: their plan exactly.

"We'll go with you," the stately Norwegians say, almost in unison again, for they sense a fun adventure coming on, and, besides, they are hearing bereft tones and desperation in the lad's voice.

Taking each little boy by the hand, the older boys lead the way. Even though the little pillared house is set on the stage and is all roped off, there's a wooden walkway used by the restoration workers, convenient boards spanning the ancient flagstones, and it gets the foursome across the half-oval courtyard right up to the little pillar house. The Maltese boys can stoop a bit and easily enter, but for the Norwegians even stooping doesn't get them in.

"Never mind," the younger boys say, "we can take it from here."

Blocked from entry by their own height, the tall, blond Norwegians stand back and watch the smaller boys disappear into the little pillar house. The Norwegians kneel to see inside, and glimpse flickering candlelight and soft shadows playing across smooth dark stones where the crude, undressed wall of rocks gives way to a chamber apse.

Having delivered the little boys where they wanted to be, and gone as far as they possibly can, the lofty kneeling Norwegians then glimpse such an unexpected sight inside the candlelit pillared chamber, that they freeze on the ground before the little trilithons, caught as they are on their knees in a spectral place.

It's a flash of white on a broad back in the candlelit shadows inside the little pillar house where the weeping Maltese boys walk with uncertainty.

Then the Norwegians note thick, swollen ankles as the elusive figure in white sidles away.

"She's *in* there!" the surprised Norwegians shout while a crowd of tourists thinking them crazy watch from behind the ropes. The security guard gestures to the crazy Norwegians to come back down from there.

"Get back behind the ropes!"

The Norwegians have wandered at will for almost an hour that morning through the rubble and disarray of Tarxien, stepping over ropes and crossing wooden barriers to reach the inner places. They have nimbly climbed through low step-in windows carved like awkward doorways in limestone walls that lead toward a profusion of apses that appear to connect to each other, but don't.

Now in shock, and still kneeling at the small trilithon, the Norwegian college boys are staring into the candlelit shadows that cloak the grief-stricken little boys when they hear their tour bus blaring its horn for them to come back at once and join the tour group waiting for them on the bus.

The boys look at each other, and say, "Nah, let's not."

Instead they try to enter the little house to find the Fat Lady. They start edging forward on their knees, they duck their heads and squeeze sideways scraping the lintel with their shoulder blades but finally they are both inside the little house – except for their legs and feet. The tourists gathered at a distance near the wooden walkway behind the ropes are gawking and laughing at the scene as if it's a theatrical performance on the little stage just for their amusement. The Norwegian boys, however, don't hear the crowd laughing at them, for the side apse which they are too big to enter has gone all quiet and still.

The joyful noise and exotic chatter from the open-air courtyard have subsided. The irate guard is yelling.

"Come out of there!" he is shouting and in the next instance, they decide they will.

For the candlelight is gone, the little pillar house is dark inside and empty, once again backed up to the unforgiving wall of rocks and rubble.

"We're coming!" the Norwegian boys start shouting to the outraged guard as they back out of the little house, get to their feet and scramble across the wooden plank toward him and the grinning tourists behind the ropes.

Meanwhile their tour group is ready for air conditioning. No one really cares any more what might have gone on inside the rubble of these fallen, crumbled walls.

Except for the two missing Norwegian boys.

This is becoming a problem for the tour group. Where have the boys gone this time? Everyone agrees the boys can catch the green bus back to the Speranza on their own. The two apparently like to take side trips anyway, so let's go without them!

Then to everyone's surprise, here come the two Norwegians, running as fast as their legs can carry them out of the ruins.

Breathlessly, the two Norwegians board the bus.

Everyone ignores them.

And back to the hotel they go, more than ready to have a catered lunch, take a nap, swim in the pool – because as they learned yesterday, afternoons all Malta closes down in the summer heat.

CHAPTER FOUR

RED SKORBA

The gleaming Malta tour bus awaits the same group, on this the third day of the week-long tour, parked by the curb at the front door of the Valletta museum.

Inside an air-conditioned lecture room, the patient museum guide is standing before a large projection screen.

"This morning," he begins, pausing for a moment to eye the mischievous Norwegian boys whose antics yesterday at Tarxien, although officially frowned upon, are a topic of hilarity among the museum staff.

"This morning," he begins again, "we will show you a brief animation of the floor plan of each of the seven temples on Malta which have been designated as UNESCO World Heritage sites. To better understand the evolution of the trefoil, that is, how the three-apse design developed over time, the Xemxija site is included in this presentation. After we see that, today we go visit three sites: Xemxija, Skorba, and Mgarr. These three sites are where it all began. The site you visited yesterday, is where it all ended.

"Let us now compare two sites."

A slide appears on a large screen as the overhead lighting is dimmed.

"Note that Xemxija is not a temple but a natural cave used for burials. It presents cave entrances that are two holes in the ground on the slope of a hill, a sight carefully carved and replicated in stone at each temple. We noted the twin holes at the entrance to Tarxien yesterday, do you recall?"

He deftly clicks for the next side.

A comparison of oval-shaped grave chamber 1 inside Xemxija is shown next to the same shape of the early Mgarr temple apses (see sketch in Zammit 1931/1994:7).

"Now I ask you: which is the temple and which is the tomb?"

"Do you se this simple connection"

"The twin circular holes so neatly carved in stone appear in various parts of all the temples but have been widely misinterpreted as 'libation holes' which were actually a much later phenomenon described by historians such as Pausanias in the 2nd Century A.D. in his travel-log of ancient Greece. The Xemxija burial caves were much earlier than Pausanias, of course, but Xemxija was in use on Malta c. 3800-3000 B.C. when the early Mgarr site was an active temple.

"Scholars believe the trefoil, that is, the floor plan of three apses, found in the two later temples at Skorba date to the Ggantija Phase (3600-3300/3000 B.C.), and evolved from the Xemxija underground chambers and replicated at the early temple at Mgarr.

"We have just seen this similarity here in the slide projection, the early Mgarr temple in relation to the Xemxija underground cave burials, as sketched in Professor Sir Temi Zammit's book."

He gently waves the little blue Sir Zammit book in the air over his head and asks the group to get their copies of it out. There is a rustle and rumbling of purses and backpacks being opened and then the museum guide resumes.

"The single-oval huts of the Red Skorba Phase, however, are believed to be perhaps the prototype of all the later temple sites, and as you will now see in the next slide, temple apses to come, for the next thousand years of temple building, repeat the shape of the underground Xemxija graves.

Tas-Silġ North

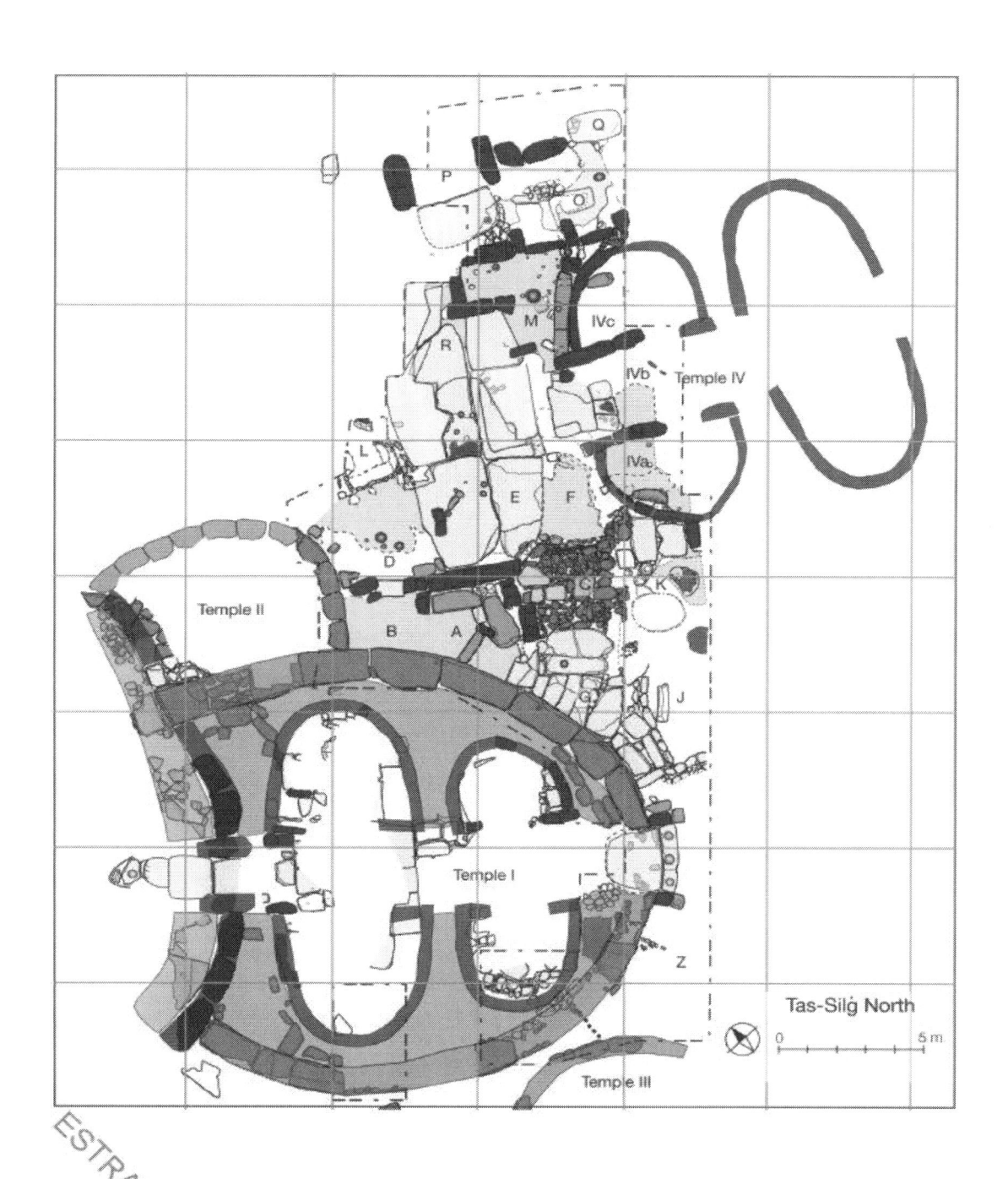

ESTRATTO

Sketch above of temple apses is from *Tas-Silg: the Late Neolithic megalithic sanctuary and its re-use during the Bronze Age and the Early Iron Age*, Scienza dell'Antichita, Sapienza Universita di Roma, 2012/2013:19 on academia.edu by A. Cazzella and G. Recchia 2012/2013:19.

"In this sketch, we can see the single oval design in Temple II, and in the large temple we can see the design of the three-apse and five-apse plan."

"The Red Skorba ovals go back as early as 4400-4100 B.C. in a Cultural Phase so named from the unique red-painted pottery such as the bowls and ladle-cups found in no other site. Since the oval huts at Red Skorba date earlier than Xemxija, what graves would they be replicating?

"The two Red Skorba conjoined oval huts were found near the two later and larger temples on the same hillside at Skorba. Both of these later, Ggantija-Phase temples feature a central courtyard and corridor leading to the three apses of the floor plan, positioned, some have said, like the head and open arms of a human figure."

He clicks for the next slide and up pops the floor plans of all seven temples on the tour (see   ).

"Before or during the Xemxija burials, there were most likely burials in other natural caves on the islands, in caves even older than Xemxija, burials that would have occurred in the Maltese archipelago for as long as it has been inhabited by humans, including the huge cave of Ghar Dalam where some layers dating back 500,000 years ago "contained the fossil bones of dwarf elephants, hippopotamcai, micro-mammals and birds among other species. This layer is topped by a pebble later, and on top of it there is the so-called 'deer' layer dated to around 18,000 years ago. The top layer , or 'cultural layer', dates less than 10,000 years and holds evidence of the first humans on the Island" (heritage.malta.org).

"And so, cave burials were a definitive presence in early Malta. In the enormous Ghar Dalam cave dating back to some 7400 years ago when humans lived there, human remains were found there, at a time way before the Red Skorba cave-shaped ovals were built, perhaps evolving from the Ghar Dalam burials.

"Thus the simple oval huts found in the Red Skorba Phase may have evolved from more ancient cave burials at Ghar Dalam, and eventually developed into the three-apse floor plan and then the five-apse and, finally at Hagar Qim and Tarxien temples the lavish six- and eight-apse design occurred by simply adding on *ad hoc* apse chambers or sub-dividing an apse as needed.

"But this begs the question: needed for what?"

The museum guide nods to his assistant and a computerized animation begins.

"Let's look for clues as to why more apses were needed by visiting now a virtual living temple from 5,000 years ago!" The museum guide beams with excitement.

The now rapt tour group gets rapidly focused on the bright light of the blank projection screen in the darkened lecture room.

The opening image of a computerized 3D virtual tour of Hagar Qim plays across the screen, and some in the tour group gasp, as they see displaying on the screen before them a moving and intensely beautiful outer view of the ancient structure by the sea, from the viewpoint of the triliton at the back of the temple, while the whole building spins and unfurls like an orbiting blueprint, a virtual Legoland of temple stones turning slowly to reveal all angles of a solid roof supported on circular and corbelled walls with stone slabs laterally placed for a completely roofed-over temple, looking like some modern-day planetarium or palace. Its lateral stone slabs balanced on corbelled outer walls hold in place an elegant roof like an umbrella cupping the inner chambers.

Then the computerized viewpoint moves to the inside of the virtual temple. It is so beautiful. Its roof is so high. The tour group is over-awed. Some are saying "Oh!" and "Ah!" at its unfolding splendor. The mouths of the entire tour group, even the Norwegian college boys, remain collectively fallen open, agape in wonder.

They see the virtual 3D temple filled inside with stone tables and apses with curving inner walls. At first the inner templ is presented in daytime with a few stray shafts of daylight stealing in through cracks in the assembled stones of the walls. There, a large cup is sitting on a stone table. There, small Fat Lady figurines are on stone tables everywhere. Then it is nighttime inside the stone walls and the virtual temple is filled with the soft light of torches and oil lamps. It is all so beautiful that the tour group is longing to *go there*.

The group is so mesmerized by the virtual tour that they hardly hear when their museum guide, so pleased he is actually beaming with a big smile at their interest, tells them they can see this stunning animation of Hagar Qim as it looked 5,000 years ago, online, any time, at:

timesofmalta.com/mobile/articles/view20120812/local/-agar-Qim-temple-as-it-was-5-000-years-ago.432456

"This virtual temple took four years to complete for a doctoral degree in Archaeo-Engineering and 3D Visualization at the University of Rome by Suzanne Psaila who is from the town of Marsascala on Malta, her 3D virtual animation of Hagar Qim is based on her study of the archaeological evidence and theories about roofing and use of the site. For example, Dr. Psaila used the small temple model found at Tarxien, which was found in broken pieces that were restored to show the whole temple in all its height and glory, so that Dr. Psaila presents a virtual façade 11.4 meters high (37.4 feet high) sheltering the curving walls of stones, with the highest point of the roof being 8.5 meters (27.8 feet) high, suggesting perhaps 'a second floor' under the inverted cup of the enormous and stately roof."

Next the museum guide clicks for slides showing photos of the floor plans first of the Red Skorba site, then Mgarr, Kordin III, Ggantija, Hagar Qim, Mnajdra, and the last temple built on Neolithic Malta, Tarxien, with its lavish confusion of multiple apses.

The tour group is raring to go. The Norwegian boys anticipate seeing their Maltese Fat Lady in stone palaces!

"The seven temples as you can see," the guide explains, "reiterate the basic inner oval apses and encircling outer wall, built over and over again almost in a dreamlike way, because taken all together, why are there so many apses? Going from the early single apse to the Hagar Qim and Tarxien multiples! Today, we still don't know why."

A guiding yellow arrow blinking like a warning alert, has taken every eye on a walking tour of each temple floor plan, the arrow wandering down walkways, central corridors, and side chambers, emphasizing the uniformity of the central corridor design, and entering the half-circle side apses that open off the central corridor, in a design that persisted for some 2,000 continuous years: from c. 4400 B.C. in the Red Skorba oval huts to c. 2300 B.C. at Tarxien when the temple building stopped.

The museum guide signals his assistant for the overhead lights to be turned back on, and the projector off.

 "And now, let's be back on the bus and heading for Skorba!"

The group likes his enthusiasm and bounds out the museum's great front door with rotating images lodged in their heads, eager to board the bus and see the first temple on Malta.

Skorba is only a few minutes away from the Mgarr site but the drive from Valletta seems uphill all the way, going up, up into a residential area on a steep hill where the tour group finds what the remains of the entire Skorba site next to a group of villas with overhanging balconies looking into the ancient rubble.

The tour group eager to see the Red Skorba ovals quickly exits the bus.

After the group has trekked off, the driver keeps the door open because as he knows, few are allowed to actually enter and walk around the site, for preservation of the strewn and scattered stones, so this will be a short stop.

Standing high on a narrow rocky ledge, the entire tour group precariously peers through wire fencing at what they think is the oldest known temple on Malta.

But it's not.

They are seeing the rubble of the two later Skorba temples with the three-apse design constructed around 3600 B.C.

They are looking for an earlier, Red Skorba site, c. 4500 B.C.

While the rest of the group pauses perplexed on the rocky ledge, the Norwegian boys saunter away. Unknown as yet to them and the rest of the group, the Red Skorba site is it not fenced off behind the wire stretched on wobbly poles on the left side of the uphill road. It is unfenced across a packed dirt road to the right.

One of the Norwegian boys grabs and shakes a nearby pole.

"We could go over the top!"

He laughs but his eyes are mesmerized by the disarray and desolation of what was once a proud temple, a palace, now spread out before them in ruins on the hillside. What is there really to *see*?

His interest fades. He views the ancient stones, as if defenseless, desecrated things, overlooked by condos with intruding balconies that overhang the sad, crumbled site, so that the desolation of the ancient site in all its humiliation is absolute.

It is almost impossible to discern a temple structure.

The young Norwegian feels angry.

Why is this place so disordered no one can tell what is what?

Ready to shake the wire fence poles again, thinking he will pull it down in protest to the ages, he glimpses by the side of the old dirt road a flash of white.

He stiffens. Oh, not again!

He stares and stares but sees nothing more.

But their guide at that instant is standing across the packed-dirt road just where the flash of white seemed to appear, and disappear, and the tour guide is motioning for the group to gather round him near the remains of an old stone wall.

It is a long and straight wall of stacked stones thought to be the oldest on Malta. The Norwegian college boys leaves the fence that he would still like to pull down, and with a sense of disappointment joins his companion to cross the dirt road and to the assembled tour group, and seeing them coming, the guide begins.

The group is led a short distance from the dirt road where they look at a stone wall near the surreal bedrock floor and outline of the lower stone walls that formed the footprint of the two simple structures in which female figurines, red slip pottery and goat skulls were found.

"This ancient stone wall actually runs *partly under* this dirt road on which we stand, going from the fenced-in disarray of the temples *behind* that wire fence, until the ancient wall disappears beneath this road and then surfaces right here, in this open.

"It is here," the guide is saying, with his own sense of awe catching a serious tone in his voice, "that two oval chambers have been found. The archaeologists call them huts. There is still some debate about what they are, and if indeed they do present what has been called a 'shrine' that could be the prototype of all the temples to come.

"The oval huts are decidedly not domiciles! For they are somewhat oddly structured, especially the bedrock floor which seems to be made from waves of stone as if in motion and moving across the chamber, as you can see, not very conducive to the comfort of home. And the huts were found without any sign of domestic hearths, one hut being larger than the other, conjoined with the smaller hut but not interconnected, without an entrance from one hut to the other. Perhaps the smaller hut was a storage outbuilding, or workplace, as found near the later temples.

"The two oval huts which were located right here, were backed up to this ancient stone wall, and inside these ovals, female figurines were found, perhaps prototypes of the Maltese Fat Lady, different but similar," the guide says with a frolicking Maltese smile.

"Some researchers have noted a resemblance to the Cyclades style of female figurines, found here among a large number of other items such as goat skulls. In fact eight boxes of the figurines, pottery and other items found in these two oval chambers are now in the safekeeping of the Valletta museum.

"Across this road behind the fence to your left," the guide continues with an audible sigh, "where we were just standing, are the remains of two later temples, built one thousand years after the two Red Skorba ovals. The two temples behind the fence were built around 3600 B.C. The oval huts where we stand now, are dated to the Red Skorba Phase beginning around 4500 B.C."

The tour group is awestruck, mainly by the weird bedrock floor, but feels disoriented by the disorder of the ancient site, surrounded as they are by the dismal array of ancient stones as if scattered by a great giant's hand on both sides of the old dirt road. The ensemble of touring visitors to Malta filled with mental weariness turns to the road and heads for the waiting tour bus with its door still open on the road below.

As the gleaming air-conditioned bus re-loads its passengers at the foot of the hill, condo balconies look vacantly down from above, and a lurking vision in white watches from the hilltop, carefully hidden from sight as the tour bus pulls away.

CHAPTER FIVE

XEMXIJA AND TA' HAGRAT

For only 9 cents Maltese, a big green #47 city bus with windows pushed all the way down goes everyday from Valletta into the countryside to Ta' Hagrat and the nearby Mgarr site. The tour group, however, is not on that bus. They are relaxing on their gleaming, two-story bus with all the windows closed and air conditioning cranked up to high.

The Ta' Hagrat area to which both buses are heading is a quiet, green land of cultivated fields. Vegetables, fruit and olives ripen peacefully in the sun. Soon a high ridge is seen to rise gently from the fields, reaching for the sea beyond. The ridge is a high sweeping hill forming a dramatic backdrop to the big stone temple entrance to Mgarr, whose huge trilithon stones are rugged and rough, compared to the smooth cement of reconstruction the tour group has just seen at Tarxien. The magnificent Mgarr entrance trilithon is still standing inact, as it was in Neolithic days, so enormous and rugged it is almost frightening, a Neolithic showcase of three huge rugged stones balanced in a trilithon entirely overwhelming to anyone approaching.

Like Skorba, the remains of the Mgarr temple lie scattered, with stones of varying size and weight fronted by the dignity of the magnificent entrance trilithon.

At the sight of it, the Norwegian boys are very pleased.

The real deal, not cement!

They note how the grounds of the Mgarr temple, compared to Skorba, are so neatly kept behind a big sturdy iron fence that all its flowers, trees and flourishing plants, growing on the carefully raked grounds, but seem to present as big a shock for the tour group as the desolate ruins of Skorba.

The tour group's ever-charming, feisty Maltese guide swiftly leads the group up to the rugged entrance to Mgarr, where the three massive stones of the trilithon dare visitors to walk through its enticing entrance.

With a quick glance to make sure the unpredictable Norwegian boys are not yet running around the site, the guide begins,

"To academic archaeology, this temple is part of 'a short transitional stage' from 3,800 to 3,600 B.C.

"Mgarr is a brief 200-year period of temple building wedged between the prototypical Skorba single-oval huts and the later, more complex temples constructed after Mgarr in the following Ggantija Phase from 3,600 through 3,000 B.C.

"However brief the Mgarr period may have been, it contained *in situ* a very important find: a miniature model of a single-oval temple which was completely roofed. No open-air central corridor in the courtyard to vent smoke from the cooking fire! The early Mgarr temple is entered through the later Mgarr temple which has three apses. The two temples are conjoined in the right-hand apse.

"And now, permit me to lead you through this Neolithic trilithon and into the inner temple."

Their guide tells the group to enter carefully two at a time. When it's the Norwegian boys' turn to walk through, they linger as long as they can under the massive lintel, marveling at the impressive bulk of the lintel stone suspended over their heads. Then they walk into the temple site. They scan the remains of the apses and go through to the early temple conjoining from the right apse.

Only minutes later, they walk out. Not much to see. Stones on the ground in disarray, as saddening as Skorba.

So the Norwegian boys are just standing by the tour bus, marveling at the rugged trilithon entrance and eyeing the big opened padlock on Mgarr's spiked iron gate, which the security guard unlocked for the group to enter, when a funny thing happens: from the cross-street leading to the temple, three corpulent elderly women can be seen walking toward them. Their thick, swollen ankles make it slow-going. The boys freeze where they are. The Fat Lady and her cohorts have found them!

But this can't be. The short, heavy-set elderly women are not wearing white robes, just the normal print of a Maltese housedress in gay summer colors. And there are *three* of them! Each Fat Lady carries a basket filled with fresh round loaves of crusty Maltese bread, bottles of olive oil and small bowls for dipping, plates of roasted vegetables and cheese, grapes and olives, platters of sausages and thick slices of honey-coated ham, bowls of hummus, strips of bread for dipping, honey cakes, and bottles of sweet Maltese wine.

The women have come to deliver a catered lunch ordered in advance, the tour organizers having taken into account the isolated rural area in the southern farmlands of Ta' Hagrat where the Mgarr and Skorba sites are found. As the three Maltese women walk toward the Mgarr gate, the Norwegians see their beautiful faces, their thick swollen ankles, their work-worn hands.

The well-brought-up Norwegian boys, getting word from the tour guide that this is their catered luncheon, swiftly unfreeze themselves and rush to carry the heavy baskets. The Fat Ladies are all shy and pleased, and gratefully hand the weighty baskets over to the two strong handsome boys who appear to be…enthralled!

They have finally caught up with (not one but three!) Fat Ladies from the museum. (And not the other way around.) So they ask themselves, what is to be feared? The Fat Ladies have come to them!

Ten minutes later, the tour guide exits the great trilithon into the outer courtyard of Mgarr and comes upon a curious site. Seated under a shady tree on a little knoll near the site, three elderly Maltese women sit as if enthroned. A blond Norwegian boy is reaching for yet another cheese slice and a clump of the crusty Maltese bread. A Fat Lady passes him more sausages, olives, fruit, a cup of wine. Everyone under the tree is laughing because the Maltese women speak only Maltese, an exotic blend of Sicilian and Arabic. Near this enchanted group, two stylish college girls traveling with another tour watch the fun with jealous irritation as the old ladies, each in a flowered housedress, hand-feed grapes to the handsome boys.

Taking it all in, the tour guide is amused.

"What in the world…?" he asks himself…and then, deciding they need a translator, rushes to the top of the knoll to join the feast.

In about an hour, after the Fat Ladies in their bright summer dresses wave goodbye to everyone, take up the empty food baskets and head home, the well-fed tour guide and his drowsy group start craving a nap.

Once they are all seated on the bus, its door closes, the air conditioning kicks in, and the guide takes the microphone to address the just-about-snoozing crowd.

"We are now heading for the Xemxjia site at the northern end of Malta," he begins, carefully looking to see if the Norwegian boys have gotten on the bus. They have, and to the guide's surprise, they are not glued to their seat window and seem to be paying close attention.

"It's just about 20 miles away," he assures them, "and we will make only a quick stop. I wish to ask you to recall the images which we saw this morning of this important grave site. Look into your memories, I ask you, or look in your tour book, and see again twin circles on the hillside that lead to the graves in this underground cave tomb."

Entrance to Xemxija cave burials, Evans 1959.

"And now, perhaps we can all take a cat-nap on our way to Xemxjia."

A short nap later and the group has been prodded off the bus and into a surreal landscape dominated by a massive hotel on top of a hill and private houses that dot the hillside for miles.

It is urban sprawl in the beautiful northern end of the island where St. Paul's Bay and rocky beaches compete for most beautiful. The tour guide starts leading the group up the hill to an excavated area sandwiched in between the big hotel and someone's house. The Norwegian boys are relaxed because this isn't a temple. Besides, now they know that Fat Ladies are actually friendly.

The group toils up the hill to the Xemxjia site.

When the guide sees them all assembled, he says,

"The similarity in shape between the Xemxjia grave ovals and the early Mgarr site does not mean that the tomb and the temple were 'used' in the same way. The purpose and use of the temple were never that of the tomb. No human burial remains have ever been found inside a Maltese temple (with one perplexing exception at Skorba cited in Trump 1966), but after c. 2,500 B.C. when the temple builders had disappeared from the islands, Tarxien became a crematorium and burial site.

"Surely the broad central courtyard and walkways that are present in every known temple on Malta in the subsequent periods after Red Skorba and early Mgarr, are there to connect the head and arms apses, in sometimes riotous union, setting apart temple from tomb, because the spacious meandering temples of Hagar Qim and Tarxien, that evolved into the lavish apse design where people could wander, were wholly meant, as we shall see, to be places for mediating the pain death brings and the sorrow of mourning."

CHAPTER SIX

KORDIN III

Disappointed that the tour group will have to miss seeing the damaged Kordin III site which was not open to visitors, and hearing that permission had to be granted by the Director of Archaeology, the Norwegian boys decide to go ask him.

They call, make an appointment, and find the academic scholar seated at a large desk heaped with reports, books, papers, in-boxes and out-boxes and flowering plants in his office at the top of an elegant flight of stairs. He explains politely that the entrance steps down into the Kordin III site are being constructed and are far too dangerous for any visitor to navigate.

"We can handle it," the boys assure him.

"You would have to go down a short but steep flight of steps made of cement blocks," the director says with a sigh, thinking of the nonexistent maintenance budget, "one block piled on top of the other. This leads downward into the site at a sharp angle. The steps and the site itself are in a fragile condition. Very much harmed by time and the elements. Why do you wish to go there?"

The boys are taken aback by his question. How can they tell him about their pursuit of the Fat Lady? (They are sure she will be at Kordin III in some surprising and tricky way.) Or, how can they express the fact that Kordin III being off-limits triggers their college-age need to go there anyway? And that they live to push limits and do what others don't dare. That their imaginations are usually running out of control. How can they explain in pleasing terms why they *have got to get inside Kordin III*?

"It's to see all seven of the UNESCO Heritage sites," one of them explains in a sincere voice that even reveals a catch in the throat, of an unexpected feeling.

"Part of our research," the other boy chimes in.

Maybe a little too quickly, the director notes.

"We need to see all seven temples in person in order to write our research papers."

"Credit for the Master's degree," the boys elaborate, in an offhand way, but practically in unison, and everyone smiles knowingly.

Actually the two are on this tour to have a good time at the Malta discos, as the director suspects of anyone their age, but ostensibly they have come to see the temples, and they are happy to bring that up now.

Educational research they say.

Just in time to get off the hook and get their way.

"All right then." The director sighs, somewhat exasperated at being overcome so easily by the obvious brashness of these boys he has heard such disquieting stories about, but, being charmed by them, their large and strong physical appearance (they can navigate the cement steps he decides) and their apparently ardent wish to see Kordin III, he reaches for a large old key, unremarkable except for its accumulated rust.

The boys break out in wide smiles.

"Kordin III," they shout, jumping to their feet as they are handed the key.

"Bring it back this afternoon," the director makes them promise, and they are off. Back down the elegant stairs and outside to a bus stop.

It was not easy to get the key to Kordin III, but it was easy to get there from Valletta on the old green Number 3 Malta bus.

The temple site is located on the heights above the Grand Harbor where the invasion of Europe was stopped in 1565 by the Knights of Malta in a fierce battle against the Ottomans. But today the view to the sea is obstructed by blank but low clouds and the boys recall retro TV scenes from the 1950s *Industry On Parade*.

Because on every horizon fronting the temple site, the boys see the blunt instruments of industrialization. Even the usual blue sky is not happy today but overcast with an industrial smog-like haze. The boys breathe in the dismal atmosphere and decide that the remains of Kordin III sit amid one of the most unspiritual places on earth.

Then they notice the grim face of an old military detention barracks perched on top of the ridge, looking through clouds of its own misery on Kordin Hill below.

It's a prison! The frowning old war building is a museum now. The boys think they see a bomber flying low over Kordin Hill targeting the Grand Harbor, but dropping its bombs on the Kordin temples instead, and then roaring off.

Incoming! The temples have been hit! Part of its protective wall is destroyed!

Then the horror of war fades and the Norwegian boys who have never been through a war but have played a lot of video games, with a shudder look around them.

The old green bus has duly deposited them at a busy street corner across from the site which cannot be seen from street level. With great expectations now, for what they will see, they stop their imaginings and stop scanning the menacing hilltop and walk over to the walled site with its padlocked gate.

With hands trembling in anticipation the boys wrestle to unlock the big rusted padlock (with 'Made in China' stamped on it in red) and after some struggle, the uncooperative old padlock yields and opens.

A set of concrete blocks, as described, will take the boys about three feet down into the temple site.

They pause.

Here it is.

Kordin III in all its ruinous splendor, lies – literally – at their feet!

Their guide book stated that Kordin III is 'the best preserved of the temple sites in the Grand Harbor area.' And after seeing the glorious virtual-computerized tour of Hagar Qim, they have extreme expectations of grandeur.

So the boys are not ready to see another forlorn spread of fallen stones and disorder. To make the scene even more unattractive, random items of wind-blown trash lay alongside the stunted outer walls.

The boys behold a dwarf temple, worn down to within three feet of its foundation stones, and yet the temple layout is still clearly there, the intact three-apse design showing all its old symmetry.

The real deal.

A three-apse temple!

They feel ecstatic.

But they feel uneasy. There is a haunted feeling to this place. As if important things have been stolen from it, so that its very presence has been taken away, desecrated like Skorba but more alone, with few visitors for far too long, and the old stones know it. Even to the untrained eye, it is obvious where a large stone has recently fallen.

How easy to simply put it back, but the boys feel too mischievous thinking it.

For they have been informed, and agree with both sides, of the academic debate: Should the temple site be restored, or left 'as is' – the fallen stone being 'an event in the life of the site' – or so the debate goes.

Still, the boys feel the cry of the temple.

They do not move to touch the fallen stone. Although they want to.

Instead they study the site.

Laying prone, like an amputee, the once mighty arms and head of the three-apse design are reduced to a confusion of stones.

Nonetheless, the boys are struck by the sight of the old circle outlines they can still see in the stones. They have read about this site (research!) and its importance in the evolution of the later four-apse and five-apse, and even a six-apse, and stunning eight-apse Tarxien site. From the tour book, *Malta and Gozo*, published in Scotland in 1967 by Christopher Kininmonth, which the boys had thumbed through late last night, they recall what they knew about Kordin III:

"This temple on the heights above Grand Harbor is the best-preserved of the sites scattered over this area, some of which have been completely destroyed. About sixty feet long…it still contains only three rounded chambers. It is constructed of rough blocks except for the megalithic stone screens dividing the rooms from the central court, the portals, and parts of the façade – which is once again given a concave curve (corbelling). The larger of the two rooms, on the left, was subsequently subdivided and two (recessed) niches built into the larger of the two chambers this made. Beside it stand the very damaged remains of a primitive temple which was found nevertheless to belong to the same phase (Ggantija Phase)."

Kordin III thus displays a developmental step which they can clearly see, moving from the single oval toward greater complexity of three apses and the Kordin III design of subdividing an apse.

And then the boys behold, sitting like some anachronistic display amid the rubble, near the right-side apse immediately after the entrance, is what looks to them like an elongated bathtub. Looking for all the world like a narrow tub, divided, however, into basin-like hollows carved into the stone as if individual wash basins, the boys smile as they imagine helpful Fat Ladies in white robes holding towels and assisting as people wash their hands and faces before entering the inner courtyeard to partake of the mourning feast.

"Wash your hands before dinner!" they say to the long tub of wash basins.

Then they remember that what looks like a long stone tub or perhaps a kayak or canoe is actually an elaborate arranegement of querns, used for grinding wheat for example into flour.

They envision many sets of hands grinding.

Food prep for the big feast.

Then the boys recall the words of Sir Zammit in his 1931 report (assigned reading for the tour) on his own personal excavations and the work of his corps of local volunteers who helped him excavate several of the temple sites. Looking upon the disarray and the great fallen stones before him, Sir Zammit's words make the boys feel better:

"These megalithic buildings," Sir Zammit wrote, "are now the bare skeletons of once magnificent structures, mostly roofed over, paved, and tastefully decorated…Food and drink were carried about in these buildings in exquisitely made jars, cups, and dishes, of which the specimens collected during the excavation, and now exhibited in the Valletta Museum, are as marvelous as the builders themselves" (Zammit 1931/1994).

Yes, indeed, now they can see in their imaginations, a bustling corps of Fat Ladies moving like doting grandmothers, grinding grains and seeds and then cooking in the big stone temple firepits as the flames crackle and the smoke rises to the sky.

Then the boys sigh as the thought fades, and they wonder where their Fat Lady is today, but since they actually *are* doing research, they absently note that segments of the outer walls of Kordin III exhibit corbelling and, as they stand there at what remains of the curved wall, they are actually awaiting the glimpse of a broad figure in white, perhaps hobbling toward them, an appearance that today is not to be, but they agree that the profusion of yellow jasmine against a swaying beige expanse of wild wheat and wild oat plants growing waist-high in some chambers and all around the outer walls, lend a lovely epitaph, as if in a Rembrandt paintingm to their absent Fat Lady and the sadness they feel in the temple's remains.

As the boys board the #47 bus back to Valletta to return the key that opens the padlocked gate, they don't see behind them in the hollow of Kordin III a white robed figure, crying.

CHAPTER SEVEN

POST-KORDIN III

The director heard the boys coming up the stairs to his office.

"An ornery pair," he thought, not really looking forward to seeing them but glad they came back with the key.

Then there they stood, quietly, and rather subdued the director thought, poised as they were in his doorway, and he wondered if they were the same boys he had seen that morning.

Gone was their bravado, their show-business exaggerations in language and gesture absent now, and he saw, and sensed in the two a sadness.

So he said,

"Come on in! How did it go? At Kordin?"

Wordlessly handing him the old key, they told him,

"It was gone. It was once great but now it's gone."

Then the boys inquire about the stone boat. The director confims, soothingly, as if to appease some errant child, that no, it is not a boat and not a wash basin but, yes, indeed it is a quern.

To grind.

The boys seem pleased to hear this, and a spark of interest seems to light up their gloom as the idea of them using the huge grinding quern together with several friends at the same time passes a thought between them, and the director senses with relief that they are a bit pepped up.

But even so, their brash approach from the morning has vanished and they seem, well, how to put this, the director thought, they seem more serious, more *mature but disappointed*.

Maybe they're just tired, the director surmises, as the boys thank him and make a hasty exit to catch the next green bus back to the Speranza.

CHAPTER EIGHT

GGANTIJA

Torre Tal Giganti

The next morning bright and early their guide walks up to the open door of the tour bus. He is ready to do a head count. After the breakfast buffet poolside, the group will take off on the bus to resume its week-long tour of the seven UNESCO World Heritage temples. The temple they will see today is as gigantic as its name implies. It is the largest temple anywhere in the islands.

Really big.

It is Ggantija.

Torre tal Giganti, the ancient locals would say.

Tower of the Giants.

From when giants lived on Gozo.

Ggantija is so big because it was built by a giant, a woman, so the story goes, a woman giant who lived here with other giants on this adjoining island to Malta in the multiple island archipelago. It will be a drive to get to the ferry boat from Malta to Gozo and time is getting short. Before the gleaming bus can take off, everyone must be on board.

Has everyone finished breakfast and are seated to go?

The tour guide climbs the steps into the bus and looks up the broad aisle.

Only two people are seated and their heads are bowed.

Their blond heads.

What?

On every other morning, the tour bus had to wait for the blond Norwegian boys who were the last to board, and in fact, the tour guide recalled one morning when the boys were running so late they were almost left behind!

Now here they sat, on time, even early, and quiet.

Perplexed, the tour guide wades up the aisle to their seats and, smiling broadly, says,

"Who are you and what have you done with the Norwegian boys?"

The boys look up and share a quick laugh with the Maltese guide. They think he has been watching too many crime shows on American TV.

He sees their heads were bowed to read a little book assigned for the tour.

"How are you finding this book?" the guide inquires. "You are liking Professor Sir Zammit?"

Their answer is yes. Very informative, they both declare.

Wannabe archaeologists, the guide chuckles to himself, but notes a strange and serious tone crouching like a tiger in the boys' reply.

No funny answers, no mocking smiles.

What *has happened* to them?

He ponders for a moment, then decides that Malta has happened to them.

He smiles, because Malta has happened to many of the visitors he has met. Malta has taken over. The impact of Mediterranean sun and lapis lazuli skies! He is pleased to be a small part of the transformative push that the temples have always, anciently, offered.

Now there is a hubbub of voices approaching the door to the tour bus, and the guide's bemused reverie is over.

He heads back up the aisle.

The boys resume reading.

Soon the guide stands before his dutifully seated tour group, microphone in hand, and before beginning to speak, looks toward the blond-haired boys, just to satisfy himself that they really are on board and seated normally like the others, and then the guide begins,

"We have now visited three of the seven UNESCO temples, and some of us have visited four out of the seven. Boys, what can you tell us about the Kordin III site?"

The boys snap to attention and describe the off-limits temple site to the gaping group and how they saw a long, long bathtub! Actually a thing for grinding grain!

Everyone wants to ask why they didn't get to come along but mention of the bathtub which looks like a kayak but is really a huge grinding quern distracts them and they just say,

"Ah, how strange!"

The stack of concrete blocks that were the steps down into the site, which had to be navigated about three feet down, in order to get into the site, put a perfect damper on any jealous comments, so that the boys were then free to describe the site's two apses plus a subdivided apse, making it three apses, and compare it all to the grounds of rubble and ruin at Skorba and Mgarr.

The boys leave out the part about the dismal hopeless sky and industrial horizon, nor do they tell about the looming military prison turned museum, poised on the ledge above Kordin hill like an intruding monster from the past, but they do describe the stunted worn-down walls, the terrible disarray of the stones, and do not tell the group that a sentimental sadness permeates the damaged site.

Many in the attentive group nod their understanding that Kordin III is just another field of rubble, glad they didn't have to climb down those steps to see it.

While the boys were at Kordin III, the rest of the group visited a cathedral and were shown a 16th-century painting by Caravaggio, a fugitive on the run from Italy and sheltered by patrons on Malta.

And so, everyone had been presented a unique gift from their day, and ended up satisfied with their yesterday on Malta.

Their tour guide feels relieved. No complaints, no unrest. But an eagerness to see the next site.

Perfect!

Now in the present moment, the guide sits down in a front seat as the bus pulls out and turns to face the group with microphone in hand and, as the bus moves on, he says,

"Today we go to Ggantija. In our Christopher Kininmonth guide book, which you all have been given to read, we find that he says,

'In parts the walls still rise to heights of seventeen feet; some of the largest slabs of coralline limestone used in any of the temples are incorporated in the outer wall. Here you do not walk through sketches of rooms, but enter chambers whose roofs alone have fallen…." (Kininmonth 1967/1987)

The Norwegian boys are elated.

Walls still standing!

Really thick, really tall.

"Only the timbered roof is gone," the tour guide says.

Satisfaction soars. No more stunted temples!

No more fields of scattered rubble. No more trilithons made of cement!

In fact, they will see more than one trilithon.

This is because for the two temples built side by side at Ggantija, each temple has its own trilithon entrance and an inner wall that divides them, although both temples are encircled by the same great outer wall where some of the megalithic standing stones in the wall weigh 50 to 70 tons.

The tour guide reads on,

"This enormous temple has the appearance of being the most rough-hewn of the seven extant UNESCO temples, perhaps due to the awkward thickness of Ggantija's outer walls which lend a crude impression to skillfully placed, 'gigantic' 50-ton and 70-ton undressed stones (the biggest in any temple) that form its outer wall. The big importance of this temple which gave its name to the Ggantija Period is that it contains the earliest known five-apse temple floor plan on Malta, a layout which Hagar Qim, Mnadjra, and Tarxien temples later also all repeat in great complexity." (Kininmonth 1967/1987)

Describing all of this, the guide's voice drones on and on, putting some visitors into a short sleepy nap as the bus rolls on, but to the Norwegian boys the information is music to their ears.

"The temple on the left side of the site is the older structure of the two. It is the largest temple anywhere on the three islands. This temple has five apses. Its inner chambers form the old trefoil or three-apse design, but are built on such a large scale that the first two apses connect with the courtyard corridor to form an additional chamber. Altars with engraved spiral designs and the little houses with their little entrance trilithons are set on both sides of the chamber entrance.

"The smaller temple on the right side of the site contains an elaborate altar located in the far back apse and facing its own entrance trilithon.

"As for the gigantic stones that form the outer wall, excavations of the site have shown the presence of rounded stone rollers, some of which were found lodged in place beneath the multi-ton standing stones. In his book, *Neolithic Engineering*, Professor R.J.C. Anderson calculates that, '…the minimum hauling party for moving stones upon rollers is two men per ton on level ground, and nine men per ton for hauling up a gradient of nine degrees.' (*Antiquity*, Vol. XXXV, 1961 in Zammit 1935/1994).

"Just a reminder also that the great Pyramids of Egypt were not yet built as the Ggantija Period began, c. 3,600 B.C., nor was Stonehenge yet standing on the English moors. Meanwhile on Malta, the biggest stones in any Maltese temple or any place in the world were being moved into place on carved stone rollers here at Ggantija.

"Important to the unsolved mystery of what was going on inside the Maltese temples are two sculpted heads that were found in situ at Ggantija, the missing link, so to speak, that make a perfect fit into the notched hole in a headless Fat Lady figurine. This clue was found *in situ* inside Ggantija." (Kininmonth 1967/1987)

The Norwegian boys exchange an anxious look.

Headless!

The tour guide concludes,

"Luckily for archaeologists, sketches were made of the Ggantija temple at a fairly early period in their abandonment.

"It is fortunate in piecing together the temple design today, that prehistorians, archaeologists and art historians can refer to sketches and watercolors, made by Jean-Pierre Houel in 1789, of the great Ggantija standing stones before the destructive clearance of debris was done and before excavations began. After the 1827 excavation of Ggantija, drawings of the site were also made by Charles de Brochtorff in 1829."

The tour guide passes around copies of the drawings.

As soon as the tour bus glides to a stop in the large visitor parking lot, while the others gather their cameras, water bottles, and carry-all bags, the boys jump off first, in their old sprightly way, and hit the ground running toward ancient Ggantija.

As they usually do, the boys separate from the rest of the group and follow their own agenda.

They reach the enormous structure and start walking the perimeter.

They stand at a wall 18-feet-high in places where several bottom slabs are propped in place by metal poles, but the poles do not distract the boys from feeling small against the thickness and rough exterior of the undressed hard coralline stone that has not crumbled. They note to each other how old these stones look, kind of rumpled and tired. But the wall is still standing. And they see the corbelling. Their sad concern about the ruins of Malta has abruptly turned to awe.

For they had seen such ruin, grounds of rubble and plunder, a fleeting glimpse of what had once been a statement clothed in majestic stones but now fallen, damaged and edged out of existence by an encroaching world of their own generation. But here at Ggantija the grandeur of the ancient statement is still embedded in high megalithic walls encircling the intact design of five apses in two separate temples.

As they walk the outer grounds, the boys note more corbelled stones curving the hard limestone protectively around the two temples inside it. They walk the entire perimeter, starting to their left where the huge standing megaliths beckoned their attention.

Now they stood in front of a trilithon entrance.

In the near distance, they see people entering the other trilithon that led into the other temple.

"Tell you what," one Norwegian suggests to the other, "I'll go in this entrance and you go in that one, and we'll meet in the middle."

But this would not be possible.

As the boys find, the two temples here, so unlike the interconnected Tarxien site, are completely separated. There is no connecting corridor or step-through window slab, or any walkway at all into the adjacent temple, only a stone wall between the two presenting no entry from one temple to the other.

Nonplussed, the Norwegians, each inside a trilithon, look eagerly around them.

Inside the right-hand temple, which is smaller than the extra-large and older temple to the left, the lone wandering Norwegian ambles along the central corridor, running clear through the center of the temple, which was as it should be, according to the floor plans of the temples he has already seen. Today inside the smaller Ggantija temple, the floor plan is clear.

The Norwegian feels a wave of pleasure just walking on the ancient corridor. Here, things are as they should be. Like, orderly. Compared to the great disarray he has seen at Skorba, Mgarr, and demolished Kordin Hill.

Now standing head and shoulders above anyone else on the corridor, he has an easy view to the far apse that sits like the head of the temple at the end of the corridor, and glimpsed an elaborate altar.

It was apparent that what seemed a triple altar set in the far end apse had been restored, but as the Norwegian boy approached it, he was glad. Because the long set of tables, three of them, were an *orderly* arrangement. He was sure he had seen a photo of this same arrangement inside the Hal Saflieni Hypogeum and of course, had close contact within it at Tarxien. He feels a little giggle coming on with the memory.

Tarxien inner courtyard, Copyright 2016 Ross-Edison.

Pausing before the triple altar, the Norwegian notes how the inner walls are also corbelled, in some areas, like parts of the outer walls, and neatly so, he thought, and then recalled hearing the tour guide say that although the huge outer wall was made of hard corralline limestone, undressed and rough, the inner walls are made of the softer, easily carved, globerigina limestone. Easy to gouge little dotted holes into slabs of the softer limestone, or carve a spiral design, which he now started noticing.

He could not remember seeing many dotted stones at Tarxien. At least not as many as he saw here in the smaller Ggantija temple set in its own private world, the Norwegian mused, still safe and protected within the hard-limestone wall, as all four apses stretched behind him, here at the triple altar, like open arms welcoming and available, and here the fifth apse is the head.

Pleased to see the ancient floor plan of the temple builders, and a clear statement, pretty much intact and recognizable, in the orderly array of stones at Ggantija, the Norwegian boy takes a deep breath of satisfaction and makes a hasty exit to find his friend and trade up to the bigger temple.

The two Norwegians cross paths outside the massive outer wall, like dutiful sentries exchanging places. Each swiftly disappears into the adjacent but separate inner corridors.

Through the trilition of the older temple, the Norwegian has one reaction:

So *big*!

The first set of apses exhibited the trefoil design on either side of the central corridor and looked, well, gigantic! The area of this big temple is 100 square feet.

Beyond this front area of two apses, according to the ancient floor plan, is a second set of apses, also stretching like welcoming open arms on each side of the central corridor, but the two are smaller apses, nevertheless making a total of four. The fifth apse is like the head of the temple, regally arising as the top of this large imposing structure. Here at the entrances into the apses were altars, one altar on each side of the apse entry.

And as if having a checklist, the Norwegian notes the niche recesses and the drilled little dots on the altars at Ggantija, and spirals that he had seen so many of, at Tarxien, caught his attention.

Tarxien had mostly been a lark. The first temple visited on the tour. It had turned into great fun running around the site with the little lost boys at Tarxien who were tearfully wandering about, and he clearly recalled seeing so many spirals there. Some little drilled holes also there, yes, but a lot of spirals.

Then his Norwegian friend was standing next to him saying they had better run for the bus.

The afternoon sun was beating down on the waiting tour bus and the uncovered head of their tour guide waiting for the Norwegian boys to appear. He needed an American baseball cap, like the boys wore, he decided for the umpteenth time. Maybe a Yankees cap, or Cubs or Royals, maybe Dodgers. A cap from any team, pretty much any, right now, to shade his eyes from the intense sun.

He had just done a head count. Everyone was on the bus and seated.

Except the Norwegian boys.

The guide narrowed his eyes behind his Ray Bans to squint into the near distance, and saw movement. The bus was idling. Air conditioning was running. Ready to go.

And here came the two blond boys running at top speed through the clingy humid air toward the bus.

"About time!" the tour guide shouts but the boys couldn't hear and kept on coming. Now that the driver sees them, he keeps the door open but prepares to put the bus in gear and start a slow roll out of the parking lot.

With a burst of effort, the two boys laughing and jostling leap through the open door, stumbling up the aisle to scattered applause and a few cheers as the tour guide announces on the microphone,

"The boys are back in town!"

Falling into their comfortable seats, the two boys breathe the cooling air and regain their breath just as their eyes start closing.

Then the tour guide came to talk. He had perceived on the boys' tired faces something new.

"How did you find the temples?" the guide asks.

The boys said that their Fat Lady had not been there.

"Must be the wrong island!" the guide says, even as the two boys are overtaken by exhaustion and fall asleep

Taking the front seat just behind the driver, the guide wonders out loud,

"How to prepare them for Hagar Qim?"

The great gleaming tour bus, washed down every day by the driver, majestically lumbers out of the parking lot and then picks up speed to catch the ferry that will take them back to Malta.

\

CHAPTER NINE

HAGAR QIM

Sated by seeing the impressive strength and order of the Ggantija temple, the entire tour group is eager to climb aboard their waiting tour bus early the next morning.

This is the final day of the tour. They have now seen five of the seven UNESCO World Heritage temples by entering the protective embrace of Ggantija's thick walls and ancient apses.

Today is the final day of busing around Malta. Tomorrow night the tour will end at the weekend Qendi Village Festa featuring a marching brass band in the streets and intense fireworks in the sky that no other place on earth can equal.

Right now, however, the group is looking forward to busing to the southwest coast and two temples by the sea.

Their tour guide is finishing up an enticing lecture during breakfast by the pool at the Speranza, detailing some helpful information. They are handed a photograph to pass around showing a small temple model, but unlike the model found at Mgarr, this model shows a layered outer wall that towers high over the broad, stately trilithon at Hagar Qim.

"Some restoration work was done in the 1940s on the lintel, the coping stone at Hagar Qim," the guide is saying. "And from this early sketch of the site, you can see that the rubble and ruin of this temple was extensive."

The tour group finishes breakfast, boards their usual gleaming tour bus, and are on their way to Hagar Qim. Their guide with microphone in hand is seated up front and twists in his seat to face them.

The group is reminded by their patient and jovial Maltese guide that the Hagar Qim site was explored in 1839 by J. C. Vance of the British Royal Engineers. Within two months, Vance had drawn a floor plan of the entire site and had sent to the National Museum of Archaeology in Valletta a stone altar, a decorated drilled stone slab, and a stash of headless Fat Lady figurines discovered beneath a stone step near the trilithon entrance; all of these items found in situ in the rather rambling site where non-symmetrical apses 'run wild' on the temple floor, as if bursting free from all previous designs. Their guide waves a little blue book at them, by Sir Themistocles Zammit, asks that they bring it with them into the complicated site they will now tour, and notes that,

"In this book we have the floor plan detailing the many apses and corridors, 'windows' and steps inside Hagar Qim, compiled by Sir Themistocles Zammit in his excavation report of 1931."

The Norwegians carry Sir Zammit's slim little book in one hand and a bottle of spring water in the other. In his book, Sir Zammit presents the usual floor plan of temples from Red Skorba through the Ggantija Period, compared to the profusion of apses, corridors and low-set 'windows' inside Hagar Qim.

By then the group is thrilled to arrive in a parking area, and all disembark with great alacrity, eager to walk to the temples, one constructed slightly above the other on a seaside cliff.

They can sense the presence of the sea.

The boys note that they and the rest of the group are now approaching the magnificent outer wall and restored tilithon, fronted by a paved courtyard as if an entry foyer.

Sir Zammit's little book describes it. Everyone is asked to please stand and read a few paragraphs before entering the site.

"A wide forecourt lies in front of a high retaining wall, through which a passage, flanked by two sets of deep apses on either side, runs through the middle of the building….This simple plan was, in this particular case (Hagar Qim), considerably modified. The N.W. apse was replaced by four enclosures independent of each other, and reached through separate entrances." Footnote Zammit

The guide points out that Sir Zammit marked his Hagar Qim floor plan into separate Areas, and in each Area numbered the specific place where in situ artifacts were found, such as Fat Ladies and decorated stone tables. The Norwegian boys study it carefully.

The guide adds, "Area A on Sir Zammit's floor plan yields important *in situ* artifacts," and reads Sir Zammit's words,

"The obese stone statuettes, known all over the world, the stone altar with deep carvings representing a plant, on each of the four sides, and a stone slab with spirals in relief, were all found standing about in this place (Area A, positions 1,2,3)."

The boys break from the group and race through the trilithon to that place.

The guide reluctantly watches the rest of his group speed through the trilithon to follow the boys.

He tries to gather them again to point out a few more important facts.

He needs to tell them that Hagar Qim, like Mnadjra temple about a half mile down the hill, exhibits extensive 'drilled hole' patterns (which Sir Zammit calls 'pitmarks'), many of which even in Sir Zammit's era in the early decades of the 1900s were in the process of vanishing, from the action of time and weather on the soft globigerina limestone. For Hagar Qim is predominantly built of this softer white stone, easier than coralline to carve and drill, but far more susceptible than the harder coralline to 'flaking' from weather erosion over time.

Finally the guide has rounded up everyone, even the two playful blond boys. Just big happy kids, the guide thinks with a shrug and then tells the group,

"Sir Zammit writes of 'the most striking instance of this extensive 'drilling' at Hagar Qim positioned in his floor plan as in-between Area B and Area C, where 'mushroom altars' positioned as #4 on his floor plan, are located as the entrance to the passageway leading to Area C.

"'To the left of this passage ('B') is the entrance to an interesting annexe ('C'), very elaborately constructed with well-smoothed slabs. These, originally, were lavishly decorated with pitmarks, but time has effaced most of the pitting and eroded some of the slabs themselves.

"'This small enclosure was, evidently, the holiest part of the Temple. On each side of the doorway stands a stone altar of peculiar shape, with an oblong top and a solid rectangular base. The edges are rounded and raised. The foot of one of the altars is pierced by two elliptical holes, one above the other.

"'The entrance to 'Area C' is well-paved with neatly flanked slabs on end. The threshold is provided with a couple of conical pits (holes) connected at the apex as if they were meant for a rope hole…similar rope holes being bored in numerous other places.'

"Sir Zammit speculates that the rope holes were used to tether animals until used for the sacrifice, as the bones of pigs, goats and oxen have been unearthed at Hagar Qim.

"But this is unprovable. It is more likely that animals were not brought inside the temple.

"'This corridor vista in drilled stone is replicated at nearby Mnajdra temple where a trilithon portal with drilled pitted holes (but without the mushroom altars) is found.'"

Perceiving that no one is listening to him anymore, the guide tells the group to go where they please. He looks to see where the Norwegian boys will be heading, but they are nowhere to be found.

The boys have moved on to Sir Zammit's Areas F, G and I, on his Hagar Qim floor plan, and Norwegians read that at positions #5 and #7 in these chambers several small Fat Lady figurines were found. In Area I and F, Sir Zammit describes some carved rectangular 'windows' set low in standing stone slabs, and in Area F is a 'window' which is large enough to use as a step-through door into another more inner chamber. Area F itself is a special elevated place, with a set of stone steps going up from Area A. Naturally the two boys climb the steps and stand in a higher place.

There they read Sir Zammit's words:

"At the end of the Western apse (of Area A) on the left, is a flight of four steps leading to a room (Area F) at a higher level….Four steps lead to a well-paved entrance, flanked on both sides by the usual series of slabs on end, and into a room which, to the right, is 10.7m long and 4.6m wide, whilst on the Eastern side it ends abruptly in a slight curve….Most of the (drilled) pitting on the blocks in the room has practically disappeared, but we know that it did exist by what remains on the footstone to the side of the doorway.

"To the South, in front of the main entrance, the wall forms a deep recess built up into a polygonal niche by vertical slabs. This recess, once probably covered, is reached through a window-like opening cut into a vertical slab."

The blond-haired boys share a knowing look.

They've got this. They know how to climb through that window.

Yet, they don't.

They are through playing inside these structures.

They sense that the high chamber where they stand, the low step-through window, he drilled dots now disappearing all hold a precious secret, and they hope to find out what these old stones know that they don't.

Not yet anyway.

So the two follow Sir Zammit's lead and simply go where he is describing.

"Coming down from the upper room, a gap between two wall slabs opens into an oval hall at a lower level. This large hall is the second one of the four-apse dependencies off the main (part of the) temple…The wall of this room is made of megalithic slabs, some with the broad face in a line with the wall, others wedged at right angles between the former, with the edge projecting into the chamber. The slabs vary in height between 1.8m (about 5.4 feet) and 2.4m (about 7.2 feet) and from 0.9m to 2.1m (about 6 feet) in width. The ashlar masonry which once topped these slabs is in part displaced, and in part encumbers the floor to this day (1931).

"That this room was of considerable importance may be inferred from the remains of a decorative frieze, on one of the slabs of the outer chamber wall. The stump of a big vertical slab, still in place, shows in relief the feet and lower part of the legs of two corpulent figures…."

Exchanging a look of surprise, the tall blond boys say too loudly, so that members of their tour group who have been trailing them are startled when they hear the boys shout,

"Two of them!"

The boys race down the steps into the large chamber.

They come across another well-formed niche and low step-through 'window' along the Northeastern outer wall (Sir Zammit's Area L).

"On leaving the fourth room (Area I) one reaches further to the east, the entrance to the main building in a line to the main passage to the Southeast. This entrance is solidly paved and has a substantial threshold. Flanked by strong high slabs, it is very imposing… From this point onwards, the outer wall of the temple displays a remarkable solidity and has a very stately aspect. To ensure their stability, enormous blocks of stone, which to the casual observer appear to be outcrops of the rock, are purposely sunk at their feet.

"Wedged between the second and third slab, a roughly hewn pillar (#8 on the floor plan) 5.2m (15.6 feet) high, towers over the ruins; its base is hollowed out so as to allow the use of a lever for placing it in position. Other huge slabs follow until one gets to a very interesting niche built into a recess (Area L) of the wall. A conical pillar broken at the top stands in this niche. A trapezoidal pitted slab stands on its smaller base before it. The niche is flanked by two large pillars, one on each side. To the left of the niche, a deep recess (Area M) like a small cabin is formed between the slabs and the wall pierced at the back by a large oval hole, seen in the Eastern apse (Area B). This chamber served, probably, the purpose of an oracular room which, originally, was well-concealed.

"Close to this shrine, the remaining part of the outer wall consists of one single slab on end. This is the finest stone of the temple, 2.7m (8.1 feet) high, and fully 7m (21 feet) long. It stands majestically at the end of the wall, and like its less bulky companions, is propped up by huge blocks of stone buried at its foot. In two of these stones, sunk at the base of the block, large double rope holes are to be found.

"Bones of numerous sacrificial animals (oxen, pigs, sheep) were found during the excavation of Hagar Qim, a fact which clearly shows that sacrificial animals were constantly required in the temple…."

The boys decide to go count the number of rope holes. Could animals have been tied up by roping a loop through the holes? Animals tied up to await slaughter with large flint knives? Being vegetarians, the boys find this thought sickening but make the rounds of all the chambers to count the alleged rope holes carved into the stones.

CHAPTER TEN

MNAJDRA

In late morning, their rope-hole tally having been announced to the rest of the tour group, who received the news blankly, the boys eagerly line up with the group for a simple trek to the seventh and last temple they will see on this tour, majestic Mnadjra.

Their guide is saying,

"The feeling in Mnajdra temple is a much more compelling and complete statement than in the ruins of Skorba and Mgarr at Ta' Hagrat and on Kordin Hill. More elegant than the thick and awkward outer walls of Ggantija, or the confusion of added-on apses at Tarxien. At Mnajdra we enter the embrace of a completely represented statement, preserved in signs, symbols and elaborately decorated entrance portals. We just don't know what that statement means."

From the trilithon forecourt outside the entrance to Hagar Qim, where they stand on a rise of land slightly above the Mnadjra temples, the tour group can see the site standing open to the fresh sea air and glimpse the polished stones of Mnadjra.

Before they shuffle off, their guide reminds them what to look for, and reminds about the limestone,

"Although Hagar Qim on the rocky ledge above Mnadjra is surrounded by the softer white globigerina limestone, from which Hagar Qim temple is made, the land sloping down to the sea and surrounding the Mnadjra site is composed of the more compact, bluish-colored coralline limestone from which the three Mnadjra temples were built. Coralline limestone is a harder, heavier stone and this gives the outer walls and trilithon portals at Mnadjra a more 'rugged' look than the smoother, softer stones forming Hagar Qim. Inside the coralline walls of Mnadjra, however, globigerina limestone slabs and stones were apparently brought down the hill from the Hagar Qim area, rubbed smooth, polished, decorated, and extensively drilled to create Sir Zammit's 'pitmarks.'

"Three temples were excavated at the Mnadjra site in 1840 but no written account of the work survives. In 1902 an accurate floor plan of the temples was made by Dr. Albert Mayer, and in 1910 professionals from the British School in Rome carried out further work at the site, which resulted in some of the temple contents being taken for preservation, and exhibition, at the National Museum of Archaeology in Valletta.

Sir Zammitt recorded his own observations, and some of those made in the 1902 and 1910 efforts, in his archaeological report of 1931 where he writes,

"'Mnajdra temple displays extensive drilled-hole patterns and carved low-set 'windows' that open through a wall into a recessed inner sanctum. In one chamber, huge drilled stones form a trilithon portal that leads into a dark recessed area like a small cave. The Mnajdra site's importance other than its multi-apse design, is its assortment of drilled holes and carved rectangular 'windows' leading into other rooms.'

"And now, I turn you loose on Mnajdra!"

Before the group a concrete foot path slopes gently down to the Mnajdra site by the sea, just one kilometer (about half a mile) from the great outer wall of Hagar Qim. The guide is motioning for them to go down the slope, and starts waving his hand with great vigor.

And with that, the tour group starts walking toward Mnajdra, with great expectation.

Path from Hagar Qim to Mnajdra,Copyright 2016 Ross-Edison

CHAPTER ELEVEN
INSIDE MNAJDRA

Ambling along on the path from Hagar Qim down to Mnajdra, the Norwegian boys come across the museum director who had permitted them to enter Kordin III. They exchange surprise and cordial greetings and then the Norwegian boys get invited to a big to-do that night inside Hagar Qim.

The feast tonight will be a special thank you to about a dozen donors who so generously support the museum and preservation work on the temple sites, the director explains, a private affair, so glad if they could attend.

Delighted to accept, the boys rush to make their apologies to their tour guide, as they will be staying here for the evening and not getting back on the tour bus, and promise that after the Hagar Qim festivities that evening they will meet up with the tour group later in the streets of Quendi which have already been decorated for the past several days with colorful flags and banners in the old-time Malta tradition, in a village preserved from the old days, dominated by multiple churches with ringing bells.

Then the boys deftly lose their tour group. They want to be the first to explore the site, on their own, as only they can.

The ever-curious college boys can't wait for the big festive gathering of VIP Maltese this very night. They know in their very bones that they will find the Fat Lady there in the disordered mix of apses and rubble. And then they will know her mystery first-hand.

Skipping along, staying ahead of their group, the boys find themselves at the end of the downhill path and alone on a raised platform in front of three temples.

They have found Mnajdra standing open to the fresh sea air and the slanting golden beams of the afternoon sun that have lit up the surface of huge polished slabs of standing stones forming a trilithon portal to a dark recessed inner sanctum. Even from the platform they can see an assortment of drilled or pitted holes and small carved window openings in the stones.

The feeling they sense in the Mnajdra site even before they enter was much more compelling and complete a statement than the ruins of Skorba, Mgarr, and Kordin III. And more elegant than the thick and awkward Ggantija. At Mnajdra the boys feel the great embrace of a sophisticated statement in symbols and elaborate entrance portals.

They feel a quiet calm pervading the ancient site and its incredible existence in a modern world, at the edge of an ancient sea.

They decide to start with the smallest of the three structures.

The boys know, thanks to their tour guide, that the important areas of temple activity as documented by Sir Zammit in each of the the two later five-apse temples are at the center of the temples, that is in the immediate upper right and left of the two apses in the center of the temple where the 'lower' two side apses meet the 'upper' two. The boys shuffle through the pages in Sir Zammit's little guide book, which is his excavation report of 1931, which their tour guide insisted that each visitor bring to this site today, and they see that Areas 6, 4, and 2 in the Sir Zammit floor plan of the Mnajdra site show where recessed altars and and the intriguing rectangular 'windows' are sited.

But what about activity in the smallest of the three temples?

And why does the small temple and the other two temples look somehow different from the Hagar Qim structures perched high on the clifftop?

Sir Zammit's little book explains that although Hagar Qim on the rocky ledge above Mnajdra is surrounded by the softer while globigerina limestone, from which the Hagar Qim temple is built, the land sloping down to the sea and surrounding the Mnajdra site is composed of the more compact, bluish-colored coralline limestone from which the three Mnajdra temples are built.

Coralline limestone is a harder, heavier stone than globigerina and this gives the outer walls and trilithon portals at Mnajdra a more 'rugged' look than the smooth walls and apses of Hagar Qim, where the softer globigerina limestone decorated by the ancients with pitted dots has been flaked away by natural causes such as hot dry sunshine, and wind and rain. Inside the coralline walls of Mnajdra, however, the soft globigerina slabs and stones were apparently brought down to Mnajdra from the Hagar Qim area, and rubbed smooth, polished, and some decorated with extensive drilling.

"Let's find some of those drilled pitholes," they exclaim as they climb the seven steps to look over the floor plan. They see a simple three-apse design surrounded by a circle of stones, constructed and used 3600-3000 B.C., and described by Sir Zammit in his 1931 report as "neat and pretty."

The blond boys cock their heads quizzically as they look.

Too pretty, too neat.

This site has been extensively reconstructed.

But remains similar to the corbelled apse plan at Kordin III.

Kind of.

More or less.

The boys both hastily start thumbing through the pages of Sir Zammit's handy little book where a sketched floor plan and his descriptions sum up his 1931 study of the small structure. After skimming the pages on Mnajdra, they decide to turn to the South and look for an apse with big pillar stones. First though, they re-read the description.

"A narrow doorway looking South is lined by slabs on end, originally decorated with pitmarks. This leads to an area of which the walls have practically disappeared. At the back, an apsidal space, lined with small stones, has in front three slabs, and a pillar on each side.

"The pillar-stones are decorated with pitmarks drilled in horizontal rows on the inner surface. This quaint decoration must have been either unfinished or the work of a novice who had no proper pattern in mind but simply exercised his hands in this peculiar sort of decoration."

Probably stoned, the boys say, savoring the double entendre with a laugh.

They take a moment to look at the odd decoration on the pillar stones.

Something about the dotted design spooks the boys. They suddenly can't see straight. A vision of pulsating dots starts distorting normal perception.

"Let's go somewhere else!"

They decide to look for the area in this small temple where Sir Zammit said the walls had disappeared.

And went to look.

What they did find was a neatly restored outer wall. It encircled the three-apse design. The outer wall was built up to a height of about 1 meter (3 feet and 3.37 inches). To restore and erect the outer wall of the smallest temple, the floor's existing torba was used to determine the placement. The ancient torba, a crushed stone mixture used to pave the Neolithic floor, was used by restorers to figure out the temple's floor plan. The remaining torba of the ancient floor readily suggested where to reconstruct the temple's outer wall.

The inner area in the smallest temple where its wall had disappeared was excavated in 1840 but no report exists of that work, then again in 1902 and 1910 and after that, its outer wall was rebuilt. In fact, this entire site was so much restored and so thoroughly reconstructed that it is described today as "an interpretation" of the ancient structure (megaliths.com).

Yet the boys are getting it, *the idea,* of the activity in the smallest Mnajdra site, in which only three areas are ancient, and in which only some of the original ancient stones remain: at the portal entrance, at the axial screen and apse (middle center of the site), and a section of the inner wall of the northeast apse.

An additional apse which is no longer present may have been included in the Neolithic design of this small temple. At the center or axis of the temple is a wall of stones flanked on each end by vertically standing stones or orthostats. Stones may have been added during restoration.

The boys soon lose interest and move swiftly outside to find themselves standing on the connecting platform again, and look from side to side. They see how the platform appears to connect all three temples but actually does not. These three structures were built at different times (the small site 3600-3000 B.C. and the two larger sites 3000-2500 B.C.) with the center temple built last. For only the little temple they have just toured, and the far temple to their left, are actually *on* the platform which is raised about 1 meter (3 feet and 3.37 inches) above the forecourt on which it stands. The larger middle temple is not included on this platform. They decide to skip it.

Because it is the third temple that is the most interesting to them. It is the oldest of the three temples and within its apses, the boys hope they will look into an apse and find there, awaiting them, the white-robed Fat Lady they have so ardently sought all week.

They rush into the third temple.

They are standing on a passageway lined with huge upright stones running the entire length of the temple. They note immediately a rectangular room with double altars in deep recesses, one to the left and one to the front of the chamber. Sir Zammit declared this chamber a Sanctuary. Drilled pitmarks seem to appear everywhere.

But mainly the boys are seeking the elusive old woman in white, a glimpse at least, lurking and taunting them, and half-concealed, as usual, behind a stone or other enclosure, somewhere in this temple, in the embracing arms of an apse. They are on the run from apse to apse when they encounter a trilithon that stops them where they stand.

The boys have stopped in front of a dotted trilithon, covered *all over*, really, with incised drilled pits, like Neolithic polka dots, shadowing a dark recess just beyond its center.

As if expecting them.

Waiting.

Without having to look at each other, they know they're both spooked. The ancient dotted pitmarks, the deep incisions covering the entire surface area of the trilithon, seem to be staring back at them, and has transfixed them. They stand as if glued to the spot, because the drilled dots are morphing into an insistent buzzing, as if hundreds of bumblebees with a dramatic angry presence which starts pushing the boys inside the dark recess within the great drilled stones.

The two college boys suddenly can't see straight. And feel their cognitive minds go dizzy. It's a vision of ancient surreality, luring them beyond normal perception.

They slap each other on the shoulder and shout in mock frantic voices, giggling but startled,

"Altered consciousness!

Laughing, the boys exchanged a high five.

"Parallel universe!

Then an exuberant fist bump.

"Dude!"

They stood staring at the mirage.

The buzzing seems angrier, louder.

Consciousness altering, Copyright 2016 Ross-Edison

Then abruptly, their mockery fades and they start backing up, in wavering steps, away from the hypnotic hold of the bees ready to buzz-dive and attack them from the formidable pitted trilithon, whose ancient angry dots are already buzzing them, a frightening power over perception, as the furious bees search out the hidden nectar inside the stone enclosure, and push the boys with them into the dark recess.

The boys don't even try to laugh it off anymore but turn around and start scrambling down the remains of the old cracked steps, to break free from an ancient grip, and start screaming,

"We are *out of here*!"

And together they lope off and away.

Then they see they are shouting to no one, for the temple site has closed for the day and there is not a soul around.

Dumbfounded, the tall, blond boys start looking for their tour group which they had so deftly evaded. Hearing a mumble of voices from up the hill path, going away from Mnajdra, which is what they want to do, because affixed with confusion where they stand to the Mnajdra forecourt, without another moment of hesitation, the two Norwegians race back up the hilly pathway to Hagar Qim, until they stand breathing heavily on its broad empty forecourt, then sink exhausted on the quiet strength of its great stone benches.

CHAPTER TWELVE

THE LITTLE HORSES OF MALTA

Skeletal remains of a species of horse have been excavated from Neolithic sites such as Hagar Qim (and) Xemxija Tombs…The few adult bones found at Xemxija compare well in size with those of the Dartmoor Pony…Remains of a small horse or donkey…have been excavated from Maltese Pleistocene deposits. shadowservices.com, *J.D. Evans, 1971.*

Appearing as if out of nowhere, the museum director comes up to the sprawled Norwegian boys to say hello.

Dreaming as they were of chasing after the Fat Lady that night, both boys do a little startle jump and stand to face the genial gentleman. He asks if they could help him.

They answer, "Yes!" as a procession in the courtyard carrying folding tables and chairs, starts trundling them inside the old stone circles at Hagar Qim.

"Could we help set up?" the tall, blond boys ask the director, unable to veil the excited tone in their voices.

"That's for later," the director says, a bit vaguely the boys think, as he scurries off to direct the tables and chairs to a storage place.

And then they all hear a clip-clop, clip-clopping on the hillside walkway.

"Horses!" the Norwegian boys cry and run to watch a curious sight unfolding.

For a pair of small Maltese horses with dark and kindly eyes are being led toward the trilithon entrance. Attached to each horse is a looped rope holding up the front end and back end of a stretcher which swings slightly between the two horses as they walk slowly onward. The boys are so stunned they go uncharacteristically speechless and just stare.

"This is what I need your help with, please, if you will," the museum director says.

"Of course," the boys agree, eyeing the draped bundle slung on a stretcher between the two horses, and have to ask,

"What is *this*?"

"Part of tonight's event," the director says.

"Do you need us to help carry it in?" the boys ask.

"Yes, please, just inside to the middle of the courtyard, if you would be so kind."

"Of course! Let's get it done!"

Liking the enthusiasm he hears, the museum director joins several men leading the two horses and, together, with the boys assisting, they carefully lower the draped bundle from the stretcher, all six of them supporting it as they lift and hold it up, before it touches the ground. Like pallbearers, the boys think, we are bearing this into the heart of the temple.

A table of stone slabs piled waist-high has been positioned in the center of the courtyard. The six stretcher bearers place the bundle upon the stones.

Then they all go back out through the trilithon and see, to the great delight of the two Norwegian college boys, that the little horses have been tethered to rope holes! Drilled so long ago into outer stones that front this temple.

"Rope holes!" the boys cry, surprising the others standing around them

"Yes, indeed," the museum director reassures them in a bemused tone,

"Rope holes, indeed!" The Norwegians chant with delight.

"And later, my dear friends," the director smiles to the boys in his endearing Maltese way, "we could use extra hands to set up the tables for tonight's feast."

"No worries," they answer, "we'll do it!"

Then suddenly, as though dreaming, the Norwegian boys see their dream come true.

And then some.

Because not one but five Fat Ladies in white have arrived and stand pausing, for dramatic effect the boys think, on the outer forecourt, back-lit by the sun beaming low on the sea beyond the great trilithon door.

The boys see five old women all wearing white toga robes, just like their Fat Lady wears, who begin to glide their way through the old stone portal, listing majestically to the right, to the left, on their thick swollen ankles as they approach the draped bundle in the center of the outer courtyard where a distraught woman and two young boys stand waiting.

A large tub is brought forward, and the Fat Ladies fill it with clear rainwater fetched from the stone cistern up the hill. The five elder ladies in white have carried out red pottery jars with long-handled ladles and placed them on the stone table. The jars are filled with oils so heavily scented that the Norwegian boys catch the wafted scent of sweet spices and herbs yards away from where they stand.

Without further ado, the draped bundle is stripped of its concealing material and the five old women with surprising alacrity begin daubing the body of the deceased with fragrant cloths which they rinse in the tub, and then wash again, until finally they proceed to pour on the scented oils while the bereaved woman and her two little boys stand nearby, staring and weeping.

The Norwegian boys are aghast.

They dash into an empty apse and hide.

CHAPTER THIRTEEN

IN THE TEMPLE OF MOURNING

The Norwegian boys know the museum director is watching but being so spooked, they couldn't care less. They settle down on the floor of the apse to wait it out.

Then, another surprise.

They glimpse from their hide-out four men who step up to the central inner courtyard. They carry the horse-drawn stretcher and silently wait while the deft care-worn hands of the five old women wrap the deceased, head to toe, in pure white cloth and step back.

Then the four men position the deceased onto the stretcher and against the family's saddening cries, as the widow's low keening sound gets amplified by the great acoustic stones and starts echoing off the inner walls throughout the temple, the men hoist the stretcher and carry it out through the great somber trilithon.

The curious Norwegian boys get up and follow.

The Fat Ladies scurry together and form an entourage that encircles the bereft little family and escorts them out onto the forecourt where mourners are waiting, dressed as they are for the somber occasion in woven brown clothing that looks like the rough burlap of sackcloth. All stay where they are while the stretcher is tied front end and back end to the two small horses.

And then the little horses with the large kindly eyes and long black mane are moving in a stately way, tossing heads and arched hoofs held high as they move off, in the sculpted beauty of flowing grace.

Everyone starts walking, mournful and silent, behind the horses, toward the far Hypogeum at Hal Saflieni, and the ancestral tomb, some five miles away.

The Norwegian boys fixated with disbelief watch them go.

Then rush back into the concealment of their apse.

CHAPTER FOURTEEN

FIRST FEAST OF THE EVENING

The blond boys are feeling tired and drowsy after plopping down on the remnants of torba inside their apse, but in a heartbeat the museum director pops his head into the hide-away and cheerfully announces it's time to get to work.

"What?"

"*Now* we set up the tables!" the museum director says with vigor and turns to go oversee the set-up, but abruptly turns to assure the boys,

"Don't worry, they'll be back!"

Then with unusual alacrity for a man of his weight, the director ran into the central courtyard where, already, there is a bustle of movement.

Walking out of their hide-out apse like awakened zombies, the Norwegian boys set to it and soon the boys and the catering staff have arranged chairs at tables set with pale yellow cloth and bowls of the yellow jasmine flowers of Malta, all ready for the feast.

Soon the guests are pouring in, well-dressed VIPs of modern-day Malta wearing stylish black evening clothes, some with gold accent jewelry studded with tanzanite as blue as the nearby sea, there a necklace of pink tourmaline and diamonds, and there a single strand of pearls.

Nodding greetings to the museum director and warmly embracing him, the elegant guests start seating themselves and hoisting bottles of local Maltese wine to pour the intense dark liquid into crystal stem glasses and drink to the prehistory of Malta and to the Maltese love of life itself. Now the catered feast is being served.

The boys are not hungry.

They need to talk with their Fat Lady.

There, they see her!

She is standing on the sidelines beyond the busy tables, as if too shy to be seated with all the grand folk in their sophisticated jewels and black evening wear while she is wearing only a simple white robe that might even look like a toga to most of the fancy folks there that night, and she without jewelry, and besides, she is engaged in conversation with a small man ill-dressed for such a warm summer night in a tweed suit and sporting an old-time handle-bar mustache and rimless glasses that give the little man the agonized look of a suspicious owl.

The Norwegian boys recognize him at once, from their first day on Malta, when they were in pursuit of the Fat Lady on the hot twisting streets of Valletta! It's that guy again! The one the Fat Lady ran away with! Now the boys hope they have a second chance.

A dark-haired younger man is also standing with them, almost invisible in the dark empty shadows near an array of apses. He's not dressed for the fancy dinner either, wearing as he is that plain woven clothing again, which is, the boys note with surprise, smeared with clumps of moist clay and red stains, dried mud, and the fine white powder from drilled stone, as if a common workman.

Oh, wait, it's that stone mason guy from Valletta.

He is smiling at them in friendly recognition. The boys had almost forgotten how they had admired him that day, an artist in stone cutting, and then they hasten to join the beckoning threesome which makes no move to be seated for the feast but instead begin a jovial conversation with the two blond boys in the warm moist air as twilight nears in the temple by the sea.

The Fat Lady is mesmerizing the tall blond boys. She is accepting them, and their friendly interest, but, still, she carefully looks them over, and stands her distance, smiling at an amusing excavation story that her old friend, Temi, has been telling.

The boys are charmed when she and Temi start giggling.

The stone mason does not laugh. He seems to never lose his awesome dignity, but stands smiling in a detached but genial way, and the Norwegian boys are happy to be included in this group. They have found their Fat Lady and she has not rejected them. She has not run off with Temi this time!

They adore her.

Then a voice breaks the spell.

"There you are!"

It's the bustling museum director.

"You must join my table! I have archaeologists waiting to talk with you about your research! Come on now while the night is young!"

Surprised by the director's rude behavior, as if he has not even seen the Fat Lady or the stone mason, or, the biggest *faux pas* of all, has not given one word of greeting, period, to the Fat Lady's friend Temi, but the boys shrug and start to follow the genial director to his waiting table anyway.

They turn back to say goodnight but the Fat Lady, the stone mason, and Temi have vanished into the night.

CHAPTER FIFTEEN

COMING BACK FOR DINNER

After the feast and entertainment by a surprise guest and trio of young tenors all wearing black and brought to Malta by boat from Italy, the well-dressed VIPs of Malta start making their way from Hagar Qim to the visitor parking lot just beyond, where their limos and cars await them. The Norwegian boys and the museum director stand outside on the broad forecourt watching them go.

They have all said their goodbyes, made promises to do lunch soon, and now their exit from the site continues, led by museum staff holding electric torches.

"What an evening!" the director says.

"Thanks so much for inviting us," the boys say.

"Well, boys, it's not over yet."

They follow his gaze into the vast darkness on the distant cliffs. They can just make out fiery torches held high, bobbling and moving on the path near Mnajdra below them, and hear amplified by the clear sea air the patient clip-clop of horses.

"They're coming back!" the director exclaims and the boys hear excitement in his voice.

There is movement behind them and the three turn to find the boys' special friend, their Fat Lady, with the handsome young stone mason, and the little man in tweed.

The Norwegian boys quietly admire the retro tweed vest and bow tie. And this time, the boys are relieved to see the museum director politely and warmly greeting all three, acknowledging their presence for the first time that night.

"We left the tables and chairs set up for you."

In reply, the Fat Lady embraces him.

The crowd of mourners has walked back from Hal Saflieni with the children and their mother riding on the horses. The crowd has become larger and can now be seen and heard as the bobbling torch light approaches the brightly lit temple in the shadows of the night. Some mourners head for the large bench slabs that run across the corbelled base of the outer wall and throw themselves down on the ancient seats in exhaustion.

A man starts tethering the horses by slipping a rope through the carved double-V holes in the large stone on the forecourt, then goes uphill to the stone cistern to fetch fresh water for the horses to drink, before he starts brushing them down.

Men in sackcloth lift the little boys and help their mother dismount from their perches on blankets spread atop the little horses.

The older boy is crying, but the younger boy is not; he is just feeling perplexed.

In all his five years, he has never seen anything like this. It must be the middle of the night but all these people are awake and walking around. The young boy clutches a red cup, worn at the lip of the bowl from much use. This cup has a special long, long handle that is topped by a bird's head. His father would use it as a dipper sometimes and sometimes a bowl.

He feels confused again.

Why do they have to come here?

It had been a long, tiring walk to a great stone entrance. Other people had walked alongside the two little horses and the grieving family. Different people would pick him up and carry him. Finally his father's draped body was lifted carefully from the stretcher-sling, swinging gently between the little horses, and the boy watched men carry it through the looming three-stone entrance, into the dim, flickering lamplight that could not dispel the darkness.

Inside the layered cavern, everyone had walked cautiously down a hewn path whose surface is strewn arbitrarily with rocks as if carelessly tossed there from the looming depth of the place. First off, the deceased was carried in and placed inside a deep recess hand-cut with axes and antler-picks into the soft stone of the ground, and the crowd of mourners looked to the little family holding carinated bowls against their wildly flailing hearts.

Almost time to throw and break them.

Only, where *is* the little boy?

The boy's mother looks around in surprise.

He is not there.

Everything just stops as she rushes as best she can back up the rocky way. She reaches the great stone entrance with fear in her mind, but, there he is, sitting on one of the little horses.

No one had noticed when he deftly lagged behind as the procession of mourners walked into the scary darkness, led by the flickering light from hanging lamps swaying gently in the night air at the dark trilithon, stationed overhead on carved wooden poles at intervals along the path, showing the mourners the way down.

"No way *I'm* going in there," the little boy said to the backs of the descending crowd, as he fades further into the shadows at the entrance trilithon, and takes off to find the little horses.

CHAPTER SIXTEEN

INTO THE DARK

The first to notice the boy, after the mourning party has trailed into the creepy darkness below, are two of the men who had loaded the stretcher-sling at Hagar Qim, and, upon arriving at the solemn trilithon into Hal Saflieni, stayed there at the Hypogeum entrance to care for the horses. And there the child stood, and they see he is motionless and silent, a little boy in shock, they see, cradling a duck-billed ladle.

So they sat him atop the little horse. He seemed content then, not crying at all but strangely lost in thought. They figured his mother did not want him to come to the burial and told him to wait here.

"Funny," one man said to the other, in a low tone so the boy wouldn't hear, "seems like he's not sad."

They peered at the child.

He tightened his grip on the long-handled cup and looked back at the men, fiercely.

"Defiant," they agreed, just as the boy's mother came running.

She began to scold the boy for not coming with her, thanked the men for watching him, and then felt how grown-up her child seemed when he said,

"I'm not going in there."

His mother smiled sadly at the boy.

The little boy asked his mother, "Where did he go?"

His mother, pale and weary with sorrow, looked at him, wordlessly.

"I'll be back soon," she said to the boy and the men, and rushed back down the rocky way.

Down below the grave goods were quickly put in place when she got back to the burial. A large, beautifully ornamented shallow bowl incised with white-paste dots and animals and painted top and bottom in two shades of red held the gift of cooked food, for the journey, then a greenstone axe amulet was added, a matching shallow cover was placed over the bowl of food, red ochre was sprinkled profusely over everything, and when all was in place, the little boy's mother was the first to throw.

She tossed the studded bowl she carried, with an angry heave for her husband's untimely death, and as it hit the stone wall backing up to the ancestral grave, the beautiful, artistic bowl broke into large jagged pieces.

The older brother threw the bowl he carried without tears or any sound, and it shattered. Into smithereens. Tiny sherds of all shapes flew defiantly through the near distance in and around the tomb. Then after a pause, the mourners filed back up and out, soon assembled in the cool fresh air of the night. Everyone was eager to get out of there, and the caravan of mourners, drivers and little horses at once begin the walk back to Hagar Qim.

The little boy riding on the strong little horse with his brother remains lost in thought.

The walk continues. Men loft torches toward the night sky. The horses plod on. Soon enough, the bright electric lights set up inside the great standing stones for the evening's gala VIP affair make Hagar Qim arise in a circle of light, while hanging oil lamps in the outer courtyard softly glow anyway, like an upstaged pre-dawn hour.

Inside and out, the ancient temple is alight. Ready to receive its second wave of guests, this time ancient people are coming to feast, heading into the unusually bright modern light, and soon the temple itself will soothe them with its strong healing presence after their long walk from Hal Saflieni in the fierce firelight of torches carried anciently against the starless night.

The little boy atop the little horse can discern about a dozen dinner-party guests, lingering n the outer courtyard, stylish stick figures back-lit and dark, dressed in black gowns and tuxedos, only their diamonds and gold jewelry glowing in the ancient lamplight as they move about in the near distance. He watches as more dinner guests file out of the bright, illumined inner temple and meld into the soft glow of the outer courtyard, greeted by museum assistants hovering with electric torches to guide them to the visitors center where the limos await.

But the little boy is not amused by the animated stick figures now scurrying away. He is brooding and confused as he clutches his father's old red ladle cup to his chest.

A generous size, this cup. A good serving.

He frowns and sighs. He can't figure out what has happened in the dark place where his father has gone.

He's got to ask someone, but *who*?

His mother is pale and silent. His brother won't know anything.

Then he sees an old woman standing quite still. He sees how she is caught in a shining stream of light, emanating from the great temple door.

The little boy studies the old woman's white robe, and sees her thick swollen ankles that must hurt, he thinks, and be painful to walk on, but there she is, standing on the paving stones at the massive portal to the temple, as if waiting for someone.

Is she waiting for *him*?

Maybe it's Grandmother.

Yes, it *is* Grandmother! And she knows everything. The child runs to her side.

The Fat Lady looks down upon the little boy holding an old cup worn with use and featuring a long handle on one side, topped off by a bird's beak.

She has been watching for him.

The child clutches the folds of the Fat Lady's robe, and asks his burning question,

"Where did he go? Grandma! Where did he go?"

The boy is not weeping, but inquiring, and the Fat Lady says,

"Come with me. I can show you."

CHAPTER SEVENTEEN

THE MOURNING TOUR

The old woman in white and the little boy wait at the trilithon entrance for his brother and mother to join them. Then the Norwegian college boys coming up behind their Fat Lady behold a curious sight.

Led by her older son, a woman made of wood is approaching.

It is the widow. Her face is so blank it's beyond expressionless, a still and fixed whittled face, carved by an artisan who sculpted her features, smooth and lovely, except for the furrowed brow of grief which creases her forehead and carves a dark strike between her eyes, as if cleaved irretrievably in half, by some terrible thrust of fate.

The furrows on her brow are all that is left of her.

She is hollow. Inside she has the sensation of falling. She thinks nothing, feels nothing. No anguish, but worse, nothingness.

Although pictures flood her mind.

From today and the day before.

She had energy then.

To get through the frantic time.

Yesterday she had gone running, not walking, everywhere. She had held her beloved in her arms and stroked his head as he silently left her forever. The picture stuck now, and re-running through her blank mind was her beloved, wrapped in a woven cloth and carried out of their mud-brick hut by three strong men.

And then the family was there. Everyone sad and shocked.

Then getting ready for the trip to the ancestral burial chamber at Hal Saflieni. She'd been there before tonight. That occasion was the removal and disassembling of bones from a previous family burial. She wondered vaguely if she would be there again when the time came to disassemble the bones of her beloved.

As these dark memories recede, bright pictures filled with late summer sunshine came in a gentle rush to replace them. She watched herself running yesterday with the women in her family from their village of Qrendi and to the nearby temple of Hagar

Qim. There they will talk to the temple assistants about the food to be prepared as grave goods and food for the mourning feast.

Then everyone is carrying food into the temple outbuilding. The temple assistants already dressed in their ritual white have gathered much food and even now the querns are in use and a hubbub of activity is underway for the mourning feast to come.

Enough food is being prepared for a full house of 32 people, using every stone baking cup on the premises in addition to the bigger stone cooking bowls.

Then, all arrangements being made, the widow's family women gather round her on the broad temple forecourt.

The plan is made to leave early tomorrow afternoon for the walk to Hal Saflieni where the just emptied ancestral tomb awaits about five miles away.

The next day the journey absorbed the sorrow. Pictures of it now encircled her mind. She saw slanting beams of sunlight as the journey started out, in the late afternoon light so normal, so calming, as if nothing abnormal could ever or had ever happened. Then she remembered thinking that they had reached the tombs too soon, even though the sun was fast sinking by then and an early darkness began falling all around them.

Then pictures of the grave site fell upon her mind. And the panic of her missing boy. She saw herself running, trying to out-race her fear all the way back up the dim-lit path, to look for him. Breathing hard she reached the great stones of the trilithon entrance to Hal Saflieni, where she found her boy contentedly sitting on a horse.

Then she saw herself rushing back down the rock-strewn way to the grave where her family and friends stood waiting. How had she done all that running?

Now she was done in.

But it was more than the great fatigue that the past two days had brought her. Tonight, soon, when everything was over, she would find herself alone, with the loss that could never be restored. The hollow feeling would never end.

Now, through all the shock and exhaustion, memory pictures still racing through her mind were disturbing her physical balance, so that she could barely walk and move forward as she now had to do.

Seeing this, with a tumult of the heart her little boy leaves the Fat Lady and rushes to her side.

Now both sons are escorting her toward the old woman who is watching with a matter-of-fact expression. The widow woodenly approaches. Her two young sons have finally steered her there.

The Fat Lady gathers them all in her arms.

Now sheltered in the bear hug of the benign old woman, the little boys and their mother are gently turned by the Fat Lady to face the entrance trilithon to make their way into the inner temple.

The curious Norwegian boys trail along behind them.

Once inside, they pause on the central corridor which runs all the way through the temple, past paired side apses, on either side of the corridor, and they can see straight to the end of the great circle where an exit trilithon faces them. The Fat Lady stops their progress toward the back door and pauses near a dark recessed niche within a side apse.

The Fat Lady steers the curious little boys, who at this moment show no fright or worry, forward to a low-set window which opens on an inner portal. The portal is fronting a dark recess carved in the stone behind it.

The bereft little boys run to the low window and clamber through it, much as the Norwegian boys had done at Tarxien. The tall and gangly blond boys chuckle seeing this and remember how these tearful little boys easily got into the small trilithon when they were lost at Tarxien.

Then they see that the two little boys have become fearful. They will go no further. They will not enter the dark recess that faces them with unknown emptiness.

The Fat Lady takes over.

She awkwardly begins to follow the little boys. She tries to climb through the low window when one plump leg and thick swollen ankle get caught behind her and she is stuck! The sight is so comical that it makes the little boys giggle at the total lack of grace in the Fat Lady's lumbering attempt to push herself through the small space. The bereft little boys remember how the same thing happened to the tall Norwegian boys when they tried to follow the little boys at Tarxien!

Soon enough as they watch the Fat Lady wriggle free, the little boys forget everything and are smiling broadly, being simply awestruck as the Fat Lady proceeds into the portal beyond the window, leading to the dark recess.

Then the Fat Lady is easily inside the dark recess and seats herself on a mushroom stone positioned there just for her, and she lights the dried grass and tallow inside a shallow swale carved into a hand-sized piece of limestone, and for a heartbeat all revel in the soft glowing light,,and then the Fat Lady speaks.

"He is only sleeping. He will visit you in dreams. He has gone to sleep inside a circle, a circle just like these. Love is the circle, and a circle has no end."

Then she tells the little boys they can go explore all the circles while she talks with their mother, but the electric lights from the previous party have been dimmed now and the young boys have become sad and fearful of the shadows now circling around them and say they would rather stay by the Fat Lady's side, even as the first aromas of the mourning feast arise with the smoke from the cooking fires and float upward through the open courtyard like wishes into the warm night sky.

CHAPTER EIGHTEEN

THE BROKEN CUP

The Norwegian boys in their Bermuda shorts and baseball caps turned sideways on their fair blond heads are watching the crowd, in which most people are wearing the plain brown clothing that the stone mason wears, and now the crowd is standing patiently together, in a line that goes through the central axis of the temple where it's SRO (Standing Room Only), surrounded as they are and hemmed in by the catering company's tables and chairs.

But the tables have been cleared of dishes and wine bottles and the long-stem crystal glasses into which the sweet dark wine of Malta was so freely poured. So that the tables now appear inviting, and so lovely, with glowing oil lamps set on pale yellow cloth and the yellow jasmine flowers that still bedeck the tables.

The line to see the Oracle that night is aimed at a recessed niche at the top of a set of steps where the glimmer of oil lamps and the light from a hanging bowl are glowing like promises.

Everyone waiting must ascend the steps to where the Oracle customarily sits.

The mourners standing in line in their coarse clothing seem to the Norwegian boys like ethereal souls displaced from the earth, and hungry for an answer and a feast, while the Fat Lady with two spooked little boys hanging on to each of her arms and holding tight to the folds of her white robe, walk together with the solemn widow to the stone steps leading to the upper chamber.

Soon after they have climbed to the top of the steps, everyone at the tables can hear smashing and breaking and a boy's voice, crying.

He has broken to bits the long-handled ladle cup that was his father's cup.

Quickly the tall, blond Norwegian boys move away from the concerning cries of the boy's tumultuous anger, and join the inner courtyard crowd, where they start watching Temi conversing with the stone mason.

The Norwegian boys think the stone mason is a cool guy. There is something all-knowing and ageless but never arrogant about the handsome young artist whose job is to restore and preserve the stones of the temple sites. At this moment the stone mason dressed in his usual dull brown weave, is running his fingers over the edges of an ancient, smooth-cut window, its low carved edge as soft as silk to the touch, as always, tonight and every other ancient night in the temple of mourning.

When the little boy's crying has ceased, the entire corps of temple attendants are on the move, on the inner courtyard floor, bringing to each table a large amphora of sweet local wine and strategically placing on each table beside the wine, plates of cheese, olives, olve oil and bread, so that very soon the wine is being hoisted all around the tables. Soon every cup is filled and tipped to the lips of the entire mourning crowd and the spell of grief is abated. A cordial buzz of sedate conversation begins to fill the inner courtyard.

CHAPTER NINETEEN
WOMAN OF WOOD

The Norwegian boys take off their baseball caps and sit down at a table.

Soon the grieving little family enters the central courtyard and attendants help them get seated at a flower-bedecked table. Plates of food are placed before them.

Instead of eating, the two little boys abruptly fall asleep, their heads slumped onto the pale yellow cloth on the table. Each boy clutches in hand the figurine of a Fat Lady. The Norwegian boys are feeling a great relief for this bereft family which seems to have found peace, when suddenly the widow starts panting.

"Uh, uh, oh," she begins saying as if in some great physical pain, "oh, uh, uh," she says and clutches at her heart.

The Norwegian boys watch with concern turning to panic.

"Call an ambulance! Call 911. Call a bus!" they shout but no one moves to do so.

They realize too late that they have watched too many American TV crime shows and the ancients at the tables have no idea what they are talking about.

Then the stone mason sidles behind them, at this weird moment, his face a mask of empathy, and says in a whisper,

"It's the sorrow."

"Uh, oh, uh," the woman keeps saying, in a disconnected keening sound, as if her voice is physically far removed from the emotions of grief stinging her like pricking pin points in every synapse in her body.

A temple attendant brings a cool damp cloth. The widow is offered a cup of water. Finally she rests one elbow on the pale yellow table cloth and puts her head in her hand.

And sits quietly.

"She was being stabbed by grief," the stone mason explains to the staring Norwegians who in their young lives have not yet known sorrow.

"What do you mean?"

Just as the stone mason decides that these boys cannot understand, the Fat Lady appears and asks if the widow is ready. A temple assistant sits to watch over the sleeping little boys as their mother lifts her head, stands up and follows the Fat Lady to steps leading to the upper oracle chamber.

There they will talk.

The Fat Lady knows that when she speaks in a high-pitched voice, the acoustical stones will not pick up her words. So when they are both seated on the specially decorated mushroom stones inside the oracle chamber where tallow candles already glow, the Fat Lady first off tells the widow that her beloved had an easy passing and is looking upon her at this moment. He wishes to tell her something.

"He says he is no longer suffering. He says to tell you the passage of time will cover this wound, because each day is a bandage to wrap the harm of such pain as you feel now. He also would like to ask: do you remember when we found the lost goat?"

The widow, sagging and defeated, abruptly sits straight up, at sudden full attention as if slapped in the face.

"Yes! Yes, I remember! That day on the cliffs where we found her! She had fallen and gotten stuck in some vines! The billy goat led us to her!"

The Fat Lady watches the young widow's surprised laughter, before continuing:

"He says he will always be watching over you and the boys. Whenever you light a candle for him, his presence will be there."

The wood-carved expression on the widow's face has changed to an ecstasy.

Then the Fat Lady lowers her tone to a deep decibel and speaks in a very loud voice to make sure the acoustical stones pick up her words and that all in the courtyard may hear,

"His message is,

"'Come back to life.'"

The widow has become as quiet and calm as the stones.

In the courtyard the Norwegian boys appear bewildered at hearing these words. The stone mason wants to help them understand.

"Grief therapy..." he says, and then wanders away mumbling the rest of that sentence, *sotto voce.*

It would be too embarrassing to say aloud.

The odds are that the Iberian's words would never be understood by anyone.

Too abstract.

So he quietly says it to himself, absently touching the pouch by his side for the reassurance of the old flint blade wrapped in a leather strip, the cool glassy obsidian, the cache of red ochre, and then adds very softly so that none would hear,

"….for the broken-hearted."

CHAPTER TWENTY

THE ORACLE

The Fat Lady was hungry.

Now that the grieving widow has been seated for the mourning feast, now that the little family has moved through the initial shock and denial and, hopefully, resolved the defiant anger of the little boy, the Fat Lady feels a profound weariness seeping through her. She has been emptied of her powers. Her head is reeling. The little boy has worn her out.

But it was all in a night's work.

She had led the little family tonight through the ancient circles.

Her head is aching. Her distended ankles are tingling as though pricked by the points of a sharp, ground-bone pin, and her poor toes are numb from walking through every circle and clambering through every window in this temple. Usually on such a tour, she doesn't clamber through every low window, but she had done it for the boy. She had brought a smile to his somber face.

Now it seems that every muscle in her elderly body is sore and inflamed.

And there is still work to do.

The Fat Lady seats herself heavily on a cool stone bench, placed there just for her, and bows her head on her arms resting on the decorated mushroom table.

A temple attendant who looks very much like the Fat Lady, approaches with a cloth. She waits until the Fat Lady raises her head in acknowledgement, then hands over the dampened cloth and the Fat Lady wipes her fevered brow. Then a bowl of water is brought. She washes her face, her aching arms, her hands.

She changes into a clean fresh robe of white. An attendant helps her.

Now she is ready to eat.

Another attendant enters with food. She unfurls a woven cloth onto the stone table and sets out fresh round loaves of crusty Maltese bread, a flat bowl of olive oil and a plate of feta cheese, roasted vegetables, grapes, olives, an ornate bowl filled with hummus, sliced strips of finger-bread for dipping, and honey cakes, and wine.

Hungrily and with great concentration, the Fat Lady partakes of the special vegetarian meal and, after eating it all, every last bite, her energy and powers of divination are restored.

A garland of jasmine encircles her forehead. Her hair is long and loose, set free from the ornate bone clasp that always held it up and away from her eyes and face, but now her hair is flowing in torrents of gray and silvery curls and past her shoulders in great disarray.

She hardly looks like her everyday self when she wakjs ibto the inner courtyard but the Norwegian boys recognize her immediately and try to race to her side, but are stopped when their Fat Lady raises her arm and holds up her palm waist-high, and they halt in mid-stride.

The Norwegians watch as the temple attendants escort their Fat Lady into the center of the packed courtyard. The boys count 30 guests seated at the tables.

No one says anything.

Then in the silence in the temple, the Fat Lady says,

"The mourning feast will now be served. But does anyone else wish to see me? Come, I will answer your questions?."

She pauses and nods to the Norwegian boys, waving to them to come with her.

The boys step back a few paces.

"No, we're good."

The tall blond boys gape at this friendly Fat Lady. Never in their wildest dreams did they imagine that she was the legendary Oracle of Hagar Qim.

Then the boys hear her chuckling at the look on their faces.

CHAPTER TWENTY-ONE

ONE ANCIENT EVENING

AND ALL THE ANCIENTS WEPT

Even before the stone mason has finished his secret abstract sentence, which no one heard anyway, there is a stir among the crowded tables and everyone starts talking at once, in low, excited tones, for they see just entering the central courtyard four handsome young men dressed in black.

Three of them wear black turtlenecks, black slacks, white shirts, colorful ties, black shoes, and black blazers. The fourth young man looks slightly different, as if he doesn't go with the others. Wearing black slacks, a faded blue shirt with a dark blue tie, the fourth man doesn't wear a blazer and appears in polished leather boots. They stand together for an instant, all radiantly handsome, with dark eyes so intense they shine like sharp black obsidian, but so alive and tender with feeling, and their soft curly hair is as black as the starless night.

The mourners and guests know three of them right away. They are the famous trio from Italy, one baritone and two tenors whom the Norwegian boys and the stone mason and everyone at the mourning feast recognize at once. The museum director appears right behind them, hands each singer a cordless microphone, and, as an ancient harp made from ibex horns is strummed, a bone flute sounds, and the museum director holding his own microphone with one hand, with his other hand claps the fourth singer on the shoulder and leads him forward.

"Ladies and Gentlemen," the director begins and cannot tone down his great excitement, "tonight we have the distinct pleasure of a young singer from afar, opening for the famous trio we all know and love! This young man standing before you tonight is here with us for his first tour of Italy with our beloved trio. He is here tonight to perform his new hit song, *Tell Your Heart to Beat Again*.

"Sing it for us, Danny!"

As the excited museum director steps aside, and the Norwegian boys hear the ancients muttering,

"Who the heck *is this guy?*"

But then the song began.

The Norwegian boys are stunned by the power of the song and swept away by the emotion of the singer. Then they look to the museum director standing in the wings in a side apse. Tears are streaming down his face. They look to the tables and see that all the ancients wept.

There was only a short pause for wild impassioned applause before the legendary trio stepped up and began to sing.

Mas Que Amore, Grande Amore, they sing and the mourners stand up en masse.

The blended voices of the three young men are virile and the strength is soothing, as their harmonies hypnotize the listeners. Their music awakens the acoustical energy in the reverberating stones inside the nighttime temple, radiating life in the somber face of death, and life makes a bold stand. The trio sings like heroes in a valiant fight.

Then all the ancients spontaneously sing the familiar words along with the trio, and as the singing continues while the mourning feast is being served, the Norwegian boys see that the temple is transforming itself before their very eyes.

The inner walls are getting higher, as if a growing thing of nature, and as the walls soar upward into layers on layers, its top layer becomes roofed with wood and daub. Apse walls are now plastered smooth and painted with red ocher. Statuettes of the Fat Lady are positioned on stone tables next to burnished red cups with elongated handles, with jars of olive oil, and large covered bowls of fruit, plates of hummus and sliced finger-bread placed on the extravagantly decorated tables featuring incised holes, bas-reliefs of plants and spirals. Fragrant garlands of wild flowers bedeck the embracing circle of inner walls. All the apses are now roofed over, but the courtyard is left open to the sky and, this night, not a star in sight.

Aromatic smoke from cooking fires disappears into the warm sea air.

Everyone is standing and singing.

Then the singing stops. Everyone at the tables and the musicians lift their cups and drink to the life of the deceased. Then with more of the sweet Maltese wine, everyone shares a toast to the singers and someone stands to say they are here to celebrate life itself.

Everyone sits.

The Norwegian boys' special Fat Lady has finished her oracle duties and comes to ask if the boys would help store some figurines beneath a stone step which needs to be lifted.

The tall blond boys jump up and do so and return to their seats. The mourning feast is served in the beautified temple before them. The Fat Lady with her hair pinned back up and the garland of jasmine flowers gone from her brow, has come to sit with the Norwegians and Temi and the stone mason and they are just savoring the delicious and abundant food when they hear a familiar voice,

"There you are!"

Everyone stops eating and turns to look.

CHAPTER TWENTY-TWO
WHERE DID THEY GO?

It's the bustling museum director.

He's shouting something.

"Boys! Come out of there!"

The Norwegian boys sit up abruptly and begin to understand that they are alone and stretched out full length on the broken torba of an apse, where they were hiding, until they fell asleep.

They look around them in total confusion.

"Il Volo!" the sleepy Norwegians say, in a kind of ragged unison,

"Where is Il Volo?"

"Not here," the director says.

"Have you been dreaming?"

The director chuckles knowingly.

"While you were in there snoozing, the tables and chairs got picked up and taken away by the catering staff, so there's nothing for you to do but go to the Festa!

"They're expecting us, the car is waiting, come on out of there!"

Like survivors from a dream world, at a loss as to where that world has gone, the blond boys exit their hide-out and look around.

And try to shake off their astonishment.

Gone are the towering walls and roofing. Gone are the plastered inner apses painted red, vanished are the statuettes and jars and bowls of refreshment on the ancient stone tables. Even the drilled holes of decoration have vanished from the surface of the soft flaking stone tables. Courtyard smoke no longer rises to the sky.

The musicians are gone. The harpist, flautist, the trio, their opening act. Gone.

And gone are the Fat Ladies.

But where is *their* Fat Lady?

Their special Fat Lady, the Oracle of Hagar Qim….

Where is the hip stone mason, and the little man in tweed?

Where are the sad young boys they met at Tarxien? Their grieving mother, the crowd of mourners, that singing guy, the trio, the little tethered horses?

"Let's get a move on," the museum director is saying.

And so, feeling perplexed but somehow restored, as if from a pleasant night's dream, the Norwegian boys leave the temple of mourning humming a song they heard at the feast last night, and in a contented daze they don't understand, they head to their next and final adventure on Malta, the village Festa at Qrendi.

CHAPTER TWENTY-THREE
"GOODBYE, MALTA"

With visions of the mourning feast and singing ancients resounding in their heads, the Norwegian boys arrive at Qrendi in a limousine with the museum director and some of the well-dressed VIP crowd from the dinner party. The limo stops, the doors open, and everyone says good-bye to go their separate ways.

The boys look for their tour group in the throngs of people on the twisting village streets. Everyone in town is out on their balconies or leaning from open windows and French doors flung wide open to watch the Qendi band club approaching with an enthusiastic crowd of followers streaming along the streets behind them and overflowing into the gutters and onto the sidewalks. There are plenty of brass horns and big booming drums in this band and the music is energetic and exciting.

The boys are gleefully marching along in time with the band and the blaring, joyous music when they find the museum director marching behind them. He laughs with delight and invites them to come watch the fireworks tonight at a rooftop party hosted by two prominent Maltese who were at the Hagar Qim dinner that night.

"Here we go again," the director says and they hurry to a large elegant villa to watch a grand masterpiece of Maltese fireworks, close up. Below the rooftop balcony is a courtyard of sumptuous orange trees. Standing on the rooftop balcony above the bright green leaves on the orange-dotted trees, it seems possible to reach out and touch the exploding stars and mushrooming colors pounding above their heads like thundering cannons of war as the fireworks explode over the Malta Festa, close coming, fast and intense, packing the sky with energy and joy.

"God loves us!" an elderly man exclaims, and someone in the crowd shouts,

"And we love God!"

But the old man shakes his head,

"No, that's not it," he said and shuffled off with a certain world weariness to refresh his plate of hors d'oeuvres and find more wine.

The next morning the tour group is both happy and sad. They have had their fill of temples and history but the pull of the island still beguiles them, and they want to stay. Tears are secretly shed as the tour group prepares to board Air Malta for the short flight to Heathrow and home. As the Norwegian boys wait to board, they watch as a little group approaches.

Two little boys lead the group, jostling for their turn to carry a canvas carry-all filled to the brim with the farewell gifts of fresh loaves of crusty bread, containers of hummus and tomatoes, cheese, a bottle of Maltese wine, jars of Maltese honey, tins of olive oil, and two special gifts wrapped in plain brown paper.

Hobbling behind the two small boys is a heavy-set old woman in a white dress, tottering along on thick swollen ankles and supported on the arm of a small man in a tweed suit. With them is a pale and somber woman in dark glasses and a black dress. Strolling behind them is the cool stone mason, and seeing them all the Norwegians rush to them with great joy at seeing them one more time, the tall blond Norwegians abandoning their luggage in the boarding line and dramatically running down the boarding ramp.

The Fat Lady giggles as she always does at the antics of these adorable boys. Then she reaches out her hands to stop them and motions to Temi and he motions for the two little boys to bring the big canvas bag. They do so with alacrity and Temi takes from the bag the two gifts in brown paper.

Excitedly the paper is swept away, revealing for each of the Fat Lady's devoted Norwegian college boys a handsome clay cup on a high pedestal.

"Thermi!" they cry, in unison as usual, laughing as they chant,

"Greek or local?

"Thermi! Thermi!

"Greek or local?"

"Greek or local?"

The watching tour group starts laughing.

They are holding the handsome pedestal cups like trophies high over their heads and start dancing around.

Their colleagues in the tour are pointing and saying,

"That's our boys!"

The Fat Lady watches with delight, smiling at their exuberant reception of these gifts from the museum shop that are saying she would like them to remember Malta.

"We'll drink our morning coffee from these cups and write a book about you and the temples," the blond boys promise. "We have photographs. We'll never forget you."

Meanwhile the rest of the tour group, their line already inching forward to board, look for the two Norwegians, who left their baggage and wandered away, as usual, and then spot them in the near distance.

Are they singing and dancing? Are they holding pottery over their heads?

The tour group is not at all surprised to see the Norwegians dancing around all by themselves, on the broad passenger walkway, and talking to thin air.

Then the museum director appears as if out of nowhere and waves to the tour group. He'll be on their flight to London.

He follows the gaze of the entire group.

There in the passenger walkway he cannot help but see the Norwegian boys dancing around, apparently singing, while waving some cups above their heads.

All by themselves on the empty walkway.

The director is bemused, and mutters to himself,

"Time to get those boys back home!"

Then he sees the young stone mason who will be traveling with the museum director to an antiquities preservation conference in London, standing next to the Norwegian boys on the walkway, as usual carrying his soft leather shoulder pouch and wearing his usual home-spun clothes, coarse woven and dull brown, like burlap or sackcloth, the director never knew which, and watches as the stone mason gently touches the Norwegian boys on their dancing shoulders, a signal that it's time to go.

With a little wave goodbye to the young boys and their mother, to Temi and the Fat Lady, the stone mason turns to hear the museum director calling out to the Norwegian boys in a teasing tone,

"Goodbye, Malta!"

The blond-headed college boys stop dancing and look up startled, as if awakened too abruptly from a pleasing dream.

The stone mason claps them on the shoulders and turns them toward the boarding ramp. They want to say one last thank you and farewell to the little group, Temi and the Fat Lady, the little boys and their mother, but when they turn to look back, the Maltese contingent is gone.

And so the tall Norwegian boys carefully rewrap their Thermie cups, place them back inside the big canvas bag and join the boarding line. They grab their baggage, and clutching the canvas tote of farewell gifts begin moving forward on the boarding ramp with eyes aglow, armed with the true gift from Malta, the determination to enjoin the feast of the rest of their lives.

"Your tour of Malta has come to an end," the director is saying to the tour group, as they move along and board, but his sing-song voice cuts through the Norwegian boys like an unknown pain.

So smug, the boys think, he gets to come right back to Malta.

"This is the end!" The director sounds gleeful.

"But we have been in the Maltese circles…," the boys begin, in an irritated tone, but the stone mason is right behind them in the boarding line and intervenes just in time to smooth all the odd feelings of good-bye, and says in unison with the boys, this time wanting everyone to hear,

"… and a circle has no end."

"Yeah," everyone who heard that mutters agreement and, even understanding, as the entire tour group files on board Air Malta.

As the plane ascends, the tour group press their faces to the little porthole windows at their seats, looking for one last glimpse of the seven temples below.

But Malta is enveloped in mist.

"It's like Brigadoon," a woman says, "we know it's there, we just can't see it."

The Norwegian boys reflect on that.

They had seen elaborate palaces of stone built for feasting. They had found out the Fat Lady's secret. But most of all, with the mourners they had learned to step away from the tomb and, come back to life.

"And a circle has no end…."

PHOTO CREDITS

For the Sleeping Lady of Hal Saflieni Hypogeum, coyrtest the Bradshaw Foundation, The Temples of Malta and Gozo, Prehistoric Archaeology of the Temples of Malta, 2011, on bradshawfoundation.com

For Temple sketch of Tas-Silg, Cazzella, A. and Recchia, G., *Tas-Silg: the Late Neolithic megalithic sanctuary and its re-use during the Bronze Age and the Early Iron Age*, Scienza dell'Antichita, Sapienza Universita di Roma, 2012, and Global Print Press, October 2013 on academia.edu

For pottery and other items in the National Museum of Valletta, as indicated in the text, Evans, Sir J. D., *Ancient People and Places: Malta*, Praeger Publishers, New York, 1959. Ellis, Richard, Photograps of Holy of Holies,Hal Saflieni Hypogeum, 1910.

Photograps of Holy of Holies, Hal Saflieni Hypogeum, Ruchard Ellis,1910.

For pottery and other items from the National Museum of Valletta, as indicated in the text, Evans, Sir J. D., Prehistoric Antiquities of the Maltese Islands: A Survey, London: Athlone Publishing, 1971.

For temple images, by Ross-Edison Copyright 2016, Tarxien and Hagar Qim photographs, from a Study Abroad on Malta, as indicated in the text.

For sherds found in the Holy of Holies chambers, Hal Saflieni Hypogeum, Tagliaferro, N., *The Prehistoric Pottery Found at the Hypogeum at Hal Saflieni, Casal Paula, Malta*, Annals of Archaeology and Anthropology, the Institute of Archaeology, Vol.III, University of Liverpool, The University Press, London: Constable & Company Ltd., 1910, digitized by Internet Archive and Microsoft Corporation, 2007 on archive.org

For twin holes at Skorba, Trump, D., *Excavations carried out on behalf of the National Museum of Malta, 1961-1963*, Reports of the Research Committee of the Society of Antiquaries of London, No. XXII, Oxford: the University of Oxford Press, 1966.

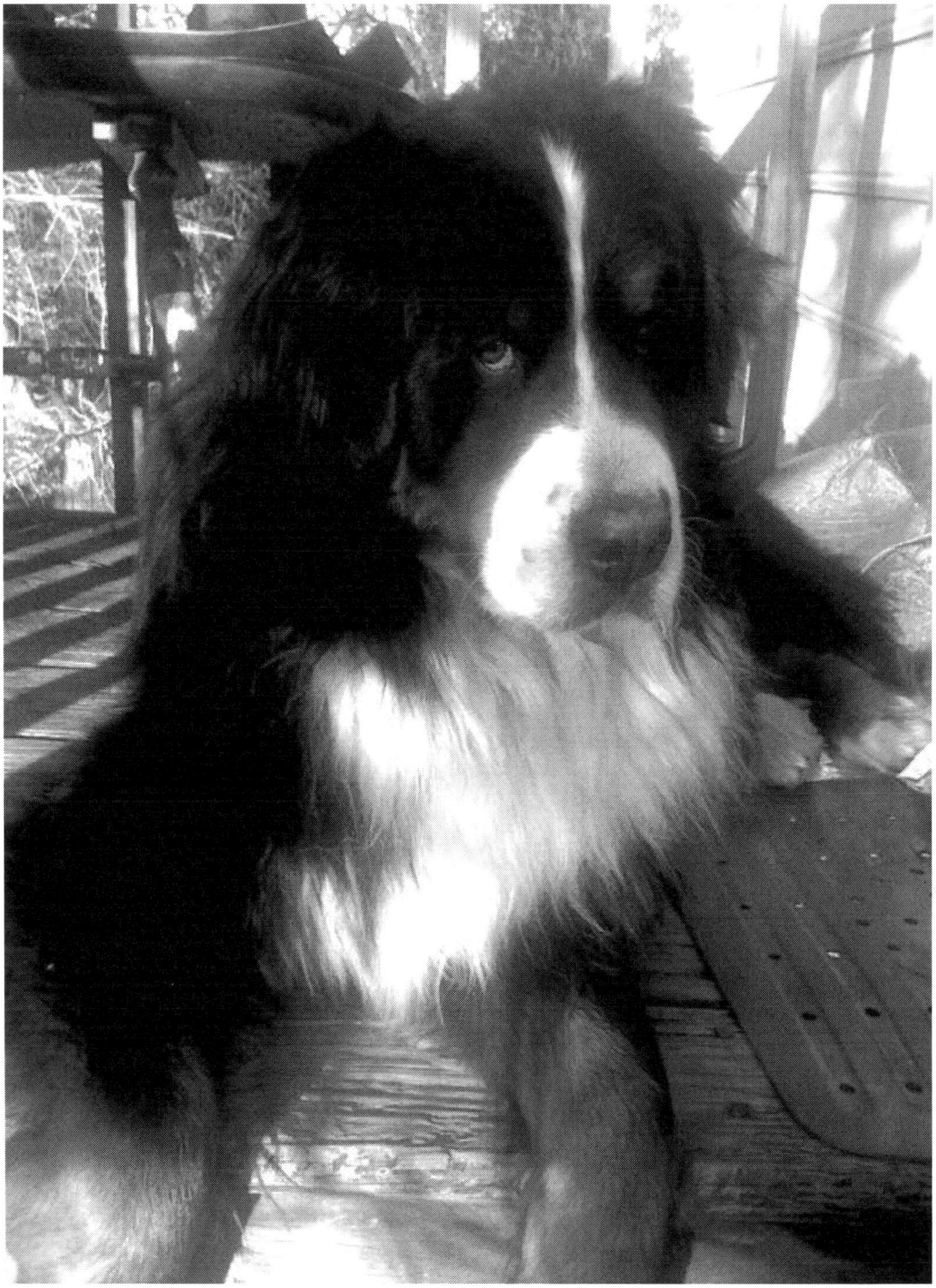

END NOTES

The Mystery of Malta

The more you read about Malta, the more you need to read.

Yet this is Neolithic Malta's great gift: the research will never stop.

This is because no one can ever know, not for sure, not from this preliterate time, not even with all the archaeological clues that abound in the temples and tombs on Malta, no one can ever know what the ancient mourners inside the temples were actually *doing*.

Therefore anyone and everyone can try to understand, from reading the online profusion of readily available sources, and from legendary books written about the temples and tombs, what went on inside the seven megalithic structures toured in this book.

Of all the many sites and sources of information on Neolithic Malta read for this book, there were six most valuable. These sources of archaeological facts and speculative theory are: two books by Sir John D. Evans with photographs and drawings (1959 and 1971); one book by David Trump on Skorba (1966) with photographs; one report by Professor N. Tagliaferro (1910); and two reports by Sir Themistocles Zammit on Hagar Qim and Mnajdra (reprinted 1994) and Sir Zammit's Museum Report on Mgarr (1929/1935). These works will thrust the first-time visitor and researcher into the thick of things and the heat of battle.

A note on the Oracle: answering questions from kings and military generals as well as from everyday people is documented in the historical accounts of Thucydides and Herodotus of the 5th centur B.C. Greek Oracle of Delphi/

Meanwhile, unanswered questions beg for research.

About prehistoric boats.

About Neolithic music.

About imported chickpeas ground for hummus on querns in the outbuildings.

About honey exports.

About the hanging lamps and ancient oil lamps.

About the far-flung inter-regional trade in the Mediterranean basin.

About real-Greek Thermi Ware, made in Greece or Troy, versus local-Thermi Ware made after 2500 B.C.

About the added-on apses, why so many.

About the large number of temples on two small islands.

About the name 'temple.'

About a temple ritual.

About male priests.

About oracles and Fat Ladies.

The list of questions goes on…

And so, at the end of this present and fanciful book, questions remain which are a legacy for the first-time visitor to explore, for the repeat visitor, for the new researcher to study, and who are hereby all invited to straddle the old questions as if a stubborn horseback-rider charging a Quixotic windmill, seeking like Don Quixote, something true about the temple builders.

Such as: Who *were* the temple builders?

Why did they leave? Where did they go?

"The discovery of the Hypogeum at Paula, whatever may have been the exact use of its mysterious chambers, with their strangely curved walls, adds another and most important testimony to this theory of an early Western Mediterranean civilization (…in Sardinia, in the Balearic Islands and in the South-East of Spain, suggest the growth of a civilization never attaining such advanced culture, but persisting through long ages with striking tenacity and individual character, and surviving as a lingering tradition to this day), which Professor Mayr traces from Malta, beyond the limits named above, to the northwestern coasts of France, England and Ireland, and as far North as the Orkney and Shetland Islands." *Newspaper article from the Omaru Mail, New Zealand, 10 June, 1911.*

There is plenty of research still to be done but our Walking Tour has now ended, with sadness for not knowing for certain what might have been.

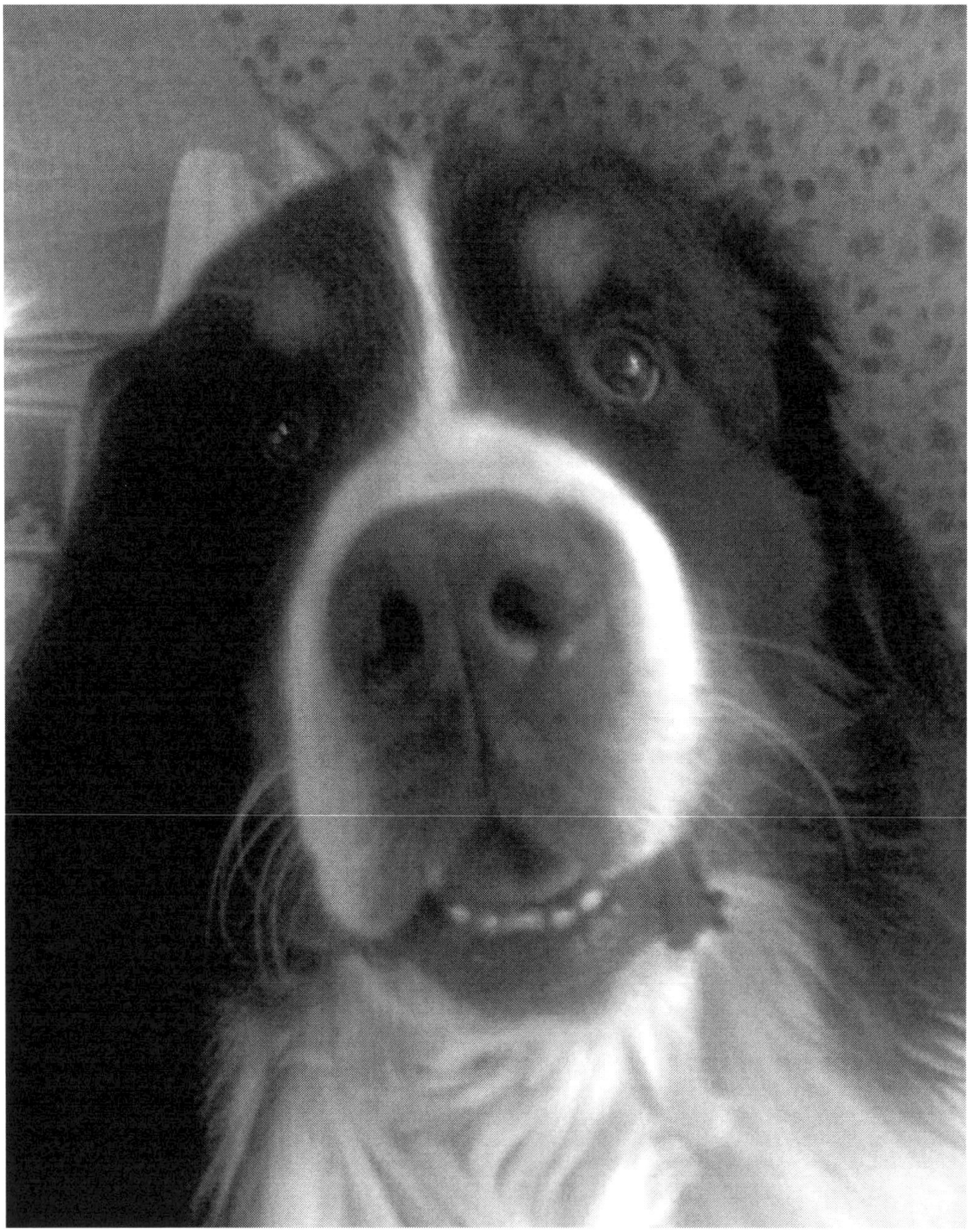

BOOKS AND ONLINE SITES

Abell, N., *The Role of Malta in Prehistoric Mediterranean Exchange Networks*, Department of Classics, University of Cincinnati, Ohio, 2007, on etd.ohiolink.edu

Ancient 4,500-year-old (59-foot) Boat discovered in Egypt, Fox News Science, February 03, 2016, on foxnews.com

Ashby, T., Bradley, R.N., et al., *Papers of the British School at Rome*, 6, 1913, on megalithics.com

Avino, P., Rosada, A., *Mediterranean and Near East obsidian reference samples to establish artefacts provenance*, Heritage Science Journal, December 14, 2014, on link.springer.com

Axiaq, P., Borg, G, Alight Technologies, *Kordin III Temple video Panorama*, Schoolnet Malta, on maltain360.com

Bonanno, A., Bartolo, J., Mintoff, M., *Malta, An Archaeological Paradise*, M.J. Publications, photoset by Interprint, Ltd, Valletta, Malta, Fourth edition, 1993.

Bonanno, A., Malone, C., Trump, D., Stoddart, S. and Gouder, T., *The Death Cults of Prehistoric Malta*, Scientific American, December 17, 2004, on scientificamerican.com

Borg-Manche, E., *A Lawyer's History of Malta*, 2011, on maltahistory.info

Bostrom, P., Late Stone Age Axes and Celts Style Variation Worldwide est. 35,000 Years Ago to Present Day, February 28, 2014, on lithiccastinglab.com

Bradshaw Foundation, *Mediterranean Figurines, Cycladic Sculptures of Greece*, 2011, on bradshawfoundation.com

Bradshaw Foundation, The Temples of Malta and Gozo, Prehistoric Archaeology of the Temples of Malta, 2011, on bradshawfoundation.com

Cartwright, M., *Neolithic Axe Heads, Photos*, Ancient History Encyclopedia, August 2014, on ancient.eu

Caskey, J., *Excavations at Lerna 1952-53, Plates 1-11*, The American School of Classical Studies at Athens, on ascsa.edu.gr

Cazzella, A., Pace, A., and Recchia, G., Cultural contacts and mobility between the south central Mediterranean and the Aegean during the second half of the 3rd millenium B.C., Chapter 11, in Mediterranean Crossroads, Prehistoric Archaeology and Mediterranean prehistory, Pierides Foundation, 2007 and University of Malta PDF on academia.edu.

Cazzella, A. and Recchia, G., *Tas-Silg: the Late Neolithic megalithic sanctuary and its re-use during the Bronze Age and the Early Iron Age*, Scienza dell'Antichita, Sapienza Universita di Roma, 2012, and Global Print Press, October 2013 on academia.edu

Chickpea Etymology, History, Description, Uses, Nutrition, Production, edited 2016, on en.m.wikipedia.org

Conservation and Restoration of ceramic objects - Why Pottery Breaks, 2016, on en.m.wikipedia.org

Copat, V., Danesi, M., and Recchia, G., *Isolation and Interaction Cycles, Small Central Mediterranean Islands from the Neolithic to the Bronze Age*, Shima: The International Journal of Research into Island Cultures, Volume 4, Number 2, 2010.

Copat, V., Danesi, M., and Ruggini, C., Late Neolithic and Bronze Age Pottery from Tas Silg Sanctuary: New Research Perspectives for the Maltese Prehistoric Sequence, Dipartimento di Scienze Dell'Antichita, Sapienza Universita di Roma, 2012.

Cope, J., *Skorba, Ancient Temple*, Malta Day Trip, The Modern Antiquarian Guide Book, 2000-2016 on themodernantiquarian.com

Danforth, L., photograpghs by Tsiaras, A., The *Death Rituals of Ancient Greece*, Princeton University Press, Princeton, New Jersey, 1982.

Daniel, G., and Renfrew, C., *The Idea of Prehistory*, Edinburgh University Press and Butler and Tanner, Ltd., Somerset, England, 1988.

Dengli, R., *Death in Malta*, a novel, Jacobyte Books, Australia, 2001.

Dogan, I., Michailidou, A., *Part I: Tracing Trade Activities in the Archaeological Record and Part II: Tracing Trade and Traders through Textual Evidence*, in Trading in prehistory and protohistory: Perspectives from the eastern Aegean and beyond, Aristotle University of Thessaloniki, on helios-eie-ekt.gr

Duyck, B., *The obsidian roads – 1. Around the Mediterranean Basin*, overblog, on earth-of-fire.com

Editors of Encyclopedia Brittanica, *Orkney Islands, Council Area, Scotland, U.K., Orcades*, Encyclopedia Brittanica, last edited January 29, 2015, on brittanica.com

Editors, World Archaeology Magazine, *Tas-Silg, Malta from Prehistoric Temple to Byzantine Church*, excerpt in Features, Issue 59, June 4, 2013 on world-archaeology.com

Freund, K., *The Politics of Obsidian Consumption in the West Mediterranean*, doctoral degree thesis, McMaster University, September 2014 on macsphere.mcmaster.ca Gokey, D., "Tell Your Heart to Beat Again," on YouTube.com

Gray, M., *Neolithic Temples of Malta*, copyright 1982-2015, on sacredsites.com

Grima, R., *Monuments in Search of a Landscape. The Landscape Context of Monumentality in Late Neolithic Malta.* For Doctor of Philosophy degree, Institute of Archaeology, University College London, 2005. UMI Dissertation Publishing, ProQuest LLC, Ann Arbor, Michigan: 2005, on discovery.ucl.ac.uk

Heritage Malta, *Hal Saflieni Hypogeum Management Plan, Consultation Document*, Prehistoric Sites Department, January 2012 on heritagemalta.org

Holkham, T., *Phoenicia*, on en.m.wikipedia. org

Il Volo, Mas Que Amore, Grande Amore, on Youtube.com

Kingdom-Hocking, M., Sailing Boats through the Ages – History of Sailboats, August 2013, on YachtPals.com

Kininmonth, Christopher, *The Travellers' Guides, Malta and Gozo*, revised by Robin Gordon-Walker, Thomson Litho, Ltd., East Kilbride, Scotland, 1967, revised 1987.

Kipper, K., logo designer and Meicel, P., illustrator, *Skorba, Ghar Dalam, Malta*, The Adventures of Archaeology Wordsmith, 2002-2016 on archaeologywordsmith.com

Kordin III Temple, National Inventory of the Cultural Property of the Maltese Islands, 1998, published 30 March, 2012 on culturalheritage.gov.mt

Kordin Temples, I, II, and III, 2016 on en.m.wikipedia.org

LePage, K., Modeling Reverberation Time Series for Shallow Water Clutter Environments, Malta Plateau, Ragusa Ridge, ONR, NRL Review, 2007 on nrl.navy.mil

Lourakis, editor on February 2016, *Cycladic Art*, on en.m.wikipedia.org

Luke 24:5 on KingJamesBible.org

Malone, C., Stoddart, S., Trump, D., Bonanno, A. & Pace A. (eds.), *Mortuary Ritual in Prehistoric Malta. The Brochtorff Circle Excavations (1987-1994)*, 361-384, Cambridge: McDonald Institute, 2009.

Malone, C., Stoddart, S., *Maltese Prehistoric Religion*, Chapter 47, 758-774, in The Oxford Handbook of the Archaeology of Ritual and Religion, Insoll, T., editor, Oxford: Oxford University Press, 2011.

McKirdy, A., *Orkney and Shetland, A Landscape Fashioned by Geology*, Scottish National Heritage, Dualchas Nadair na h-Alba, and British Geological Survey, Battleby, Redgorton, Perth, 2010, on snh.org.uk

Megalith, Megaliths worldwide, 2016 on en.m.wikipedia.org

Megalithic Malta 4, Video, Ta'Hagrat Temples, Mgarr on youtube.com

Mnajdra, color photograph of Mnajdra South temple drilled and pitted trilithon and niche, 2016, on en.m.wikipedia.org

Mommsen, H., Bonanno, A., Bonavita, A., Kakoulli, I., Musumeci, M., Sagona, C., Schwedt, A., Vella, N., Zacharias, N., *Characterization of Maltese pottery of the Late Neolithic, Bronze Age and Punic Period by neutron activation analysis*, University of Malta, The Geological Society of London, Special Publications 257:81-89, 2006.

Montalto, Nicola A., *The Characterisation and Provenancing of Ancient Ochres*, Ph.D. Study, Cranfield University, Bedfordshire, U.K., 2010, on dspace.lib.cranfield.ac.uk/bit

Omaru Mail, *The Mystery of Malta. The Strange Hypogeum at Malta*. Volume XXXIX, Issue 10789, page 3, National Library of New Zealand, issue 10 June, 1911.

Pace, A., *Chapter on the Tarxien temple model*, in Cilia, D., Malta Before Prehistory- The World's Oldest Free Standing Stone Architecture, 2004 on ancient-wisdom.com

Pausanias, *Description of Greece, Volume 1*, Translated by W.H.S. Jones, Litt.D., St. Catherine's College, Cambridge, William Heinemann, Ltd. Publishers, London, 1918 first printed, reprinted 1978.

Psaila, S., *Hagar Qim Temple 5,000 Years Ago, 3D Virtual Video, The Times of Malta Newspaper*, on timesofmalta.com/mobile/articles/view20120812/local/-agar-Qim-temple-as-it-was-5-000-years-ago.432456

Queen Bees from the Honey Island, on melitabees.com

Quern-Stone, edited 2016, on en.m.wikipedia.org

Robb, J., *Island Identities: ritual, travel, and the creation of difference in Neolithic Malta*, European Journal of Archaeology, Vol.4(2): 175-202, Sage Productions (London,

Thousand Oaks, California and New Delhi) and the European Association of Archaeologists, 2001, on academia.edu

Savona-Ventura, C., Maltese Ungulates (cattle, goats, pigs, sheep, horses, deer, hippopotamus, dwarf elephants, mastodon, aurochs), The Maltese Islands, the Natural Environment, Multimedia Encyclopedia, Malta, 2001.

Schembri, P., *Physical Geography and Ecology of the Maltese Islands: A brief overview*, in Busuttil, S. (editor), Lerin, F. (editor), Mizzi, L. (editor), Malta: Food, agriculture, fisheries and the Environment, Mediterranean Options, Montpellier: CIHEAM, 1993: 27-39 on om.ciheam.org

Sen, S., Barrier, E., and Crete, X., *Late Pleistocene dwarf elephants from the Aegean island of Kassos and Dilos, Greece*, Ann. Zool. Fennici 51: 27-42, Finnish Zoological and Botanical Publishing Board, 2014 on sekj.org

Sinnigen, W. and Boak, A., *A History of Rome to 565*, 6th edition, New York: Macmillan, 1965: 8-15 and Grant, M., *History of Rome*, Scribner's 1978: 14, *Prehistoric Peoples of the Italian Peninsula*, on jaysromanhistory.com

Skeates, R., Pounding and Grinding Stones in Prehistoric Malta, The European Association of Archaeologists, The Institute of Archaeology, Czech Republic, Issue No. 29, Summer 2008:7-8.

Skorba, Heritage Malta, Reasons to Visit, on heritagemalta.org

Skorba Photos: Shrine Hut Figurine, and Seated Figurine from Xaghra Circle, and damaged Standing Statue of the Tarxien Fat Lady 9 feet high (2.75 m.), with its base 3.6 feet high (1.11 m.) and 4.3 feet wide (1.30 m.), Photos, on web.infinito.it

Skorba Temples, About Malta, Excursion Information on ChooseMalta.com, and heritagemalta.org/sites/skorba

Skorba Temples, Excursion Tours, Pearl of the Mediterranean Sea, Web Edition, Ltd., 2011 on malta.com

Skorba Temples, National Inventory of the Cultural Property of the Maltese Islands, 1998 and December 2011 on culturalheritage.gov.mt

Smith, Roff, photography by Richardson, J., *Before Stonehenge, Scotland's Stone Age Ruins*, National Geographic Magazine, published by the National Geographic Society, Canada and U.S., August 2014 on ngm.nationalgeographic.com

Society for Interdisciplinary Studies, SIS, *Sicily to Tunisia*, March 2012, on sis-group.org.uk; shadowservices.com/nature/Maltese/Geomorph/geograp.htm; and bestofsicily.com/history1.htm

Stoddart, S., *Neolithic and Bronze Age Malta and Italy*, Chapter 14, 302-311, in World Archaeology at the Pitt Rivers Museum: A Characterization, edited by Dan Hicks and Alice Stevenson, Archaeopress, 2013, on archaeopress.com

Stroud, Katya, A *Visit to the Maltese Megalithic Temples*, Oxford Archaeology, Occasional Paper No.16, Recent Developments in Research and Management at World Heritage sites, Oxford Archaeological Unit, Ltd., printed by the Alden Group, Oxfordshire, U.K., 2007, on library.thehumanjourney.net

Stroud, Katya, *Hagar Qim and Mnajdra Temples, Malta: A History of Conservation*, Oxford Archaeology, Occasional Paper No.16, Recent Developments in Research and Management at World Heritage sites, Oxford Archaeological Unit, Ltd., printed by the Alden Group, Oxfordshire, U.K., 2007. on library.thehumanjourney.net

Ta' Hagrat Temples, last edited October 2015, on en.m.wikipedia.org

Ta' Hagrat Temples, National Inventory of the Cultural Property of the Maltese Islands on culturalheritage.gov.mt

Tagliaferro, N., *The Prehistoric Pottery Found at the Hypogeum at Hal Saflieni, Casal Paula, Malta*, Annals of Archaeology and Anthropology, the Institute of Archaeology, Vol.III, University of Liverpool, The University Press, London: Constable & Company Ltd., 1910, digitized by Internet Archive and Microsoft Corporation, 2007 on archive.org

Tarxien Temple Photos and Plan of the Temple Complex, 1998 on art-and-archaeology.com

The Megalithic Temples of Malta, Odyssey Adventures in Archaeology, June 14, 2012 on odyssetadventures.ca

The Temple of Skorba, Reach Malta in the Heart of the Mediterranean, Excursions on reachmalta.com

Thorpe, W., Warren, S., Courtin, J., *The distribution and sources of archaeological obsidian from southern France*, Journal of Archaeologic

The Times of Malta, *Archaeologist is on a roll with tale of ancient bread, Interview with David Trump*, 2014 on TIMESOFMALTA.COM

Traditional Food of Malta, 2016, on visitmalta.com

Trump, D., *Excavations carried out on behalf of the National Museum of Malta, 1961-1963*, Reports of the Research Committee of the Society of Antiquaries of London, No. XXII, Oxford: the University of Oxford Press, 1966.

Van der Werf, V., *In the Shadow of Megaliths, the forgotten tools and implements from Malta's Prehistoric Temples*, Leiden University, the Netherlands, June 17, 2013, on openaccess.leidenuniv.nl

Vassallo History, Bee Keeping and Maltese Honey, Maltese Heritage, 2015, on vassallohistory.wordpress.com

Vella, C., Distribution patterns of imported lithic tools in Early Neolithic Skorba, Ta' Hagrat and Skorba Ancient Monuments in a Modern World, Heritage Malta and Structural Funds Programme for Malta, 2008, on academia.edu

Wells, H.G., The Earliest Ships and Sailors – The Outline of History by H.G. Wells, 15.0 Sea Peoples and Trading Peoples, 15.1 The Earliest Ships and Sailors, from A Plain History of Life and Mankind, on outline-of-history.mindvessel.net

Whitelaw, T., *Digging in the Archives: Re-discovering the Excavations of John D. Evans*, Day of Archaeology, July 10, 2012 on dayofarchaeology.com

Whitaker, A., *Skorba: (Temple Complex),* and *Hagar Qim (Temple Complex),* The Ancient Wisdom Foundation, April 2012, on ancient-wisdom.com

World Heritage List, *Megalithic Temples of Malta*, United Nations Educational, Scientific, and Cultural Organization (UNESCO), Date of Inscription 1980, Extension 1992, Minor Modification 2015, on whc.unesco.org

Zammit, Prof. Sir Themistocles, *Malta, The Prehistoric Temples, Hagar Qim and Mnajdra*, 1931, photographs and drawings by Ing. Karl Mayrhofer, photoset and printed by Interprint Limited, Malta, 1994.

Zammit, Prof. Sir Themistocles, *Museum Report on Mgarr*, 1929, reprinted 1935.

ACKNOWLEDGEMENTS AND THANKS

Thanks and gratitude to Lois and Anne for making the time and place possible for researching and writing this book.

Special thanks to Terry and Poppy for Ingrid and to Cuthbert who always led the way.

With gratitude to the archaeologists at Cambridge University and the University of Sapienza, to the Bradshaw Foundation, to Heritage Malta staff, all of you for the encouragement of promptly answering my confused emailed questions,, and thanks, profusely, to the National Museum of Archaeology in Valletta.

CUTHBERT, REST IN PEACE

Manufactured by Amazon.ca
Bolton, ON